THE
MEXICAN
GOURMET

THE MEXICAN GOURMET

RECIPES: *MARÍA DOLORES TORRES YZÁBAL*

TEXT: *SHELTON WISEMAN AND JOSÉ N. ITURRIAGA*

AUTHENTIC INGREDIENTS AND TRADITIONAL RECIPES FROM THE KITCHENS OF MEXICO

THUNDER BAY
P·R·E·S·S

Published by Thunder Bay Press
5880 Oberlin Drive, Suite 400
San Diego, Calfornia 92121

Produced by Weldon Russell Pty Ltd
107 Union Street, North Sydney NSW 2060, Australia

A member of the Weldon International Group of Companies

Chief Executive: Elaine Russell
Publisher: Karen Hammial
Managing Editor: Ariana Klepac
Editor: Libby Frederico
Editorial Assistant: Cassandra Sheridan
Design Concept: Judy Hungerford
Designer: Stuart McVicar
Illustrator: Kathie Smith
Ingredients and Location Photographer: Michael Calderwood
Recipe Photographer: Andrew Furlong
Food Stylist: Marie-Hélène Clauzon
Indexer: Garry Cousins
Production: Dianne Leddy

Library of Congress Cataloging-in-Publication Data

Torres Yzábal, María Dolores
    The Mexican gourmet : authentic ingredients and traditional
recipes from the kitchens of Mexico / recipes. María Dolores
Torres Yzábal ; text, Shelton Wiseman and José N. Iturriaga.
        p.   cm.
    Includes index
    ISBN 1–57145–057–2 (hardcover)
    1. Cookery, Mexican.   I. Wiseman, Shelton.   II. Iturriaga
de la Fuenta, José N.   III. Title.
TX716.M4T66   1995
641.5972—DC20
                                                    95-10918
                                                    CIP

Front cover: Photographer: Michael Calderwood

*Back cover: Uncooked Mexican Salsa (front, recipe page 26); Guanajuato-
style Guacamole (back, recipe page 27)*

Endpapers: Tomatillos: Photographer: Gerald Colley; Stylist: Kay Francis

Opposite title page: Woman selling breakfast tamales

Title page: Edam Cheese with Yucatecan Shredded Pork (recipe page 42)

Opposite contents page: Woman making blue tortillas

*Opposite: Corn Tortillas (back center, recipe page 53); Flour Tortillas (back
right, recipe page 53)*

CONTENTS

INTRODUCTION

INTRODUCTION

CONNOISSEURS OF GASTRONOMIC MATTERS GENERALLY COINCIDE IN CLASSIFYING MEXICAN CUISINE as one of the world's great, together with French, Italian, and Chinese.

❡ The Mexican kitchen is a *mestizo* creation, the result of a union of two major elements: the native, pre-Hispanic cooking, with corn as the principal ingredient (archaeologists have ascertained that this grain had been cultivated by the natives for over 3,000 years); and the Spanish cuisine brought to Mexico with the conquest in 1521.

❡ Corn continues to be the Mexican's principal staff of life, with eleven million tons being consumed each year. In pre-Hispanic times, it was the basic food not only of the body but also of the spirit. The religious beliefs of the Aztecs were linked in many ways to corn. Conquering Spaniards often found a host of idols made of corn dough and adorned with grains and whole ears of corn in native temples. Offerings to the gods invariably included corn and objects made from it.

❡ One of the principal historians of Mexico during the sixteenth century was the Spanish Franciscan friar, Bernardino de Sahagún. His main work, *Historia General de las Cosas de Nueva España*, written

Previous pages: An export crop of tomatoes from the northwestern state of Sinaloa. Although Mexico may have given the world this versatile fruit, it remains one of the cornerstones of the cuisine at home.

Opposite: Woman selling chicharrones de harina, a fried pasta snack which derives its name from the crunchy similarity to pork crackling. The traditional accompaniment is a sprinkling of hot chile sauce.

shortly after the conquest was completed, is a valuable source of information on pre-Hispanic life. Using his influence as a man of the church, he formed a sizeable group of old men whose lives had been spent mainly in pre-Hispanic times. These men allowed Sahagún to reconstruct their history, customs, religion, and traditions from the time before the Spaniards' arrival.

❡ Several chapters of Sahagún's book deal with ceremonial celebrations by the natives in honor of the specific gods charged with each of the eighteen months of the Nahuatl year: "Also, images of their dead they placed on hoops of grass and, as day broke, they would place these images in their oratories on beds of reeds; then they would offer them food: *tamales* and *mazzamorra*, a stew made with the meat of fowl or dog and, finally, they would honor them with incense, pouring incense over coals burning in a clay holder formed like a gigantic spoon . . . And the rich among them sang and drank *pulque* in honor of these gods and of their own dead relatives while the poor could only offer food to theirs. Offerings were also placed on other tombs where other dead were buried and on each of these a *tamal* was placed. At last, all ate together."

❡ To this day, the Mexican people continue to celebrate their dead from October 31 to November 2, the "Days of the Dead," with food, particularly *tamales*, just as Sahagún describes it. These *tamales* are made from corn dough (the addition of lard in the dough came after the conquest) topped with meat or sweet-meats, and wrapped in corn husks before being steamed.

❡ The "Encounter of Two Worlds" took place during the conquest, between 1519 and 1521.

From the very outset, Captain Hernán Cortés, the leader of the Spanish, appreciated the vast riches that these lands could provide. On seeing the market of Tlaltelolco—the most famous market of ancient Mexico—he wrote: "There is a street of game where are sold all manner of birds to be found in the land. There are hens, quail, partridges, wild duck, spits, parrots, owls, hawks and eagles, vulcans, sparrow hawks and kestrels. Of some of these birds of prey, they sell the skins with feathers, heads, beaks and talons. The natives also sell rabbit, hare, deer and little dogs that they breed and castrate for eating. All kinds of vegetables are on sale, among others, onions, leeks, garlic, nasturtium leaves, watercress, borage, sorrel, artichokes and golden thistles.

¶ There are also many fruits of different sorts such as cherries and plums similar to those of Spain. Honey made by bees is sold as well as honeycomb, syrup made from corn stalks and as sweet and delicious as that of sugar cane, and syrup made from a sort of plant known in the islands as 'maguey' and quite better than our boiled grape must. From these plants they make both sugar and wine (*pulque*). Pasties filled with game and fish are sold as well as fish, both fresh and salted, raw or cooked. Eggs of hens, geese and all the other birds that I have mentioned are sold in quantities, and likewise a kind of omelet."

¶ The conquering Spanish army brought with it an extensive range of ingredients for the preparation of its own traditional cuisines, including pork, chicken, sheep, cattle, turnips, cabbage, and chickpeas. As time went by, the native and Spanish foods and cooking techniques intermixed, which vastly enriched each culture's respective cuisines with new ingredients. The Spanish had already acquired a taste for chile, Christopher Columbus having taken chile seeds back to Europe some thirty years before. The Spanish continued spreading chiles throughout the known world, first to the kitchens of Europe then, later, to those of Africa and Asia. They also introduced some new-found tastes to Old World palates. Mexico's great contributions to the rest of the gastronomic world included corn, tomatoes, chocolate, vanilla, chiles, and avocados (*aguacates* in Spanish), many of whose names can be traced to the Nahuatl language: *tomatl, chocolatl, chilli,* and *auacatl.* Vanilla comes from the Spanish name *vainilla,* a derivative of "vaina," meaning "pod." The original

Nahuatl name is *ixtlilxóchitl,* meaning "black flower."

¶ It is hard to imagine European cuisines without the tomato, or Western desserts without chocolate or vanilla, so much has the influence of these ingredients transformed the foods we eat. The sweet peppers of Europe, paprikas of Hungary, cayenne, and innumerable other chile varieties found all over the world were all generated from the original capsicum seed from Mexico.

¶ Just as for the cuisines of most large countries, it is inaccurate to speak of "Mexican food" as a single concept. There are, in reality, many regional cuisines, each with its own geographical and historical influences.

¶ The beginnings of agriculture in Mexico and the cultivation of corn have been traced by archaeologists to the high, arid Valley of Tehuacán in the southeast corner of Puebla. The markets of the area are a crossroads of three states—Puebla, Veracruz, and Oaxaca—each with its own regional cuisine.

¶ Puebla's culinary fame stems from the sophistication of two signature dishes: *Mole Poblano* (see page 168) and *Chiles en Nogada* (see page 114). Its cuisine, like its colonial architecture, is typically baroque: it was one of the first cities to be founded by Cortés after the conquest. Local habits and ingredients were influenced by European traditions brought to its convents by the Spanish Catholic nuns. The nuns, familiar with the techniques for making sweets from sugar, quickly incorporated local fruits and other ingredients into the process, hence the many sweets that Puebla boasts.

¶ The central plateau of Mexico, which includes Puebla, is characterized by an abundance of maguey and nopal cactuses. *Pulque,* the pre-Hispanic beverage, is fermented from the sap of the former. The characteristic *mixiote* of the region, mutton-filled packages steam-baked in an earthen pit oven, gets its name from the skin of the maguey arms (a sort of parchment) that it is wrapped in. From the nopal cactus come the edible nopal paddles, eaten as a vegetable, and the sweet cactus fruits it produces. The brothy casseroles of the region are often made with *xoconostle,* an acid version of the fruit from a different variety of nopal.

¶ To the south, the state of Oaxaca stretches through rugged mountainous regions all the way to the Pacific coast and down to the narrow Isthmus of Tehuantepec, bordering on the state of Chiapas. Oaxaca has one of the greatest indigenous

Banana leaves and corn husks for sale as casings for tamales. *Dried husks are soaked in water to make them more pliable for wrapping.*

populations of any state in Mexico, principally Mixtecs and Zapotecs, whose cultural traditions are very much alive. Grasshoppers (originally an indigenous food), fried in great quantities in the marketplace, are eaten like roasted peanuts or heaped into *tacos*. The large variety of *tamales* in Oaxaca stems from its ethnic diversity. Oaxaca also boasts its own rich variety of chiles, including yellow and black *chilhuacles*, *costeños*, and the large, lightgreen *chiles de agua*. These are the basis for the seven different *moles* of Oaxaca, each distinctly different from the next.

❡ To the east, stretching along the Gulf of Mexico, is Veracruz, whose cuisine is characterized geographically by the fish and seafood which abound in the Gulf. It is one of the most versatile agricultural regions of the country, producing an abundance of tropical fruits in the lowlands and coffee in its mountains. Cattle ranches abound, and it is the sole producer of vanilla in Mexico, in the area around Papantla. Nut- and seed-based sauces, whether from the plentiful peanuts grown in the area, almonds, or sesame seeds, are also very popular here.

❡ Both Spanish and Caribbean influences can be felt in Veracruz's cuisine, which is not surprising since Veracruz remained the main port of entry for 400 years after Cortés landed in 1519, and the routes of commerce would often include the Caribbean islands. The Spanish influence can be seen in dishes such as *Pescado a la Veracruzana*, which has the typically Spanish ingredients of capers and olives, and also in that many dishes are cooked with olive oil rather than the more common vegetable oil or lard characteristic in most of the country. Cooked plantains and *moros y cristianos* (Moors and Christians), a dish of black beans and white rice, reflect the Caribbean influence in cooking.

❡ Another distinct culinary region is that of the Yucatán, which is characterized by its Mayan heritage (a culture still very much alive today), its geographical distance from the main body of Mexico, and its geological make-up. It is a flat expanse of limestone where deer and wild turkey roamed (they still exist in smaller numbers today, and, despite laws forbidding the hunting of deer, venison is still eaten). The Yucatán Peninsula was often more directly connected historically to Europe than to the distant and difficult to reach capital, Mexico City, and, therefore, Yucatecan cuisine has

a strong European influence. Certain ingredients are key to this cuisine: *achiote* (*axiote* is the Mayan spelling, pronounced ah-chee-oty), or annatto, seeds which give not only a distinctive taste but also a reddish color to food; bitter oranges, used as the acid element in food and sauces where limes, vinegar, or tomato might be used elsewhere; *habanero* chiles, the fiery component of table sauces; and the large-leafed oregano of the region. Other condiments such as cloves, cumin, cinnamon, and garlic are added to many of the *recados*, or seasoning pastes, that flavor the different foods. *Chaya*, a typical Swiss chard- (silver beet-) like leaf is chopped in *tamales* or used to wrap them, and red and white onions are ever-present as a pickled condiment. The *pib* of the Yucatán, like the *mixiote* and *barbacoa* of the center and north, is the earthen pit oven which is used for cooking such specialties as *cochinita pibil* (pork wrapped in banana leaves and seasoned with *recado rojo*, the annatto-seed seasoning paste) and turkey with black stuffing. Curiously, hard-boiled eggs are added to many dishes, including this black stuffing, and are the center piece for a subtle dish called *papadzules*, where they are wrapped in *tortillas* and covered with both a green pumpkin-seed sauce and a tomato sauce and drizzled with the green oil from the pumpkin seeds. It should also be noted that Lebanese cooking has a place of its own in Yucatán, as merchants arrived in several waves and settled there.

❡ The lesser-known cuisine of Tabasco is a surprise of subtle flavors and unusual ingredients. It shows many similarities to that of Veracruz, with whom it shares the Gulf Coast to the north, such as in the use of the large, licorice-flavored *hoja santa* leaf (*Piper auritum*, called *acuyo* in Veracruz and *momo* in Tabasco) to wrap fish and flavor casseroles; and to Chiapas, farther south, in its use of both the acid *Chiapas* cheese and a profusion of interesting herbs—five different unusual herbs are blended together to make a subtle green sauce for pork or fish (one of these, curiously enough, is called *perejil*, the Spanish name for parsley, but it is a completely distinct, long oval-leafed herb which grows in small lettuce-like sprays only in the Tabascan swamplands). One of the great banana growing areas of Mexico, here plantains come into their own, whether they are stuffed with cheese, flattened and fried as a crisp *tortilla* to munch on at the beginning of a meal, or added to a banana leaf-wrapped fish

A woman uses the time-honored method to carry garlic to the Oaxaca market where people come to sell their produce.

dish called *mone* with *momo*, tomatoes, onions, and sweet chiles. Tabasco shares with the Yucatán a variety of *tamales* made with *chaya*, and a paste of annatto seeds for seasoning. One of its most unusual ingredients is a fish called *pejelagarto*, which looks like a tiny crocodile because of the shape of its mouth and the tough scales of its skin. Cacao cultivated in the area is added to ground corn as the base of a nutritious drink mixed with water called *pozol*.

❡ The north, although less influential gastronomically than the regions farther south, has many culinary aspects that set it apart from the rest of the country. To begin with, the indigenous populations of the north were primarily nomadic tribes rather than the rooted civilizations to the south, so they left little trace in the cultural upheaval to follow. In the present day, the most outstanding factor of northern cuisine is that wheat has surpassed corn as the most important grain cultivated; flour *tortillas* are more common than those of corn. Unlike the abundance of ingredients from the center, south, and coastal lands, large areas of the north are characterized by harsh, often desert, lands. However, these vast expanses do lend themselves to cattle breeding and the best meat of the country, of excellent quality, is produced from Sonora to Nuevo Leon. Using cow's milk, the hard-working Mennonites, who settled in Chihuahua, have made an industry from their special cheese, *queso Chihuahua*, or *queso Mennonita*. Peaches, apples, and pecans (so popular in Mexico that the generic word "nut," or *nuez*, refers exclusively to them), which prosper in dry climates with cold winters, are cultivated in the north. The rich red soil of Zacatecas is excellent for growing chiles, and micro-climates in Zacatecas and Aguascalientes lend themselves to the cultivation of grapes destined for making wine.

❡ It is incorrect to speak of "Mexican food" as a single concept, as each area of Mexico offers its own particular culinary characteristics and unique ingredients. However, when the corn-based cooking of the indigenous peoples mixed with the Spanish ingredients and techniques brought during the conquest, one thing was certain—one of the world's great cuisines had been born.

EQUIPMENT

Much of the cooking equipment used today in Mexico hasn't changed since pre-Columbian times. In the diaries of Bernal Díaz, a Spanish historian and soldier with Cortés, which date from 1519, he writes about Tlatelolco, the central market of Tenochtitlán (now Mexico City). There, he records that sauces were blended in the *molcaxítl* and corn was ground on a *metatl*.

The wooden stick used for frothing the hot chocolate served at Montezuma's table was probably similar to the marvellous *molinillo* used today. Other pieces of equipment, such as the versatile *comal*, show the ingenuity of Mexican knowhow. Notable concessions to modern conveniences are the blender and the food processor, used a great deal for pureeing

sauces, although often recipes instruct the cook to leave some texture so the result more closely resembles that made in the original stone *molcajete*.

Metate and metlapil (mano): From the Nahualtl word *metatl*, the *metate* is a three-legged, rectangular grinding stone made of volcanic rock. It is used traditionally for grinding grains of all kinds, corn (slaked with lime),

chiles, and roasted cacao beans to a pulp. It slopes gently downward so the grain or pulp is pushed forward as it is worked and falls into a *cazuela* (pot) placed under the front edge. In a kneeling position, the cook uses a *metlapil*, or stone rolling pin, to grind with. To grind chocolate, a candle is placed under the *metate* to gently heat it. *Metates* are still widely available, although some of

have some of its ingredients ground to a pulp in the *molcajete* to blend the flavors of the juices before the remaining ingredients are added. You can use a spice or coffee grinder for any dry grinding, while a blender can be substituted for making sauces, but leave some texture in the mixture.

Tortilla presses: The two kinds of *tortilla* press, wooden and metal, can be used interchangeably. They are used to flatten a little ball of *masa* into a corn *tortilla*, the size and shape of which will depend on the size and shape of the ball and the amount of pressure used. Two squares of plastic are used to protect the dough from sticking to the press. Once pressed, the plastic is peeled off, and the raw *tortilla* is often tossed from palm to palm *(palmeado)* to achieve that extra thinness before being cooked on a hot *comal* and eaten forthwith.

Rolling pin and board: These are used for flour *tortillas*; because of the gluten in wheat, flour *tortillas* must be rolled rather than pressed.

Cazuela: Traditionally most Mexican food is cooked and served in *cazuelas*, which are glazed earthenware pots and casseroles. These vary in size and shape according to cooking needs (see page 91).

Comal: Essentially a flat round of clay or metal, like a griddle, the *comal* is both inexpensive and essential to the Mexican cook. Large or small, it is heated directly over a flame and used for cooking *tortillas*, blistering chiles, charring tomatoes, or toasting grains and spices. It is always used dry, without any fat for cooking. Clay *comales* are first rubbed with lime (calcium oxide) to prevent sticking and hot spots. A cast-iron frying pan or griddle can be substituted.

Tamal steamer: This is a tall pot made of tin that has a removable, perforated steamer disk a few inches from the bottom. On the disk rests a three-way vertical divider, which helps the *tamales* stand upright and allows three different kinds of *tamal* to be cooked at the same time. To cook the *tamales*, the water is brought to a boil and the steamer is lined top and bottom with extra corn husks before the *tamales* are added. (A practical cook puts a copper coin in the bottom with the water: the clanging of the coin indicates whether there is still water.) To ensure a good seal, the top is usually also lined with a cloth and then a layer of plastic wrap before the top is put on. A pasta pot with a deep basket can be used instead, but more boiling water may have to be added during the cooking time.

El anafre: The ever-practical Mexican cook has a light, mobile stove, or *brazier*, made of tin that can be fired up with wood or charcoal wherever a meal is needed. Built to hold anything from a large *comal* or *tamal* steamer to a *cazuela* full of *mole*, these instant kitchens are a common sight on street corners or in the marketplace. Some foods are cooked directly over the coals, such as *tamales* of little white fish — the outer layers of the corn husks char and add a smoky taste to the fish.

Lime press: These ingenious squeezers are made to fit the small Mexican limes. Half a lime is placed in the bowl of the squeezer, cut-side down facing the holes, and pressed with the top half of the squeezer. Many newcomers try to squeeze the limes cut-side up, as the curved side of the lime seems to fit so snugly into the bowl, but they realize their mistake when they get a

nasty squirt in the eye!

Bean mashers: These are used for making well-fried beans *(frijoles refritos)*, and may be of metal (similar to a potato masher), or, more traditionally, of wood. As the cooked beans are being fried, they are mashed by moving the utensil in a circle up and down around the frying pan, until the mashed and drying beans begin to rise and fall in a single mass that pulls cleanly away from the bottom of the pan.

Molinillo: The *molinillo*, or chocolate *moulinet*, used to froth up hot chocolate, is made of wood with a hollow, carved bottom and several moving wooden rings around the base of the handle. As the handle is rolled quickly back and forth between the palms, the hot chocolate is whipped to a furious froth.

Any market worth its salt in Mexico will have a display of wooden and metal utensils that includes bean mashers, chocolate *molinillos*, flat paddles and round spoons — small enough for little table sauces or big enough to move mounds of *carnitas* (fried pork) or *mole* — and spoons with holes for frying or draining.

their traditional uses are now supplanted by the presence of public mills for making *nixtamal* (corn *masa*) and commercially processed chocolate.

Molcajete and tejolote: Made of the same volcanic rock as the *metate*, the roughness of a *molcajete* is excellent for grinding spices, and its bowl-like shape lends itself to both blending and serving table sauces. A true *guacamole* will

1. tamal steamer; 2. metal and wooden utensils; 3. metlapil; 4. metate; 5. wooden tortilla press; 6. tejolote; 7. molcajete; 8. metal tortilla press; 9. clay and metal comals; 10. lime press; 11. wood and metal bean masher; 12. wooden chocolate moulinet; 13. flour tortilla rolling pin; 14. anafre

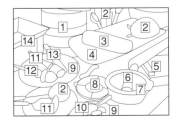

SAUCES AND SNACKS

Sauces and Snacks

THE WORD *ANTOJITO* OR SNACK COMES FROM THE SPANISH VERB *ANTOJAR*, MEANING TO PROVOKE A STRONG desire, and has come to mean the *botana*, or tidbits, usually salty, that Mexicans eat before meals, between meals, and, sometimes, instead of meals.

¶ *Antojitos* are often prepared at little street stands along sidewalks, or on charcoal braziers called *anafres*. *Antojitos* are also offered in restaurants and are prepared at home to eat before or at the beginning of meals.

¶ Almost all *antojitos* are made of corn *masa* (a dried-corn dough). The ones most frequently eaten are *tacos* (soft *tortillas* rolled around some kind of filling); *tamales* (see *Corn: The Foundation* {pages 48–61}); *quesadillas* (*tortillas* folded in half over cheese or other savory foods and fried or dry-toasted on a *comal* or cast-iron griddle); *sopes* (small *tortillas* with raised borders to retain their varied contents); *chalupas* (similar to *sopes* but usually flat); and hundreds of other *antojitos* that vary from region to region.

¶ Along with *tortas*—the Mexican version of a sandwich on a wheat-flour roll—*burritos* (large, wheat-flour *tortillas* folded around a meat filling) are one of the few *antojitos* not based on corn *masa*.

¶ A glance at the members of the *taco* family gives a good idea of the wide range covered by *antojitos*. The most common *tacos* are made of *carnitas* (pork boiled and fried in its own fat) and *chicharrón* (pork crackling). Another favorite is *tacos al pastor* made from thin, seasoned slices of pork threaded onto a vertical spit that revolves before an open flame. *Barbacoa* (mutton or goat cooked in maguey cactus arms in a hole in the ground), *rajas* (thin strips of roasted *poblano* chiles) cooked with potatoes, or onions and cream, and *chorizo* (Mexican sausage) are also popular. *Flautas*, or flutes, are long *tacos*, fried stiff, and filled with meat, chicken, cheese, or potato. *Tacos de canasta* or *tacos sudados* (basket or sweated *tacos*) are so called because after cooking they are wrapped in cloth inside a woven basket. They are often filled with potato, pork *chicharrón*, refried beans, or even *mole*.

¶ *Salsas* are chopped or blended sauces placed in little bowls on the Mexican table to be added to grilled (barbecued) meats, eggs, *tacos*, and many simple traditional foods. They should not be used with already sauced dishes such as *moles* and *pipianes*, as they would interfere with the already rich flavors.

¶ Although the most common ingredients for table sauces include chiles, tomatoes or green *tomatillos*, and onions, there are a large number of variations on this theme. The range of flavors will differ from region to region depending on the chiles available and the traditions of the local cuisine. The character of the sauce will depend on whether fresh or dried chiles are used, and whether these and the other ingredients are left raw or charred on a *comal* and cooked. Red sauces are made with tomatoes and green sauces with *tomatillos*. Other sauces have a liquid base of bitter orange, lime, or vinegar, and are more like a pickle.

Previous pages: Cheese-making is a cottage industry in the state of Oaxaca. The characteristic stringy texture is achieved when the curds are heated in water and stirred to make long threads which are twisted into balls or braids.

Opposite: Street vendor preparing fritangas, which are a popular deep-fried snack throughout Mexico.

SALSA DE JITOMATE ASADA

BROILED TOMATO SAUCE

This is a very basic and adaptable cooked tomato sauce. It is excellent on Pellizcadas *(see page 30), or with rice or beans. It is also delicious as an accompaniment to broiled (grilled) meat or chicken.*

1 lb (500 g) tomatoes
1 serrano *chile*
1 clove garlic, peeled
½ teaspoon salt, or to taste
1 tablespoon (½ fl oz/15 ml) vegetable oil

MAKES 1½ CUPS (12 oz/375 g)

❡ On a hot *comal*, cast-iron griddle, or broiler (grill), blister each tomato skin, turning on all sides, and toast the chile.
❡ Peel the tomatoes, cut the stem off the chile, and process together briefly in a food processor with the garlic and salt.
❡ In a small saucepan, heat the oil and cook the sauce until it thickens slightly, about 10 minutes. Serve at room temperature.

SALSA CRUDA DE GUADALAJARA

FRESH TOMATO SAUCE FROM GUADALAJARA

This sauce from Suzanne Scherer of Guadalajara is typical of the region but unusual because it does not have any chile in it. Serve it on tostadas *or flat fried* tortillas, *topped with refried beans, shredded chicken, grated onion, and cheese. It is also excellent served with* Tortitas de Papa *(see page 142).*

6 oz (185 g) tomatoes, peeled, seeded, and quartered
1 tablespoon (½ fl oz/15 ml) vinegar
3 tablespoons (1½ fl oz/45 ml) vegetable oil
1 tablespoon chopped onion
1 clove garlic
pinch dried oregano
¼ teaspoon salt, or to taste
freshly ground black pepper

MAKES ABOUT ¾ CUP (6 fl oz/185 ml)

❡ Place all the ingredients together in a food processor and coarsely process.
❡ Serve in an earthenware bowl at room temperature. This *salsa* will keep for several days if stored in the refrigerator.

Left: Broiled Tomato Sauce; center: Fresh Tomato Sauce from Guadalajara; top right: Drunken Chile Sauce with Beer

SALSA DE CHILE PASILLA Y CERVEZA TIPO BORRACHA

DRUNKEN CHILE SAUCE WITH BEER

Salsa borracha is indispensable as an accompaniment to the barbacoa of central Mexico. The authentic recipe is made with pulque, the freshly fermented juice of the agave cactus. But as it is almost impossible to find this ingredient outside Mexico, you can substitute flat beer or even tequila. This sauce goes well with any kind of grilled (barbecued) meat.

10 (2 oz/50 g) pasilla chiles
1 large clove garlic, chopped
½ cup (4 fl oz/125 ml) orange juice
½ cup (4 fl oz/125 ml) flat beer
2 tablespoons (1 fl oz/30 ml) olive oil
½ teaspoon salt, or to taste
2 oz (60 g) queso añejo or dry feta, crumbled

MAKES 1¾ CUPS (14 fl oz/440 ml)

❡ Using rubber gloves and scissors, cut the stems off the chiles, slit them open, and remove the seeds and veins. Hold the chiles briefly over a flame with metal tongs or under a broiler (grill) to toast on each side.
❡ Tear the chiles into pieces and put in a blender with the garlic, orange juice, and beer. Blend briefly so the sauce still has texture, then stir in the olive oil and salt.
❡ Put in a bowl and sprinkle with the cheese.

Top left: jitomate guaje (red plum tomato); top right: tomate/tomatillo chico (small green tomato); bottom left: tomate/tomatillo (green tomato); bottom right: jitomate bola (red tomato)

TOMATOES AND TOMATILLOS

One of Mexico's greatest contributions to the cuisines of the rest of the world is the tomato. It was, of course, the Italians who were the first to appreciate this fruit's culinary possibilities. For a long time, other European and northern American cultures grew it only as an ornamental plant, believing the fruit was toxic.

Red tomatoes: Both the large, round tomatoes (*jitomate bola*) and the smaller, oblong, plum tomatoes (*jitomate guaje*) are used in Mexico for salads, sauces, and casseroles. When not used raw, they are often blistered (charred) on a *comal* (cast-iron or clay griddle). This method of cooking loosens the skin for peeling and gives them a stronger flavor. The same results can be had by broiling (grilling) them until they are soft. To peel raw tomatoes, slit the skin with a sharp knife in four cuts from top to bottom. Drop them in boiling water for 10 seconds (1 minute at high altitudes) and the skin should peel easily.

Tomatillos: Also called *tomates* in Mexico, these are green tomatoes with a dry, green husk. They are not unripe tomatoes but another species altogether (*Physalis ixocarpa*); a closer biological relative is the cape gooseberry (*Physalis peruviana*). *Tomatillos* are hard to the touch when you buy them, and have a much higher acid content than tomatoes. Both large (2-inch/5-cm) and small (less than an inch/2.5-cm) *tomatillos* are sold in the market. They are usually a uniform yellow-green, but sometimes range from a darker green to yellow to a purplish variety. Remove the husk and wash the stickiness off the *tomatillo* before using it. *Tomatillos* are ground (minced) or blended raw in uncooked, green tomato sauces, or are boiled by just covering with water for about 15 minutes for a cooked sauce; they may also be broiled (grilled).

Salsa verde (green sauce) is served with anything from eggs and meat to fish and *tacos*. Its agreeable acidity makes it a piquant accompaniment to bland foods, and it's nicely balanced by a little heavy (double/thickened) cream or cheese on such dishes as *chilaquiles* and *enchiladas*.

Front: Tomato Sauce; back: Cooked Green Sauce

SALSA DE JITOMATE

TOMATO SAUCE

This tomato sauce contains no chile and has the unusual addition of basil to flavor it—a pungent herb seldom used for cooking in Mexico. This sauce is delicious served with Chiles Poblanos Rellenos de Queso y Envueltos en Pasta Hojaldrada *(see page 106).*

6 tomatoes, skinned, seeded, and quartered
3 tablespoons (1½ fl oz/45 g) vegetable oil
½ onion, sliced in half moons
2 allspice berries
2 black peppercorns
½ teaspoon salt, or to taste
1 bay leaf
1 sprig thyme
1 tablespoon fresh basil leaves, finely sliced

MAKES 1½ cups (12 oz/375 g)

❧ Chop the tomatoes coarsely in a food processor. Heat the oil in a saucepan and sauté the onion until translucent. Add the tomato, allspice, peppercorns, and salt. Cook over medium heat for 5 minutes, stirring occasionally. Add the bay leaf and thyme and simmer until the oil rises to the surface, about 10 minutes. Before serving, remove the herbs and spices and discard. Add the sliced basil and serve.

SALSA VERDE COCIDA

COOKED GREEN SAUCE

A traditional favorite, salsa verde is served as a condiment in most Mexican restaurants to accompany many dishes and snacks such as sopes, quesadillas, *and* flautas.

10 fresh or canned tomatillos (11½ oz/360 g)
1 or 2 serrano *chiles*
3 cups (24 fl oz/750 ml) boiling water
1 small onion, chopped
1 clove garlic
1 tablespoon cilantro (fresh coriander), minced (finely chopped)
½ teaspoon salt, or to taste

MAKES 1 CUP (8 fl oz/250 ml)

❧ Cook the *tomatillos* and chiles in the water until soft, about 20 minutes. (If using canned *tomatillos*, cook only the chiles.) Drain, reserving the liquid.
❧ Combine the *tomatillos*, chile, onion, garlic, cilantro, and salt in a food processor. Process briefly with some of the reserved liquid until thinned but still coarse.
❧ Can be refrigerated for up to 3 days but it will become gelatinous, so reheat to liquefy before serving at room temperature.

SALSA DE TOMATE VERDE CRUDO

UNCOOKED GREEN SAUCE

This is one of the great table sauces of Mexico. The crisp, fresh flavors of the tomatillos, cilantro (fresh coriander), *and chiles make a wonderful accompaniment to* tacos de carnitas *or grilled (barbecued) meat. One of the most simple ways to enjoy it is in a hot tortilla with nothing more than a little* queso panela *or fresh farmer's cheese. Canned* tomatillos *cannot be substituted in this recipe.*

12 oz (350 g) fresh tomatillos, chopped
1 onion, chopped
½ oz (15 g) cilantro (fresh coriander) leaves
3 serrano *chiles* (⅓ oz/10 g)
½ teaspoon salt, or to taste

MAKES 2 CUPS (16 fl oz/500 ml)

❧ Put the *tomatillos* in a food processor, then add the remaining ingredients. Pulse briefly so that the texture remains coarse.
❧ Set aside for 1 hour before serving to let the flavors meld. The sauce can be refrigerated for up to 3 days.

SALSA NEGRA

BLACK SAUCE MADE WITH CHIPOTLE CHILES

This sauce, which is also known as salsa de chile seco, *is a specialty of Veracruz, where* chipotle *chiles are called "chile seco" (dry chiles). It is delicious with dishes such as* Infladas de Frijol *(see page 70), but it is very spicy, so watch out!*

8 oz (250 g) chipotle *chiles*
1 cup (8 fl oz/250 ml) water
4 cloves garlic, peeled

½ teaspoon salt, or to taste
6 tablespoons (3 fl oz/90 ml) vegetable oil

MAKES 2 CUPS (16 fl oz/500 ml)

❡ Toast the chiles on a hot *comal* or cast-iron griddle, then soak them in hot water until soft. Remove the seeds and veins. Puree the chiles in a blender with the garlic and a little fresh water to make a thick paste. Add the salt.

❡ Heat the oil in a frying pan over medium heat and fry the sauce, stirring regularly, until it bubbles. Allow to cool.

❡ Serve at room temperature in a bowl. It will keep in the refrigerator for 3 to 5 days.

Front: Uncooked Green Sauce; back: Black Sauce Made with Chipotle Chiles

Front: Uncooked Mexican Salsa; back: Guanajuato-style Guacamole

SALSA MEXICANA CRUDA PICADA

UNCOOKED MEXICAN SALSA

Green, white, and red like the Mexican flag, this salsa is the most popular of them all. Although the recipe is subject to some regional variations, the name of the salsa is always the same, except in the Yucatán, where the Mayan name is x-ni-pec, or "dog's snout"—because it is made hot enough there to make your nose run.

1 lb (500 g) firm tomatoes, chopped
1 small onion, minced (finely chopped)
4 small serrano chiles, minced (finely chopped), and 2 deveined for less spiciness

½ teaspoon salt, or to taste
½ cup (4 fl oz/125 ml) cold water
8 sprigs cilantro (fresh coriander), chopped

SERVES 6–8

¶ Mix all of the ingredients together just before serving; everything except the cilantro can be prepared ahead of time.
¶ To prepare the *salsa* as it's made in northern Mexico, coarsely chop the tomatoes and mix with a minced (finely chopped) garlic clove. Add the water mixed with a little lime or lemon juice.
¶ For Yucatecan-style *salsa*, add lightly toasted yellow chiles and replace the water with orange juice; you can also add a dash of olive oil.

GUACAMOLE GUANAJUATENSE

GUANAJUATO-STYLE GUACAMOLE

In this recipe, devised by Claudia Alfaro de Petriccioli, fruits and vegetables are combined with the avocado, and the pomegranate seeds add a touch of color. This recipe, from La Cocina Regional de Mexico *published by the Bancomer Volunteer Group, has been translated with the kind permission of María Eugenia R. E. de Guajardo.*

2 ripe avocados, pitted and skinned
1 clove garlic, minced (finely chopped)
4 guavas, seeded and cut into ½-inch (1-cm) cubes
2 firm peaches, skinned and cut into ½-inch (1-cm) cubes
1 cup (5½ oz/170 g) cucumbers, minced (finely chopped)
1 onion, minced (finely chopped)
3 tablespoons minced (finely chopped) cilantro (fresh coriander)
1 teaspoon salt, or to taste
seeds from 1 large pomegranate, for garnish

MAKES 2 CUPS (16 oz/500 g)

❡ Put the avocados and garlic in a glass bowl and mash with a fork. Add all the remaining ingredients except the pomegranate seeds and mix well. Add more salt to taste, and garnish with the pomegranate seeds.

❡ Use the *guacamole* to stuff roasted, peeled green chiles or serve with pieces of *chicharrón* (pork crackling) or *tortillas.*

Chapulines (*grasshoppers*)

INSECTS

The variety of insects enjoyed as a delicacy in Mexico is as astonishing to foreigners today as it was to the Spanish during the conquest, or to travelers in subsequent periods of history. Francisco Hernández, a research doctor who lived in New Spain from 1571–1577, wrote that the Indians "don't disdain fried crickets or ants, and consider delicacies many things which no other human being in the world would eat." When confronted by the number of strange insects and animals in a Mexico City market in 1799, Simón Bolívar is quoted in Gabriel García Márquez's novel *A General in his Labyrinth* as having exclaimed, "They eat everything that walks!"

Today, maguey worms (*gusanos de maguey*), from the agave salmiana cactus, and the especially prized ant larvae (*escamoles*) are served, at a price, in the best restaurants, when they are in season in spring. The worms are crunchy when fried, and are served with avocado and *salsa* to make *tacos*. These ones are white, but there is also a smaller, red variety, which is similarly delicious. *Escamoles* are now often sautéed in butter with a little minced (finely chopped) onion and herbs and served in a small, clay bowl as a first course.

Boiled or fried crickets (*chapulines*) are sold year-round in the markets of Oaxaca, ready to be eaten like peanuts or tossed in a *taco* with a *pasilla* chile sauce. Honey ants (*hormigas mieleras*) from Hidalgo or Oaxaca are coaxed from their hills with a resinous stick; their captor then pinches off the enlarged, honey-filled abdomen, and eats it or brings the ants to market to be sold alive. Also often eaten alive are the small beetles, *jumiles*, from Cuautla (Morelos) or Taxco (Guerrero). Sold wrapped in a leaf or small paper package, they are scooped into a *tortilla* with lemon and salt or *salsa* and eaten quickly before they escape. They are also fried or, like maguey worms, toasted and ground with chile and salt as a condiment to sprinkle on food.

A great source of protein to the Aztecs, insects are often said to be the food of the future. If that is the case, Mexico will certainly be in the forefront.

Front: Guacamole; back: Coxcatlán Sauce

SALSA DE COXCATLÁN

COXCATLÁN SAUCE

This sauce, from southeastern Puebla, is traditionally prepared in a molcajete *(grinding bowl), although here it is processed lightly in a food processor. Coxcatlán sauce is usually served with* barbacoa *(see page 182), but it is also delicious with beef, chicken, or any antojito.*

10 oz (315 g) tomatoes
1 serrano *chile, stem removed*
1 clove garlic, minced (finely chopped)
½ teaspoon salt, or to taste
2 tablespoons chopped cilantro (fresh coriander)

MAKES 1 CUP (8 fl oz/250 ml)

❡ Put the tomatoes and chile in a saucepan and add just enough water to cover. Boil until the tomato skins separate easily from the flesh, then drain and discard water.
❡ Combine the tomatoes, chile, and garlic in a food processor, and process for a few seconds only; the sauce should be coarse.
❡ Pour into a bowl, season with the salt, and stir in the cilantro. Serve immediately.

GUACAMOLE

GUACAMOLE

This is a very typical guacamole, *and perhaps the best known, which can be served with rice, carnitas, chicharrón, tacos, or totopos. There are many other versions, which might include chopped tomato or* Salsa de Tomate Verde Crudo *(see page 24). Because avocados are often expensive, here's a tip for "stretching" them: Boil 2 (6½-oz/200-g) zucchini (courgettes) with a pinch of salt until tender and process in a food processor until smooth. The puree not only increases the volume, but also lends a more intense green color.*

3 ripe avocados (5 oz/150 g each), pitted and skinned
1 small onion, minced (finely chopped)
1 tablespoon coarsely chopped cilantro (fresh coriander)
2 serrano *chiles, or to taste, deveined and chopped*
¼ teaspoon salt, or to taste

MAKES 1½ CUPS (12 oz/375 g)

❡ Place the avocados in a bowl and mash them with a fork. Add the remaining ingredients (reserving some onion and chile for garnish, if desired) and mix well. Serve immediately or cover with plastic wrap for up to 1 hour before serving.

SALSA DE CHILE PIQUÍN VERDE

GREEN PIQUÍN CHILE SAUCE

In northern Mexico these little, almost round chiles are called chile piquín, *whereas they are called* chiltepines *in the northwest. Furthermore, the name* chile piquín *also refers to another type of equally small chile that is slightly longer and thinner and sold dried almost exclusively. This is a fiery* salsa! *If you like chiles and can find green* piquín, *you will enjoy this favorite which comes from Anita Domene of Monterrey.*

½ cup (2 oz/60 g) green piquín *chiles, stems removed*
½ teaspoon salt, or to taste
4 tablespoons (2 fl oz/60 ml) lime or lemon juice
¾ teaspoon olive oil
1 small onion, minced (finely chopped)

MAKES ⅓ CUP (2½ fl oz/75 ml)

❡ Grind the chiles and salt in a *molcajete* or mortar, then rinse the bottom and sides with the juice.
❡ Pour the mixture into an earthenware bowl, add the oil and onion, and mix well.
❡ Serve on the table to accompany your favorite barbecued meats.

Front: Green Piquín Chile Sauce; back: Dried Piquín Chile and Persimmon Sauce

SALSA DE CHILE PIQUÍN SECO Y PERSIMO

DRIED PIQUÍN CHILE AND PERSIMMON SAUCE

You should use a stone molcajete *to make this sauce; you can also use a metallic mortar, although the texture will not be quite the same. If you enjoy the flavor of chile with fruit, you will be delighted by this combination of* piquín *chiles and persimmon. It is often spooned onto freshly made* tortillas *to make* tacos.

1 small clove garlic, toasted and skinned
¼ teaspoon salt, or to taste
7 dried piquín *chiles*
1 (8 oz/250 g) ripe persimmon, peeled and seeded
MAKES ¾ CUP (6 fl oz/185 ml)

❡ Grind the garlic with the salt and chiles in a *molcajete* or with a mortar and pestle.
❡ Add the persimmon and continue grinding, being sure to thoroughly mash the hard parts of the fruit.
❡ Serve in a *salsa* bowl with *tortillas*.

TAQUITOS DE REQUESÓN EN TORTILLAS DE HARINA

RICOTTA CHEESE TACOS MADE WITH FLOUR TORTILLAS

An invention of the creative cook Berta Legaspi de Arroyo, these taquitos are excellent when served with drinks as a botana, or hors d'oeuvre. The wild herb, epazote, adds a particularly pungent taste, but if it's not available in your area, you can just omit it.

5 oz (155 g) requesón or ricotta cheese
2 teaspoons minced (finely chopped) serrano chiles
2 tablespoons minced (finely chopped) epazote, optional
½ teaspoon salt, or to taste
6 (5½-inch/14-cm) Tortillas de Harina (see page 53)
2 tablespoons (1 fl oz/30 ml) vegetable oil

MAKES 6 TACOS OR 18 TAQUITOS

❧ In a bowl, mix together the *requesón*, chiles, *epazote*, and salt.

❧ Heat the *tortillas* briefly on a *comal* or cast-iron griddle to make them pliable.

❧ Spoon one-sixth of the cheese mixture onto each *tortilla* and spread it in a straight line near one edge, being careful to keep it slightly clear of the edge so that none can spill out or burn during frying.

❧ Each *tortilla* should then be carefully rolled tightly into a cigar-like shape, and secured firmly with a toothpick along the side.

❧ Heat the oil in a frying pan and brown 3 *tacos* at a time, turning on each side. Drain on paper towels to remove any excess oil.

❧ Remove the toothpick, cut off the ends, and serve either whole or cut into thirds.

❧ The *tacos* can be fried up to 2 hours before serving and reheated in the oven.

PELLIZCADAS

MASA SNACKS

Pellizcada literally means "pinch," as the edge and cen-ter of these thickly formed tortillas are pinched together to form a ridge to contain the sauce. Although they can be made larger, these ones are bite-size. Serve them with Salsa de Jitomate Asada (see page 22), or any green or red chile sauce, and top with a little minced (finely chopped) onion or shredded cheese.

CHICHARRONES DE HARINA
(Fried "pork skin")
These fried pasta snacks are eaten like peanuts in Mexico. They are sold as thin, hard, translucent pasta in a myriad of shapes, from squares to wheels. When deep-fried, they puff up and become crunchy and light. Called flour chicharrones for their similarity to pork crackling, once fried, they can be eaten fresh or packaged, with or without a sprinkling of hot chile sauce.

½ lb (250 g) masa harina
1½ cups (12 fl oz/375 ml) warm water, approximately
½ teaspoon salt, or to taste
3 tablespoons (1½ fl oz/45 g) vegetable oil
1 cup (8 fl oz/250 ml) Salsa de Jitomate Asada (see page 22)
1 small onion, minced (finely chopped)

MAKES 35 x 2-inch (5-cm) PELLIZCADAS

❧ In a bowl, mix the *masa harina* with the water, form into a ball, and allow to rest at room temperature for 10 minutes.

❧ Divide into little balls about ⅓ oz (10 g) each. Using your hands, flatten the balls into patties approximately 2 inches (5 cm) thick.

❧ Heat an ungreased *comal* or a cast-iron griddle over medium heat. Place several patties in the pan at once.

❧ Turn after 1 minute, then turn again as soon as the bottom starts to become speckled with brown flecks.

❧ Turn once more to toast the other side again slightly before removing from the pan. The total cooking time should not exceed 3 minutes.

❧ The side with the brown flecks (called the side with *la telita*, or the thin skin) is the side you should pinch. As soon as the patties are cool enough to handle (but still warm), pinch up the sides to form walls and pinch a ridge in the middle of each patty.

❧ If desired, the patties can be frozen in a plastic bag at this point, then brought to room temperature before proceeding.

❧ To serve, put the *pellizcadas* on a hot *comal* or cast-iron griddle. Put several drops of oil on each and heat until the oil starts to sizzle.

❧ Spoon about 1 teaspoon of the *Salsa de Jitomate Asada* on each. Remove to a serving plate and sprinkle with a little of the minced onion.

❧ Serve immediately.

Front: Ricotta Cheese Tacos Made with Flour Tortillas; back: Masa Snacks

Savory Christmas Rolls

TORTAS DE NAVIDAD

SAVORY CHRISTMAS ROLLS

From Laura Esquivel's famous book Like Water for Chocolate, *this recipe features baguettes filled with an unusual stuffing of sardines and spicy sausage. Although this recipe calls for a baguette, you can substitute small crusty rolls. It is a custom in the north of Mexico to eat these during the Christmas season.*

12 oz (350 g) chorizo or kielbasa sausage, skinned and roughly chopped

1 x 15-oz (425-g) can sardines packed in tomato sauce or 3 x 4½-oz (125-g) cans, with 3 tablespoons of the tomato sauce reserved

2 onions, minced (finely chopped)

1 x 4-oz (125-g) can pickled serrano chiles, or jalapeño chiles, drained and chopped

1 teaspoon salt, or to taste

1 baguette, 12 inches (30 cm) long

MAKES 15 x 2-inch (5-cm) SLICES

❡ Fry the *chorizo* over a low heat until cooked, being careful not to brown. The fat it renders is part of the recipe, but if there is an excessive amount, discard some of it.

❡ Remove the skin and bones from the sardines. Mix them with the reserved tomato sauce, the *chorizo*, onion, chiles, and salt.

❡ Cut the baguette in half lengthwise and hollow it out slightly. Fill the bottom half with the mixture and cover, if desired, with the top half of the baguette.

❡ Wrap in a cloth and let stand overnight in a cool place so the fat from the *chorizo* is soaked into the bread. If you are in a hurry, a few hours will suffice.

❡ To serve, slice the baguette into 2-inch (5-cm) pieces. Serve on its own as an *antojito* or with a salad to make a light lunch or dinner.

TOSTADITAS DE CAVIAR

LITTLE CAVIAR TOSTADAS

This dish is a very elegant hors d'oeuvre from La Noria Restaurant in Monterrey, Nuevo León. It is important that the tortillas be cut very small so the tostadas are bite-size. The combination of beans and black caviar is marvellous.

5 *corn* tortillas
6 *tablespoons (3 fl oz/90 ml) vegetable oil*
1 *cup (8 oz/250 g)* Frijoles Refritos *(see page 150)*
½ *cup (4 oz/125 g)* requesón *or ricotta cheese*
Sevruga, or any good black caviar

MAKES 20

❧ Cut the *tortillas* into approximately 1½-inch (4-cm) circles to make 20 circles.
❧ Heat 5 tablespoons of the oil in a large frying pan over medium heat and fry the *tortillas* until crisp. Drain on paper towels.
❧ Heat the remaining oil in a separate frying pan and fry the beans. If they are too thick, add a little bean broth or water to make a good spreading consistency. Spread 1 teaspoon of beans on each *tostada*, then add ½ teaspoon of the *requesón* on top.
❧ Garnish with caviar, and serve immediately.

TACOS RELLENOS DE HONGOS

MUSHROOM TACOS

In Mexico, these mushrooms are commonly served in a cazuela accompanied by warm tortillas to make tacos. Here they are served already wrapped in the tortillas.

3 *tablespoons vegetable oil*
2 *cloves garlic, minced (finely chopped)*
1½ *lb (750 g) cultivated mushrooms, wiped and sliced*
1 *teaspoon salt, or to taste*
2 *fresh* jalapeño *chiles, cut into strips*
1 *tablespoon minced (finely chopped) epazote leaves, optional*
12 *warm corn* tortillas

MAKES 12 TACOS

❧ Heat the oil in a frying pan over medium heat and sauté the garlic, but do not burn.
❧ Add the mushrooms and salt and raise the heat. Stir the mushrooms occasionally until they release their liquid.
❧ Add the chiles and cook until almost all the mushroom liquid is evaporated. Stir in the *epazote* and then divide the mixture equally among the *tortillas*.
❧ Wrap the *tortilla* around the mixture, and serve.

Bottom left: Little Caviar Tostadas; top right: Mushroom Tacos

THE CHEESES OF MEXICO

Cheeses, like all dairy products, were incorporated into Mexican cooking after the Spanish conquest, when these Europeans introduced cows and other domesticated animals to the New World. They are generally added to dishes as a neutral note, a backdrop to the stronger flavors of chile, *chorizo* (Mexican sausage), or the pungent herb *epazote*. They also balance the acidity of a *tomatillo* (green tomato) sauce. Cheeses are usually accompanied by cream or are a subtle complement to beans.

Perhaps their use as a neutral food in Mexican cuisine is why most of the cheeses are bland, fresh, white cheeses or mild, semisoft cheeses. An aged *Chihuahua*, on the other hand, has a wonderful, quite sharp flavor, rather like a good medium-sharp Cheddar, but it is more often sold as a milder cheese before it has matured. Fresh cheeses and the aged white cheese *añejo* are used for crumbling onto a dish before it is served. *Oaxaca* cheese is a delicious melting cheese made by the same technique as mozzarella. *Chihuahua* and *Manchego*-type cheeses are the only light yellow ones, also used young, mostly for topping and melting.

Nowadays, several French and other foreign cheeses are being successfully produced in Mexico, such as goat's cheese, camembert, and brie. Goat's cheese is a natural addition to Mexican *antojitos*, because it is similar in texture to the fresh cheese that is traditionally used.

The terminology in Mexican cheeses is very confusing, as so many of the names resemble each other and are often interchanged. This is certainly true for *queso fresco*, *panela*, and *ranchero*.

Queso fresco (fresh cheese): Fresh cheese is made from molded, fresh, white, salted curds. Whereas the French *fromage frais* has a creamy, spoonable texture, Mexican

(20 cm) in diameter. At its best, it can be like a soft mozzarella, tasty when eaten fresh and sliced; at its worst, it is watery and rubbery. If recipes call for it to be sliced to eat fresh or for melting, substitute a mozzarella. Otherwise, see the substitutions for *queso fresco*.

Queso ranchero (ranch cheese): *Queso ranchero* is a fresh cheese that has been ground (minced) to break up the curds before being remolded. It is usually found in village markets in small rounds about 1 inch (2.5 cm) high and 4 inches (10 cm) in diameter, often with a leaf wrapped around them. Use the same substitutions as for *queso fresco* or use a shredded (grated) mozzarella.

Queso de Chiapas (cheese from Chiapas): This is an acidic white cheese made in *Chiapas*. The texture is somewhere between *queso fresco* and *queso añejo*, and it is sold in rectangles covered with red or yellow celophane. Substitute Italian cacciotta or feta cheese.

Bola de Ocosingo (cheese from Ocosingo, Chiapas): Named after the town that produces it, this cheese is made in a small, oblong round that is light yellow. The rind is semihard, while the interior is soft.

Queso añejo (aged cheese): This is rather a misleading name, as *queso añejo* is more like a fresh cheese that has been well salted, pressed, and dried, rather than matured. It comes in large, tall, white rounds, sometimes with a red dusting of chile powder on the outside. Like fresh cheese, it is used for crumbling (or shredding/grating) onto dishes before they are served. It is drier and saltier, though, so the taste is stronger, and it is generally a question of personal preference which is

fresh cheese is molded to solidify it and has a texture that can easily be crumbled by hand. It is mostly used for crumbling onto dishes as they are served: *enchiladas*, beans, and *antojitos*. Substitute farmer's cheese, an Italian cacciotta, or fresh bel paese.

Panela: Similar to *queso fresco*, *panela* is often lower in fat and is molded in a basket that leaves its imprint on the cheese. It comes in soft rounds about 6 inches (15 cm) high and 8 inches

used. *Queso añejo* is sometimes called *queso cotija*. Substitute Italian cacciotta or a dry feta.

Requesón (ricotta cheese): This is the Mexican equivalent of ricotta, made from the whey left over from milk after making cheese. It has a spreadable, grainy texture and is usually sold loose by the spoonful, although in Toluca, it is pressed into round molds. It is used where a spreadable texture is required and is very common as a filling for *tlacoyos* (a street *antojito* made of *masa* in a large, oblong shape, rather like a small sandal, or *huarache*—another name for them).

Queso de Oaxaca (Oaxaca cheese): This cheese, made in the state of Oaxaca (otherwise referred to as *tipo Oaxaca*, or *Oaxaca* style) is a lovely, stringy white cheese made in the same way as mozzarella. After the curds are formed, they are heated in water and stirred to make long threads, which are then pulled and formed into braids or wrapped into balls. *Oaxaca* cheese has a pleasant saltiness; it should be shredded (grated) by hand, much like shredding chicken, so the texture of the fibers remains intact. The chewy elasticity and bite are very satisfying. It is excellent for melting and is usually the cheese preferred for *quesadillas*. Commercial brands are often inferior to the fresh cheese. You can substitute mozzarella.

Asadero (broiling/grilling cheese): Similar to *Oaxaca* cheese, it gets its name from its use for melting directly on a flat grill for eating. It is also sold braided.

Queso Tipo Manchego (Manchego-style cheese): This cheese is considerably less aged and developed in flavor than its Spanish

counterpart. It is a light yellow, semisoft cheese that is used for slicing, cubing, or melting. Its taste is very mild—a good foil for the heat of a *poblano* chile when used for stuffing or when added to a *chile poblano* soup. Substitute fontina, Tilsit, bel paese, or American meunster (a mild cheese, unlike the European meunster).

Chihuahua: The technique for making this cheese comes from the Mennonite farming community of German descent, which settled in the northern state of Chihuahua. This semihard, light yellow cheese is either pressed in large wheels (about 6 x 18 inches/15 x 45 cm), which form a skin and are excellent for ageing, or into rectangular logs. It is not uncommon in Mexico City to see male Mennonite farmers dressed in overalls, or the women in longish skirts with scarves around their heads, selling these logs on the street. *Chihuahua* cheese is slightly stronger than *tipo Manchego*, although the flavor depends on the ageing, and they are often used interchangeably. Substitute a mild Cheddar or any of the cheeses suggested for *tipo Manchego*.

1. queso fresco (Mexican fresh cheese); 2. panela; 3. bola de Ocosingo, Chiapas (cheese from Ocosingo); 4. queso añejo (aged cheese); 5. requesón (ricotta cheese); 6. queso de Oaxaca (Oaxaca cheese); 7. queso tipo Manchego (Manchego-style cheese); 8. chihuahua cheese; 9. queso añejo with chile powder

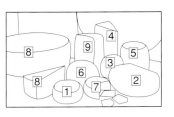

TOSTADAS DE QUESO DE CABRA CON HIERBAS FRITAS

GOAT'S CHEESE TOSTADAS WITH DEEP-FRIED HERBS

Like the Tostadas de Atun Ahumada *below, this recipe from El Tajín Restaurant uses* tostadas *made with flour tortillas.* Goat's cheese is a recent addition to the cheeses successfully produced in Mexico. Its smooth, slightly acidic flavor is subtly set off by the crisp, aromatic fried herbs in this recipe by the owner and chef Alicia De'Angeli. If the herbs used are not available, any combination of fragrant fresh herbs could be substituted.

4 tablespoons (2 fl oz/60 ml) plus 4 cups (1qt/1 l) oil
10 x 4 in/10 cm Tortillas de Harina *(see page 53)*
5-oz (155-g) mixture of chopped epazote, hoja santa, *parsley, and cilantro (fresh coriander); and minced (finely chopped) leek*
⅔ cup (5½ oz/170 g) Frijoles Refritos *(see page 150)*
⅔ cup (5½ oz/170 g) Guacamole *(see page 28)*
14 oz (400 g) fresh goat's cheese, at room temperature, finely sliced

MAKES 10

❡ Heat the 4 tablespoons of oil in a frying pan and fry the *tortillas* until crisp and golden. Drain on paper towels and set aside.
❡ Heat the 4 cups of oil in a deep-fryer. Make sure the herbs and leek are dry, then deep-fry them for just a few seconds until crisp. Drain and set aside.
❡ On each *tortilla*, spread approximately 1 tablespoon of *Frijoles Refritos*, 1 tablespoon of *Guacamole*, and the sliced cheese.
❡ Top with a sprinkling of the herb mixture and serve immediately.

TOSTADAS DE ATÚN AHUMADO

SMOKED TUNA TOSTADAS

These tostadas *were created by Alicia De'Angeli, the chef of the Tajín Restaurant located in the southern part of Mexico City. They give us a good idea of how traditional recipes are being transformed subtly to make them lighter. This recipe uses two ingredients now being produced in Mexico that have become very popular recently—goat's cheese and smoked tuna.*

4 tablespoons (2 fl oz/60 ml) vegetable oil
10 (5 in/10 cm) Tortillas de Harina *(see page 53)*
3 tablespoons (1½ fl oz/45 ml) olive oil
8 oz (250 g) smoked tuna fish, or any other smoked fish, shredded
1 cup (8 fl oz/250 ml) Salsa Mexicana Cruda Picada *(see page 26)*
½ cup (4 oz/125 g) mayonnaise
1 canned chipotle *chile*
5 romaine (cos) lettuce leaves, shredded

MAKES 10

❡ Heat the vegetable oil in a frying pan until hot, and fry the *tortillas* until crisp and golden. Drain on paper towels to remove any excess oil and set aside.
❡ Mix the tuna with the *Salsa Mexicana Cruda Picada* and the olive oil, and set aside.
❡ Put the mayonnaise and the chile in a food processor and process until smooth.
❡ Spread the mayonnaise mixture on each *tortilla*, then add the tuna mixture, and sprinkle with shredded lettuce.

CREMA ENTERA
Cream

Crema entera (cream) in Mexico is thick and slightly acidic. It is dribbled onto enchiladas or tostadas, used as a cooling foil to the highly acidic tomatillo sauce, and spread on tortas—the Mexican sandwich—instead of mayonnaise or butter. The fresh cream found in small villages or sold suelta (loose) in the markets is often superior to the commercial varieties sold in little containers. What is sold as crema ácida, or sour cream, is more acidic than crema entera but less so than sour cream as we know it. The best substitute for crema entera is a heavy (double/thickened) cream, while crema ácida can find a counterpart in a commercial crème fraîche or even a well-stirred light sour cream. Beat heavy cream just enough to slightly thicken it but allowing it to remain fluid enough to be drizzled on top of the required dish. A more recent addition in the marketplace is crema para batir, which literally translates as "cream to be beaten"; substitute it with a light whipping cream that doesn't contain any thickening agent. Generally, for any dish that calls for cream to be dribbled over the top, use an aerated light sour cream or heavy cream; for soups and so on, stir in crème fraîche, which can easily be made at home by mixing together 4 parts of heavy cream with 2 parts of either sour cream or buttermilk, and left to rest at room temperature for several hours before use.

Top: Goat's Cheese Tostadas with Deep-fried Herbs; bottom: Smoked Tuna Tostadas

FLAUTAS

FLUTES

These tortillas are called "flutes" because of their long, thin, cylindrical shape. They are usually made with special oblong tortillas, but the same effect can be achieved by slightly overlapping two small tortillas. Flautas are one of Mexico's most popular snacks, sold by street vendors all over the country.

8 oblong 7- x 4-inch (18- x 10-cm) tortillas *or*
    16 round (5-inch/12-cm) tortillas *slightly overlapping*
    to make 8 sets 7 inches (18 cm) long
1 cup (8 oz/250 g) of any one of the following: cooked,
    shredded chicken; ricotta, drained; mashed potatoes; or
    Frijoles Refritos (see page 150)
6 tablespoons (3 fl oz/90 ml) vegetable oil
½ cup (4 fl oz/125 ml) any cooked red or green
    tomato sauce
½ cup (4 fl oz/125 ml) heavy (double/thickened) cream
4 tablespoons queso añejo *or* feta cheese, grated

MAKES 8

❡ Heat the *tortillas* briefly on a hot *comal* or a cast-iron griddle to make them more pliable.
❡ Place a tablespoon of either the chicken, ricotta, mashed potatoes, or *Frijoles Refritos* near the long edge of each, and roll the *tortillas* up tightly so they don't open. (You can use a toothpick to secure them if necessary.)
❡ Heat the oil in a frying pan and fry the *flautas* on high heat on all sides, 2 or 3 at a time, for about 1 minute or until lightly golden.
❡ Drain the *flautas* on paper towels to remove any excess oil, and put on plates or a platter.
❡ Spoon some sauce over the *flautas,* top with some cream, and sprinkle with cheese.
❡ Serve immediately; *flautas* are passed around on a platter, and eaten with the fingers.

GORDITAS DE CHILE COLORADO

THICK MASA ROUNDS WITH RED CHILES

In Saltillo, in the north of Mexico, where ancho *chiles* are called "chiles colorados," chile-spiced *masa is used* to make tortillas *that are dipped in the* ancho *chile* sauce, rolled up, and topped with chopped onion and crumbled fresh cheese. Here it is used to make gorditas, *or* thick tortilla cakes. They can be eaten either for a late breakfast or as a snack before lunch.

For the *gorditas*:
1½ oz (45 g) ancho *chiles, toasted, with stems, seeds, and*
    veins removed
8 oz (250 g) prepared corn tortilla masa (see Tortillas
    de Maiz page 53 and halve quantities)
1 tablespoon all-purpose (plain) flour
½ teaspoon salt, or to taste
For the sauce:
2½ oz (75 g) ancho *chiles, toasted, with stems, seeds, and*
    veins removed
1 small onion, chopped
1 cup (8 fl oz/250 ml) water
2 teaspoons vegetable oil
½ teaspoon salt, or to taste
For the topping:
1 small onion, minced (finely chopped)
½ cup (3½ oz/100 g) queso panela, *farmer's cheese, or*
    cacciotta, crumbled

MAKES 16 GORDITAS

❡ To make the *gorditas:* Cook the chiles in boiling water to cover until very soft, approximately 5 minutes. Strain and grind the chiles in a *molcajete* or mortar to make a smooth paste.
❡ Mix together the *tortilla masa*, flour, salt, and chile paste until uniform in texture and color. Divide into 16 little balls and flatten to make thick *tortillas* about 3 inches (8 cm) in diameter.
❡ Cook the *tortillas* on a *comal* or a cast-iron

TOSTADAS Y TOTOPOS

Tostadas *and* totopos *are fried* tortillas *in various shapes and sizes.* Tostadas *are whole, flat-fried* tortillas, *usually served with a variety of different ingredients layered on top as a first course or* merienda *(light supper).* Tostadas *can vary in size from 2½ to 5 inches (6 to 12 cm) in diameter.* Totopos *are* tortillas *cut into different shapes and fried. Triangles,* tortillas *cut into eighths, are served with* Frijoles Refritos *(see page 150) or* Guacamole *(see page 28), and are used like a spoon to scoop up the mixture. Strips are the main ingredient in tortilla soup, while little ½-inch (1 cm) squares or more elegant small shapes cut with a small cookie cutter are often strewn over the surface to adorn hot or cold soups. For 6 tortillas, use about ¼ cup (2 fl oz/60 ml) vegetable oil. Fry the* tostadas *one at a time in a small frying pan over high heat. Press them down with a metal spatula to keep them flat, turning them over a few times until a pale golden-brown, then drain. They are also sold ready-made. Cut* totopos *to desired shape before frying and cook them in small batches, turning constantly with a slotted spoon; drain before serving.*

griddle over low heat, a few at a time, for approximately 2 minutes a side, or until flecked with dark patches.

❡ As soon as possible after removing from the pan, place a *tortilla* with the *"telita,"* or second side that was toasted, facing up, and pinch up the edge to form a ridge about ¼ inch (6 mm) deep. Cover with a cloth to keep warm.

❡ For the sauce: Place the chiles, onion, and water in a blender and blend until completely smooth. Add salt to taste and mix thoroughly.

❡ Heat the oil in a small saucepan and fry the sauce over medium heat, stirring occasionally for 3 to 4 minutes until slightly thickened. Use hot.

❡ To serve, reheat the *gorditas* on a hot *comal* or cast-iron griddle. Spread 1 tablespoon of sauce on the pinched side of each, sprinkle with 1 teaspoon of onion, and some crumbled cheese.

❡ Put the *gorditas* on a platter and serve immediately.

Left: Flutes; right: Thick Masa Rounds with Red Chiles

QUESADILLAS DE TINGA

MEATLESS TINGA QUESADILLAS

Tinga, *a common dish in Puebla, is a mixture of tomatoes and* chipotle *chiles usually made with shredded pork or* chorizo. *This meatless version comes from Coxcatlán, Puebla, and can be a filling for* tortas *and* tostadas *too.*

¾ cup (6 fl oz/85 ml) vegetable oil
1 small onion, minced (finely chopped)
3 cloves garlic, minced (finely chopped)
1½ lb (750 g) tomatoes, skinned, seeded, and minced
   (finely chopped)
2 canned chipotle chiles, coarsely chopped
1 teaspoon salt, or to taste
4 tablespoons parsley, minced (finely chopped)
1 lb (500 g) tortilla masa (see Tortillas de Maiz page 53)

MAKES 25 MEDIUM QUESADILLAS

❡ Heat 2 tablespoons (1 fl oz/30 ml) of oil in a frying pan and sauté the onion and garlic until translucent. Add the tomato, chiles, and salt; cook until almost dry, stirring to prevent sticking. Stir in the parsley and remove from the heat.
❡ Roll the *masa* into ¾-oz (20-g) balls and, using a *tortilla* press, flatten each ball into a slightly thick 3½-inch (9-cm) *tortilla*. Put 1 heaping tablespoon of the tomato mixture in the middle of each *tortilla*, fold over, and press the edges to seal.
❡ Heat the remaining oil to cover ½ inch (1 cm) of a medium frying pan and cook the *quesadillas*, a few at a time, for 3 to 4 minutes on each side until golden brown. Remove and drain on paper towels.
❡ Serve the *quesadillas* wrapped in a cloth napkin inside a basket.

TAQUITOS DE PURÉ DE CHICHARO Y NOPALITOS

GREEN PEA AND NOPAL TACOS

This is a very old recipe that is a favorite today among vegetarians. Serve it as an appetizer or a light supper. If you can't find nopales *(prickly pear paddles), substitute with boiled carrots cut into small cubes.*

4 cups (1½ lb/750 g) fresh green peas, or frozen peas
6 tablespoons (3 fl oz/90 ml) vegetable oil
1 small onion, minced (finely chopped)
salt to taste
2 cups (14 oz/440 g) cooked nopales, chopped into
   ½-inch (1-cm) pieces, or canned nopales

For the sauce:
2 large tomatoes, chopped
3 chiles de arbol
1 clove garlic, peeled
½ teaspoon salt, or to taste
2 tablespoons (1 fl oz/30 ml) vegetable oil
¼ cup (2 fl oz/60 ml) vegetable oil
18 small corn tortillas (4 inches/10 cm)

SERVES 6

Left: Meatless Tinga Quesadillas; bottom: Green Pea and Nopal Tacos

❡ Cook the peas in salted water until soft. Drain and puree them with a potato masher.

❡ Heat the oil in a medium saucepan and sauté the onion until translucent.

❡ Add the peas and simmer for 4 minutes, stirring occasionally. Remove from the heat and add the salt and *nopales*.

❡ To make the sauce: Puree the tomatoes, chiles, garlic, and salt in a blender until smooth.

❡ Heat the oil in a small saucepan and add the

tomato mixture. Simmer over low heat for 15 minutes, or until just thickened.

❡ Heat the ¼ cup of oil in a small frying pan and submerge the *tortillas* one at a time for a few seconds on each side. Drain to remove any excess oil.

❡ Fill each *tortilla* with a heaping spoonful of the *nopales* mixture, then roll each *tortilla* to make a *taco*.

❡ Serve immediately as the filling will soften the *tortillas*, accompanied by the sauce.

QUESO HOLANDES CON PICADILLO YUCATECO

*EDAM CHEESE WITH YUCATECAN
SHREDDED PORK*

In the Yucatán, this dish is traditionally made with a whole Edam cheese. The red wax is removed and the hollowed-out cheese stuffed with the shredded pork. It is then wrapped in muslin (cheesecloth) and steamed. This recipe is a simplified version served in individual gratin dishes.

2 lb (1 kg) pork shoulder (blade), cubed
5 cloves garlic, charred with skin, then peeled
½ onion, charred
½ teaspoon oregano, lightly toasted
1 teaspoon salt, or to taste
For the tomato sauce:
3 tablespoons lard or oil
½ onion, minced (finely chopped)
1 red bell pepper (capsicum), chopped
2 tablespoons capers
2 tablespoons raisins
15 green olives, pitted and chopped
2½ lb (1.25 kg) tomatoes, peeled, seeded, and chopped
2 teaspoons paprika
½ teaspoon salt, or to taste
pinch saffron
½ cup (4 fl oz/125 ml) tomato juice
For the *picadillo* (meat mixture):
15 peppercorns
4 allspice berries
1 cinnamon stick, 2 inches (5 cm) long
5 cloves
3 cloves garlic, charred with skin, then peeled
1 tablespoon vinegar
1 tablespoon raisins
1 tablespoon capers
4 hard-boiled eggs, white and yolk separated, and minced
    (finely chopped)
For the *kol* (gravy):
2 tablespoons vegetable oil
2 teaspoons grated onion
1 small clove garlic, minced (finely chopped)
2 tablespoons all-purpose (plain) flour
pinch saffron
1 x-cat-ik chile, optional
½ teaspoon salt, or to taste
2 tablespoons (1 oz/30 g) butter
⅓ cup (2½ oz/75 g) shredded Edam cheese

MAKES 6 GRATIN DISHES (4 inches/10 cm IN DIAMETER)

❡ In a pot, cover the pork with water and add the garlic, onion, oregano, and salt, and cook until tender. Remove the meat from the pot and reserve 1 cup (8 fl oz/250 ml) of the broth.

❡ To make the sauce: Heat the lard in a medium saucepan and sauté the onion until it is translucent. Add the next 8 ingredients and cook over high heat for 8 to 10 minutes, or until the fat rises to the surface. Divide the mixture into 2 parts. Add the tomato juice to one half.

❡ To make the *picadillo* (meat mixture): Grind the peppercorns, allspice, cinnamon, and cloves in a spice grinder. Place the spices with the garlic, vinegar, raisins, and capers in a food processor. Add the pork and process very briefly, so the meat is just broken up but not ground (minced). Place the mixture in a bowl and mix with the egg whites. Add the tomato sauce without the tomato juice and mix. Place in a saucepan and cook over low heat until almost dry, stirring occasionally.

❡ Make the *kol* (gravy): Heat the oil in a small saucepan and fry the onion and garlic briefly. Stir in the flour and cook until it starts to brown. Add the reserved broth, saffron, chile, and salt. Stir constantly until it thickens slightly.

❡ Preheat the oven to 350°F (180°C/Gas 4).

❡ Butter the gratin dishes and divide the grated cheese among them. Cover with a layer of *picadillo*, sprinkle with the egg yolks, and top with the remaining *picadillo*. Spoon the remaining tomato sauce on one side and the *kol* on the other.

❡ Place the dishes on an oven tray and bake for 15 minutes, or until heated through, and serve.

QUESO RELLENO

Relleno *used as an adjective means "filled" or "stuffed;" as a cooking term, it can relate to any number of fillings that go into the making of many well-known and much-loved vegetable, poultry, and cheese dishes. In its original form, the recipe on this page is made with a whole, rindless Edam. A ½-inch (1-cm) "lid" sliced off its top (plus a bit trimmed off the bottom, too, to insure the round cheese remains upright while cooking) and the contents carefully hollowed out, converting it into a ¼-inch (0.5-cm) shell, not dissimilar to a jack-o'-lantern. Filled with a warm* picadillo, *traditionally made of shredded cooked meat and various spices, the cheese is capped with the reserved lid, wrapped tightly in cheesecloth (muslin), and steamed until soft enough to be slightly runny but still hold its shape. For a dinner party, this dish can also be made with the small, fist-sized Edams which are fairly readily available everywhere. Serving one whole stuffed cheese to every guest makes an impressive start to a meal.*

Edam Cheese with Yucatecan Shredded Pork

HONGOS QUISHIMOS PARA TACOS

SAUTÉED WILD MUSHROOMS FOR TACOS

This recipe is an adaptation by Esther Garrido de Barrios of a Nahuatl recipe from southern Michoacán and northern State of México, where the "yolk" mushrooms, amanita ceasarea, *grow.* Quishimo *is the Nahuatl name for these mushrooms, while in Spanish they are called* hongo de yema—*"yema" meaning egg yolk—as the mushrooms are yellow and an oblong shape when the cap is closed.*

½ cup (4 fl oz/125 ml) corn oil

1 large onion, chopped

5 cloves garlic, chopped

8 poblano *chiles, roasted (see box page 112), and deveined, if you prefer less spiciness*

2 lb (1 kg) wild mushrooms, such as hongo de yema, *oyster, or chanterelles, cleaned and sliced*

2 cups (½ qt/500 ml) Salsa de Jitomate Asada *(see page 22)*

2 sprigs epazote, *optional*

2 tablespoons granulated chicken stock or 2 chicken bouillon cubes, crumbled

Left: Sautéed Wild Mushrooms for Tacos; Top: Chalupas with Goat's Cheese

2 cups (16 fl oz/500 ml) cream entera, *or substitute heavy (double/thickened) cream*

MAKES FILLING FOR ABOUT 40 TACOS

❡ Heat the oil in a large deep frying pan. Sauté the onion and garlic over medium heat until translucent. Add the chiles and cook for a few minutes. Add the mushrooms and, when they release their liquid, add the tomato sauce and *epazote*. Cover and cook for about 5 minutes. Uncover, add the granulated chicken stock, salt, and cream and heat through.

❡ Use as a filling for *tacos* using fresh, hot *tortillas*.

CHALUPAS DE QUESO DE CABRA

CHALUPAS WITH GOAT'S CHEESE

These chalupas *are a specialty of El Ciruelo Restaurant in Tepoztlán, Morelos. The restaurant offers a view of Tepoztlán's extraordinary mountains from its terrace and garden, where these snacks are often enjoyed.*

1½ lb (750 g) tortilla masa (*see* Tortillas de Maiz *page 55*)
10 oz (300 g) goat's cheese, crumbled
½ teaspoon salt, or to taste
4 tablespoons (2 fl oz/60 ml) olive oil
2 onions, minced (finely chopped)
2 cloves garlic, minced (finely chopped)
8 oz (250 g) tomatoes, roasted on a comal *or cast-iron griddle or broiled (grilled), peeled, and chopped*
1 cup (8 oz/250 g) drained and mashed Frijoles de la Olla (*see page 150*)
1 head romaine (cos) lettuce, washed and finely shredded

MAKES 30

❡ Knead the *tortilla masa* with half the goat's cheese and the salt until uniform in texture and color. Divide the dough into 30 (1-oz/30-g) oblong balls and flatten each into thickish ⅛ inch (2 mm) oval *tortillas*. Cook on a hot *comal* or a cast-iron pan over medium heat for 1 to 2 minutes on each side until they are a light golden brown. As soon as they are cool enough to handle, pinch up the sides to form a ridge ¼ inch (5 mm) high. Set aside while making the bean paste.

❡ Heat the oil in a large frying pan over medium heat and sauté the onions and garlic until translucent. Add the tomatoes and a little salt, and cook for about 5 minutes. Add the beans and cook, stirring, until they have dried to the consistency of a paste.

❡ To serve, warm the *tortillas* on a *comal* or cast-iron griddle and spread a little bean paste on them. Top with the remaining goat's cheese and sprinkle with the lettuce.

TLACOYOS

Another of Mexico's great street foods, these large, thickish, oblong tortillas are stuffed with the mixture of your choice: ricotta cheese, refried beans, cooked potatoes with onion, stringy Oaxaca cheese, and so on. The tortilla masa, of white or blue corn, is pressed into shape while you wait, stuffed raw, and then cooked on a large comal (cast-iron griddle) sitting over a brazier, usually with a wood fire beneath it. A red or green chile sauce is available for you to add, according to your taste.

CHORIZOS CON TOMATILLOS Y FRIJOLES NEGROS EN CHALUPAS

CHORIZO, TOMATILLO, AND BLACK BEANS ON MASA SOPES

These chalupas (little boats) differ from the original sopes which originated in Guadalajara in that they are smaller than usual, filled to overflowing, and intended to serve as a meal's appetizer.

For the *sopes:*
2 tablespoons lard
⅓ cup (2 oz/60g) all-purpose (plain) flour
1 teaspoon salt
1 teaspoon baking powder
2¼ cups (10 oz/300g) masa harina *mixed with 1½ cups hot water and allowed to rest for 30 minutes*
For the toppings:
1 cup drained and mashed Frijoles de la Olla *(see page 150)*
8 oz (250g) chorizo *sausage, peeled and finely diced*
vegetable oil, for deep frying
1¼ cups Salsa Verde Cocida *(see page 24)*
2 oz (60g) crumbled feta, or farmer's cheese, or other firm white cheese
1 cup finely shredded romaine (cos) lettuce
4 radishes, finely sliced

MAKES 24 SOPES

❡ Add the lard, flour, salt, and baking powder to the *masa harina* and knead with your hands until fairly smooth.
❡ Divide the dough equally into 24 portions and roll into balls. Flatten each with the palm of your hand into ¾-inch (2-cm) *sopes.* Keep covered with plastic or a damp dish towel while working to prevent dough drying.
❡ Cook the *sopes* in batches on a hot *comal,* or cast-iron griddle, for 2 minutes on each side, until lightly browned. Keep the cooked *sopes* covered with a clean dish towel while finishing the others.
❡ With the cooked side down, pinch up the sides to form a definite raised edge. Cover and repeat with the remaining *sopes.*
❡ Prepare the toppings about 30 minutes before serving. Reheat the beans and dry-fry the *chorizo* in a frying pan until browned. Drain. Keep both warm until ready to assemble the *chalupas.*
❡ Just before serving, reheat the *sopes* on a *comal* or cast-iron griddle, brush with a little oil, and cook until they start to sizzle.
❡ To assemble the *sopes,* layer the beans, *chorizo, Salsa Verde Cocida,* cheese, lettuce, and radish on the top. Serve immediately.

Chorizo, Tomatillo, and Black Beans on Masa Sopes

Corn: The Foundation

CORN: THE FOUNDATION

CORN IS THE BASIC GRAIN NOT ONLY OF MEXICO BUT OF MOST OF LATIN AMERICA. THE IMPORTANCE of corn in the Mexican diet is such that a quarter of Mexico's population depends directly on its cultivation, and it represents the single largest agricultural product.

❡ A technique was developed in Mexico more than 1,000 years ago that rendered corn more digestible and improved its nutritional qualities. This is the process of making *nixtamal*, the basic dough of *tortillas* and *tamales*, by boiling and soaking the corn kernels with calcium oxide (lime) to soften the hard, outer skin, which can then be removed. This alkaline processing has the chemical effect of improving the balance of corn's protein content and releasing its niacin so it can be absorbed by the human body. In areas of Europe where corn was introduced without knowledge of this process, and was heavily relied on as the dietary staple, poor people suffered from the disease pellagra, which is caused by a niacin deficiency. It is interesting to

Previous pages: Corn destined for tortilla *making, drying on the back patio of a small farmhouse. Mexicans prefer to store corn on the cob as there is more air circulating and it keeps better. This picture was taken in January—the corn would have been harvested during the previous October.*

Opposite: Shucking fresh corn at La Merced market in Mexico City. Boiled or roasted cobs are a popular street food, served with a dressing of salt, chile, and lime juice, or a mixture of cream or mayonnaise with shredded añejo *cheese and chile.*

note that beans make an excellent natural dietary complement to corn because they contain just those elements in which unprocessed corn is deficient.

❡ The corn for *nixtamal* was and still is ground manually on a *metate* (grindstone) made of volcanic rock, although today communal mills exist where individuals can take their prepared corn to be ground, and there are also commercial *tortillerias* where *tortillas* and the dried-corn dough, or *masa*, can be bought.

❡ The list of different foods prepared from corn dough is endless: *tortillas* and *antojitos* (corn-dough snacks) of all different sizes and shapes; sweet and salty *tamales;* and *atoles* (hot plain or fruit-flavored drinks thickened with *masa*). In turn, the *tortillas* are made into a large variety of dishes, whether filled, rolled, or cut and fried, added to soups, eggs, or used for spooning beans or dips.

❡ There are certain preparations that are both drink and basic nourishment, satisfying both thirst and hunger. In many rural areas, dried corn is toasted and ground to a powder and mixed with sugar to make *pinole*, which laborers take with them to work or on long trips. The powder can be eaten or mixed with water for drinking. In the Southeast, where *cacao* is also produced, both grain and *cacao* beans are ground to make a lightly fermented drink called *pozol*. It is usually drunk cold, neither sweetened nor salted.

❡ Although the majority of Mexico's corn production is consumed dried, fresh corn is also enjoyed on the cob, in soups, mixed with chile strips for filling *tacos*, and for fresh-corn *tamales*. Both fresh and dried corn husks are used as *tamal* wrappings, as well as the green corn leaves from the stalk.

DRY CORN

Most corn in Mexico is eaten dried; usually, in the form of *tortillas*. These are typically about 5 or 6 inches (12 or 15 cm) in diameter and ¹/₁₆ inch (1.25 mm) thick, although they vary in size, and smaller ones are often used for *antojitos* (corn dough snacks). They are made with *tortilla masa* (dried-corn dough) and cooked briefly on a *comal*, a flat, round griddle made of clay or metal, placed directly over the flame.

Traditionally, *tortillas* have always been made by hand by tossing the dough from palm to palm (*palmeado*) to form the thin disks, but at the beginning of the twentieth century, mechanical presses were designed. At first, these were manually operated machines, but in the 1940s, industrial machines were invented that were capable of processing several pounds of *masa* per minute. Although many Mexicans in rural areas continue to make *tortillas* by hand, and simple hand presses—of wood or metal—are available all over

Mexico, there are close to 40,000 *tortillerias* in the cities. These are small establishments dedicated exclusively to making and selling fresh *tortillas* to the public. However, the difference between handmade and factory-made *tortillas* is always noticeable, and the flavor of freshly made *tortillas* is incomparable.

Although people usually make their own *sopes*, handmade ones are sold by the same women who sell homemade *tortillas* outside the markets. *Sopes* are small *tortillas* with a little ridge around the edge, which is made by pinching up the sides when the *masa* is still hot. There are many variations on the theme: *garnachas, chalupas, pellizcadas,* to mention a few. There are many varieties, but they are usually filled with a little sauce, cheese, and chopped onion, and sometimes with chicken.

Totopostles are hard disks of *tortilla masa* sold in

Oaxaca. They have small holes and are about 10 inches (25 cm) in diameter.

Nixtamal is dried corn that has been cooked and soaked with hot water and lime (calcium oxide) and then ground to make *tortilla masa*. Also available in Mexico and elsewhere is a dry *tortilla* flour (*masa harina*) processed industrially from *nixtamal*. It is mixed to a dough with warm water as a substitute for fresh *masa*. It's a boon where *nixtamal* and *tortilla* mills simply do not exist, although the results may be less fine; *tamales* tend to be

less fluffy, for example, and *tortillas* less pliable. The advantage is that the flour keeps for months while fresh *masa* must be used immediately.

Most people who live off the land in Mexico produce corn and keep a portion of it for their own use during the year. They prefer to store it on the cob, as there is more air circulation than with stored kernels and the corn keeps better.

Nothing goes to waste when it comes to corn. Corn husks are rarely thrown away and are used for wrapping *tamales*. They are sold dried, cupped together in huge packages, and need only be soaked briefly before using. Even the dried corn cobs, left over after the kernels have been removed, are used as kindling to make fires for cooking or heating water.

1. fresh tortillas; 2. fresh blue tortillas; 3. dried tortillas; 4. sopes; 5. garnachas; 6. totopostles; 7. dried corn husks; 8. different varieties of dried corn on the cob; 9. different varieties of dried corn kernels; 10. nixtamal (corn tortilla masa); 11. lime (calcium oxide); 12. masa harina; 13. dried corn cobs (without kernels)

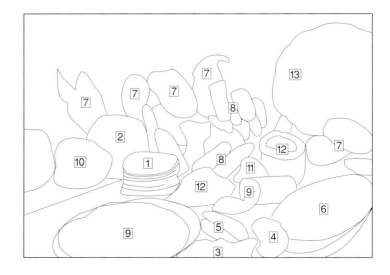

TORTILLAS DE MAÍZ

CORN TORTILLAS

While tortillas *are generally made in Mexico with fresh* masa, *which consists of corn kernels soaked with lime, this recipe relies on* masa harina (tortilla *flour). When making* tacos *or enchiladas, always make sure that the side of the* tortilla *with the thin skin (the second side to be toasted) is facing you—once you fill the* tortilla, *this skin, also called the* cara *(face) or the* telita *(thin cloth), will be on the inside. You can use this recipe for any other recipe in this book that calls either for* tortillas *or for prepared* tortilla masa, *which is needed in making* antojitos, chocoyotes, *and* tamales.

2 cups (7 oz/220 g) masa harina (tortilla *flour)*
1⅓ cups (11 fl oz/345 ml) warm water

MAKES 1 lb (500 g) MASA, OR ABOUT 15 TORTILLAS

❡ Mix the *masa harina* and water together in a bowl to form a soft dough. You may need to add more *masa harina* if the dough is sticky.
❡ Form balls of 1 oz (30 g) or the size of golf balls. Line the surfaces of a *tortilla* press with 2 squares of plastic wrap and press each ball flat, or follow the same procedure with a rolling pin. Remove the *tortilla* from the press and carefully peel off the plastic wrap. Continue with the remaining dough.
❡ Toast the *tortillas*, one at a time, on a *comal* or cast-iron griddle. Leave on the first side for about 40 seconds, or until little brown spots appear on the under side, then cook the second side for 40 seconds. Flip again and toast the first side for a few seconds more, pressing the edges down to make them inflate. Keep the *tortillas* warm in a basket lined with a cloth napkin as you proceed.
❡ Stored *tortillas* can be reheated briefly on a hot *comal* or cast-iron griddle, but be careful not to brown them.

TORTILLAS DE HARINA

FLOUR TORTILLAS

Flour tortillas *are a specialty of northern Mexico, where more wheat is cultivated than corn. They are used to accompany meals, just like corn* tortillas, *or to make* tacos. *In Puerto Nuevo, in northern Baja California, it has become a popular morning custom for the fishermen to sell flour* tortilla tacos *of freshly boiled lobster and mashed beans directly from their houses on the beach.*

In Sauces and Snacks (starting on page 18) we have included several recipes using flour tortillas, *two of which are unusual* tostadas *created by Alicia De'Angeli, who also gave us this recipe.*

2 lb (1 kg) all-purpose (plain) flour, sifted
1 teaspoon salt, or to taste
pinch sugar
8 oz (250 g) vegetable shortening (margarine) or lard, cut into small pieces
2 cups (16 fl oz/500 ml) water

MAKES 30 LARGE OR 60 SMALL TORTILLAS

❡ Sift the flour with the salt and sugar.
❡ Place the flour mixture on a table and make a well in the center. Add the shortening and incorporate into the flour mixture with your fingers, gradually adding the water to make a soft dough.
❡ Divide the dough evenly into 30 parts for large (12-inch/30-cm) *tortillas* or into 60 parts for small (6-inch/15-cm) ones. Roll the dough into balls and flatten slightly on a greased surface. Cover them with a cloth and let rest for 30 minutes. Roll each ball into the desired size on a floured surface.
❡ Cook each *tortilla* on a hot *comal* or cast-iron griddle for 30 seconds per side. If it puffs up, flatten it with a spatula. The *tortilla* will have pale brown spots on the surface when done.
❡ Use immediately or store the *tortillas* in a plastic bag. They will keep in the refrigerator for several days or in the freezer for 3 to 4 months.

Left: Flour Tortillas; right: Corn Tortillas

TAMALITOS DE ELOTE

SMALL FRESH CORN TAMALES

In Mexico, fresh corn is generally rather starchy, which works perfectly for making these tamales. American sweet corn, although delicious, tends to be too watery, so use the starchiest corn available.

6 ears corn, shucked, with husks reserved
¾ teaspoon salt, or to taste
½ teaspoon sugar
¼ cup (2 oz/60 g) melted butter

MAKES ABOUT 12 SMALL TAMALES

❡ Cut the kernels off the cob to yield about 2 cups (8 oz/250 g). In a blender, mix the corn, salt, and sugar to a paste. Put the paste into a mixing bowl, add the butter, and blend until thoroughly mixed.
❡ Using the tender inner corn husks, take 1 large, or overlap 2 small pieces, for each *tamal*. Place 1½ tablespoons of the corn mixture in the center of the bottom half of the husk. Roll the husk lengthwise to close, then fold over the pointed top half to form a neat package. Repeat with the remaining corn mixture. Tear any leftover husks lengthwise into strips to make string for tying the *tamales*.
❡ Bring water to a boil in the bottom half of a *tamal* steamer, couscous steamer, or vegetable steamer. Line the top half with some of the outer husks.
❡ Place the *tamales* snugly in the basket, arranging them vertically with the tips pointing up to prevent leakage. Cover with more corn husks and a dish towel, then with the steamer cover, and steam for 1½ hours.
❡ Serve in their husks.

INDITOS VESTIDOS

CLOTHED LITTLE INDIANS

The curious name for this recipe might be explained by the way the folded tortilla and cheese wedges, or "little indians," are clothed with the egg batter and sauce. It is a very old recipe from central Mexico that is excellent for a late breakfast or light evening meal.

1 pasilla *or large* guajillo *chile*
2 avocado leaves, optional

¾ cup (6 oz/185 g) Frijoles de la Olla *with some of their broth (see page 150)*
6 corn tortillas *(6 inches/15 cm in diameter)*
2 oz (60 g) Manchego-*style, Monterey Jack, or other semisoft cheese, cut into 6 slices about 1 x 4 inches (2.5 x 10 cm)*
1 egg, separated
½ teaspoon salt, optional
½ cup (4 fl oz/125 ml) vegetable oil

MAKES 6

❡ Slightly toast the chile and avocado leaves on a hot *comal* or cast-iron griddle. Cut open the chile to remove the stem, seeds, and veins.
❡ In a blender, puree the chile, avocado leaves, and beans with enough of their liquid to make a thick sauce. Heat well in a saucepan before serving.
❡ Heat the *tortillas*. Put a slice of cheese to the right of the middle and fold the *tortilla* over it in half; fold it again in quarters.
❡ In a bowl, beat the egg white with the salt to form stiff peaks and fold in the lightly beaten egg yolk. Heat the oil in a frying pan. Hold the *tortillas* by the point and dip them into the egg batter. Fry them in the oil, turning once, until golden. Drain on paper towels to remove excess oil and place on a serving platter.
❡ Pour the bean sauce over the *tortillas* and serve.

Top: Small Fresh Corn Tamales; bottom: "Clothed Little Indians"

Fresh Corn

The consumption of corn in Mexico is such an ancient and widespread tradition that one could say it's eaten or drunk in every possible way, whether fresh or dried. When fresh, it is called *elote* in Mexico. Although all the different varieties are eaten, white corn is perhaps the most popular. Yellow corn is fairly common, if less esteemed, but it's not unusual to find red, blue, or purple corn in rural areas of the central plateau. In Mexico, these colored varieties are considered to be rather exotic.

Cacahuazintle, or hominy, is a natural variety of white corn with large kernels, almost four times the weight of other corn kernels. It is different not only in size but also in taste, and pops open like a flower when cooked. It is very popular for making *tortilla masa*, and the cooked, open kernels are the key ingredient for a hearty traditional soup called *pozole*.

After heavy rainfall, corn may suffer from a fungus called *cuitlacoche*, which grows on the already-formed ears. It feeds off the kernels and cob, deforming and swelling the ear until it is gradually transformed into the black fungus. While in the rest of the world this fungus is disdained and contaminated ears are discarded, in Mexico, it is considered a delicacy and has been eaten since pre-Columbian times. In fact, the demand for it is so great that it can command up to twenty times the price of regular corn. During the rainy season, it is sold fresh by the ear, and part of the husk is removed to display its quality.

To prepare it, the fungus is cut off the cob and chopped after the corn silk has been removed; it should not be washed. During the rest of the year, it is available canned. *Cuitlacoche* is usually sautéed with onion, garlic, and chile as a filling for *tacos* or crêpes.

Corn husks are typically used as *tamal* wrappers: fresh-corn *tamales* use fresh husks, while *tamales* made with *masa* are wrapped with dried-corn husks that have been soaked briefly in water to make them more pliable.

The Mexican predilection for fresh corn is evident in a popular form of street food where the ears are sold on a stick after having been either boiled or roasted in their husks. Either way, two kinds of dressing are offered: the most traditional is salt, chile powder, and a squeeze of lime juice; the other, which has become popular in recent decades, is thick cream or mayonnaise, shredded *añejo* cheese, and chile powder. The same vendors also sell little cups of cooked kernels flavored with the herb *epazote*, chile powder, and lime juice.

1. white corn; 2. red, blue, or purple corn; 3. cacahuazintle (hominy), and fresh corn husks; 4. cuitlacoche (corn fungus); 5. hominy kernels; 6. white corn kernel

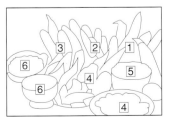

TORO PINTO

SPECKLED BULL

Called "speckled bull" because of the black spots of the beans against the white masa, toro pinto comes from Chiapas. The combination of the sauce, cream, and cheese served over the open tamal is delicious and original. This recipe, from Gloria Reséndez de Palacios, appears in La Cocina Regiónal de México, *published by the volunteers of Bancomer.*

8 oz (250 g) lard
2 lb (1 kg) tortilla masa (see Tortillas de Maíz page 53)
2 cups (16 oz/500 g) cooked soft black beans, whole (see Frijoles de la Olla page 150)
5 large banana leaves
For the sauce:
2 lb (1 kg) tomatoes
2 cloves garlic, peeled
2 tablespoons vegetable oil
1½ teaspoons salt
1 cup (8 fl oz/250 ml) heavy (double/thickened) cream
8 oz (250 g) Chiapas or feta cheese, grated

MAKES 20 TAMALES

❡ Whip the lard with an electric mixer at maximum speed for 10 minutes until it becomes creamy. Add the *masa* little by little and continue beating until a small ball of the dough will float when dropped in a glass of cold water. Fold in the beans with a spatula.

❡ Pass the banana leaves over an open flame so they become more pliable. Split them down the middle, removing the thick central vein. Cut the leaves into twenty 10- x 10-inch (25- x 25-cm) squares. Place the leaves shiny side up, put about 2 tablespoons of *masa* in the center of each, and flatten into a rectangle. Fold the 2 sides of the leaves inward to overlap, then fold the top and bottom to form little packages.

TEQUESQUITE

Tequesquite *(chloride and sodium carbonate) is a natural baking soda (bicarbonate of soda) that is sold in rock form in Mexican markets. It has been used for centuries as a leavening agent for making* tamales. *It can also be used as a softening agent for cooking beans, is sometimes used as a salt substitute, and, like commercial baking soda, can be added to boiling water to keep cooked vegetables green. It is crushed in a mortar before being used, and commercial baking soda can be substituted for it.*

❡ Line the bottom of a steamer basket with 3 or 4 leftover pieces of banana leaf. Layer the *tamales* in the basket, cover with more leaves, then a dish towel, plastic wrap, and the lid. Bring water to a boil in the bottom of a *tamal* or other steamer and cook the *tamales* for 45 minutes, or until the leaf wrappers separate easily from the *tamales*.

❡ To make the sauce: Combine the tomatoes and garlic in a food processor until smooth. Heat the oil in a saucepan and fry the tomato mixture with the salt over medium heat for about 15 minutes.

❡ Open the hot *tamales* and serve on the leaf when serving on individual plates, or leave closed when passing around on a platter. Pass the warm tomato sauce, the cream, and the cheese with the *tamales*.

❡ The *tamales* can be reheated directly on a hot griddle until the banana leaves turn slightly black, giving them a roasted flavor.

TAMALES MORENO

TAMALES MORENO

This recipe from Laura Caraza, a well-known cookbook author and teacher, has been in her family for many generations. She has simplified it, to make it more adaptable to modern times.

For the filling:
8 oz (250 g) pork tenderloin (fillet)
¼ onion
½ bay leaf
1 sprig thyme
1 sprig oregano
½ teaspoon salt, or to taste
2 oz (60 g) ancho chiles, cleaned, seeded, and deveined
1½ cups (12 fl oz/375 ml) warm water
1 large clove garlic, peeled
½ tablespoon lard
For the *tamales:*
2 lb (1 kg) prepared corn tortilla masa (see Tortillas de Maíz page 53 and double the quantities)
1½ cups (12 oz/375 g) lard
½ tablespoon baking powder
1 tablespoon salt, or to taste
50 to 60 corn husks (dried if available), washed, soaked in warm water for 30 minutes, and drained well

MAKES 30 TAMALES

❡ To prepare the filling: Place the pork, onion, herbs, and salt in a pot and add enough water to cover. Boil for 30 minutes, or until the meat is tender. Drain, reserving 2 cups (8 fl oz/500 ml)

Front: Speckled Bull; back: Tamales Moreno

of liquid, and shred the pork tenderloin. Set aside.

❡ Soak the chiles in the warm water for about 10 minutes. Puree the chiles, water, and garlic in a blender until very smooth. Heat the lard in a frying pan and fry the chile mixture over medium heat for about 10 minutes. Add the pork and adjust the seasoning if necessary. Cook for 5 minutes to heat through and thicken slightly.

❡ For the *tamales:* Mix the *masa* and the reserved liquid with an electric beater for 5 minutes and set aside. In another bowl, whip the lard at maximum speed until light and fluffy, then add the *masa* mixture. Beat at high speed for 5 to 7 minutes or

until a small ball of the dough floats when dropped in a glass of cold water. Add the baking powder and salt, and mix well.

❡ Divide the *masa* mixture among 30 corn husks, spooning the dough into the center of each along with 1 tablespoon of filling. Fold the sides of the husk together and bring the tip down to seal completely. Heat water in the bottom of a *tamalera* or vegetable steamer, line the basket with husks, and place the *tamales* on the top. Cover with the remaining husks, a dish towel, plastic wrap, and the lid. Steam for 45 to 55 minutes or until the husks can be easily separated from the filling and serve.

Finished tamales *ready to be consumed by street-side customers.*

TAMALES

Tamales are food packages where the filling, typically of corn *masa* mixed with beaten lard, and flavored with either salty or sweet ingredients, is enclosed in a vegetable wrapping and steamed. The corn *masa* is traditionally prepared from *nixtamal,* ground corn kernels soaked in lime water; it can also be made from *masa harina,* the dried *tortilla* flour available commercially in and outside Mexico, although the results of the latter are less fluffy.

Tamales are often made in large numbers: they freeze well and can be steamed to reheat. Dry-corn husks are the most common wrapping, although on the coasts and in the South, banana leaves are used. Other regional specialties may be enclosed in avocado leaves; in the large, anise-flavored leaf called *hoja santa;* in the splayed *chaya* (like Swiss chard / spring greens / silver beet), a specialty of the Yucatán; or in fresh-corn husks (for fresh-corn *tamales*) and the tender green leaves from the corn stalk.

Tamales in one form or another can be found in all of Latin America, and there are hundreds of different varieties in Mexico. These range from the tiny ones, such as those from the North that are the size of a finger and are flavored with red chile and shredded pork or beef, to the giant *zacahuiles* from the Huasteca, which can weigh up to 150 pounds (70 kg)—a single *tamal* is capable of serving all the guests of a wedding.

Although the majority of the salty *tamales* are made with pork or chicken, they can also be filled with iguana, fish, shrimp (prawns), alligator, frogs, and other animals, or with beans or vegetables.

There are simple *tamales* without flavoring other than the *masa* and lard, which are eaten in the place of *tortillas* to accompany a meal, and there are baroque creations with numerous ingredients, such as the kind from the Yucatán that, aside from the usual pork and chile sauce, has olives, capers, raisins, prunes, peas, potatoes, and chopped carrots. Still others do not contain *masa* at all, but have small, whole fish (common in the lake regions of the central plateau) that might be grilled (broiled) rather than steamed.

Another variety of *tamales* is those baked in a casserole instead of being wrapped in leaves and steamed. These will usually have alternating layers of *masa,* meat, and sauce or other flavorings.

For the most common sweet *tamales,* the corn dough is tinted pink and mixed with raisins and candied cactus *(acitrón).* Another variety is made of fresh corn sweetened with cinnamon and raisins; and yet others are flavored with anise or fruits, especially pineapple and strawberry. In the North, small *tamales* sweetened with the molasses-flavored *piloncillo* mixed with beans or pecans are a specialty.

In Veracruz, some delicious *tamales* combine both sweet and salty flavors and chile sauce. These often include *hoja santa,* whose exquisite anise flavor and aroma have been appreciated since pre-Hispanic times.

Tamales have been used since the pre-Columbian era as an offering to the dead, and it is interesting to note that the same customs exist even today, especially in rural Mexico. On the *Dias de Muertos* (Days of the Dead), the *tamales* that used to be favored by the deceased are placed on an altar next to his or her photograph, along with many other offerings, including desserts, drinks, and cigarettes. Later, the *tamales* are eaten by the living. (See Mexican Fiestas starting on page 246.)

TAMALES DE FRIJOL DULCE

SWEET BEAN TAMALES

This old recipe from the state of Sonora is usually served for breakfast or supper. Good tamales, which are light and airy, are always made with corn masa. *When* masa harina *is substituted, cornstarch (cornflour) or grits are usually added. However, this recipe, which Diana Kennedy helped make, is an exception to that rule.*

1½ cups (10½ oz/330 g) cooked pinto beans, pureed
5 oz (155 g) piloncillo, *cubed, or light molasses*
½ teaspoon ground cinnamon
pinch ground cloves
4 oz (125 g) lard
1 lb (500 g) prepared tortilla masa *(see* Tortillas de Maíz *page 55), left to stand at room temperature for 2½ hours*
⅓ cup (2½ fl oz/75 ml) warm chicken stock
1½ teaspoons salt, or to taste
1 teaspoon baking powder
50 dried corn husks, soaked in hot water until soft and dried

MAKES 20

❡ In a pan over low heat, combine the beans, *piloncillo*, cinnamon, and cloves. Simmer for 20 minutes until thick, stirring constantly. Let cool.
❡ With an electric beater, on maximum velocity, whip the lard for 10 minutes. Slowly add the *masa* alternating with the broth, salt, and baking powder. Continue beating for 5 to 8 minutes more.
❡ Spread 1 tablespoon of the batter in the center of 20 husks, and place 1 teaspoon of the bean mixture in the center of the batter. Bring the sides of the husks together and fold the tip down. The *tamales* expand as they cook.
❡ Fill the bottom of a *tamalera* or steamer with water and bring to a boil. Line the rack with corn husks and place the *tamales* in a standing position filling any gaps, with more leaves. Cover with the remaining husks, a thick dish towel, plastic wrap, and the lid. Steam over medium heat for 1¼ hours or until the husks separate easily from the *tamales*.

TAMALES DE CHILE VERDE

GREEN CHILE TAMALES

Fonda San Miguel in Austin, Texas, is among the truly outstanding Mexican restaurants in the United States. Miguel Ravago, the creative executive chef and co-founder there, devised this butter-based tamal *recipe.*

For the filling:
6 poblano *or long green chiles, roasted, peeled, seeded, and chopped (see box page 112)*
2 red tomatoes, roasted, peeled, seeded, and chopped
1 white onion, chopped
1 clove garlic, minced (finely chopped)
For the *tamal masa:*
1¼ cups (10 oz/315 g) butter, softened
½ cup (4 fl oz/125 ml) sour cream
2 lb (1 kg) tortilla masa (see Tortillas de Maiz *page 55)*
1½ cups (12 fl oz/375 ml) warm chicken stock
1 tablespoon salt, or to taste
14 trimmed banana leaves or dried corn husks soaked in hot water
banana leaves or corn husks, for lining the steamer

MAKES 14 TAMALES

❡ To make the filling: In a bowl, mix together the chiles, tomatoes, onion, garlic, and salt.
❡ For the *tamales:* Whip the butter in a large mixing bowl with an electric beater until light and fluffy. Add the sour cream, beat to incorporate, then slowly beat in the *masa*. Lower the speed of the mixer to slow. Add the stock and salt to taste, and mix until blended. Let stand for 5 minutes.
❡ Divide the mixture evenly among the banana leaves or corn husks, spreading it about ⅛ inch (3 mm) thick in the center of each. Spread 1 tablespoon of filling on top. Overlap the sides of the leaves, then fold over the tops and bottoms to create little packages.
❡ Line a steamer basket with the remaining banana leaves or corn husks and place the *tamales* upright, packed tightly together. Cover with more leaves. Place the basket over boiling water, cover tightly, and cook for 45 to 55 minutes, or until the *masa* separates easily from the leaf when opened.

Left: Sweet Bean Tamales; right: Green Chile Tamales

TAMAL DE CAZUELA CON TORTILLAS

TORTILLA TAMAL CASSEROLE

This is a modern adaptation of a recipe from the culinary historian Señora Tere Castelló. Instead of tortilla masa, or dough, the recipe calls for ready-made tortillas and is a good excuse for using leftovers. The tortillas would traditionally have been ground on a stone metate (grindstone), lending the tamale mixture a wonderful texture, so try not to overprocess.

3 medium ancho chiles
½ cup (4 fl oz/125 ml) hot water
½ cup (4 fl oz/125 ml) vegetable oil
1 lb (500 g) corn tortillas (about 25)
2 teaspoons salt, or to taste
1 cup (8 fl oz/250 ml) chicken stock
3½ oz (100 g) plus 2 teaspoons lard
14 oz (440 g) thinly sliced and seeded tomatoes
10 baby or new onions, sliced
2 chicken breast halves, cooked and shredded
½ cup (4 oz/125 g) green olives, pitted and sliced
¼ cup (1½ oz/45 g) raisins
½ teaspoon ground cumin

SERVES 8

❡ Clean the chiles, removing the stem, seeds, and veins. Soak them in the hot water for 10 minutes to soften. Drain and discard the liquid.

❡ In a frying pan, heat the oil over medium heat and dip both sides of each *tortilla* in it briefly to soften. Cut the *tortillas* into quarters and put them into a food processor with the salt. Process roughly. Add the chiles and stock, and process to blend, retaining some texture. Put the mixture into a bowl.

❡ In a small pan, heat the 3½ oz (100 g) of lard until smoking. Pour it over the *tortilla* mixture and mix well to form a dough.

❡ Grease a *cazuela* or other deep heat-proof casserole (10 x 3 inches/25 x 8 cm) with the remaining lard. On the bottom, place a piece of cheesecloth large enough to completely cover the *tamal*. Place half the dough on the cloth and cover with the tomatoes, onions, and chicken. Sprinkle with the olives, raisins, and cumin. Add the rest of the dough, cover with the cloth, and then seal with an aluminum foil lid.

❡ Place the casserole in a pot large enough to hold it. Fill the pot with boiling water to half the depth of the casserole and cook over medium heat for 45 minutes. Remove the casserole from the pot, uncover, turn onto a serving platter, and carefully remove the cloth. Cut into wedges and serve.

TAMAL DE CAZUELA DE ELOTE FRESCO

FRESH CORN TAMAL CASSEROLE

This half-sweet/half-salty tamal casserole is typical of Hermosillo, Sonora. At grandfather Yzábal's house, it was always made in a cazuela and served as an accompaniment to the main dish.

10 ears corn, with kernels cut from the cob (about 3 cups/ 24 oz/750 g)
3½ oz (100 g) queso panela or other semisoft, low-fat white cheese

3½ oz (100 g) lard

½ teaspoon salt, or to taste

½ teaspoon baking powder

1 tablespoon sugar

3 tablespoons raisins, soaked in a little hot water and drained

2 tablespoons shredded (grated) Oaxaca or mozzarella cheese

1 large poblano chile, roasted and cut into strips (see box page 112)

SERVES 6

❡ Preheat the oven to 350°F (180°C/Gas 4).

❡ In a food processor, process the corn and cheese until smooth.

❡ With an electric mixer, beat the lard for 5 to 7 minutes until light and fluffy. Add the corn mixture and beat for another 2 minutes, adding the salt and baking powder at the end.

❡ Butter an 8-inch (20-cm) *cazuela,* or any ovenproof dish with high sides. Divide the mixture into 2 parts, adding the sugar and raisins to one of them. Spoon this mixture into one side of the mold.

❡ On the other side, spoon half of the corn mixture, then the shredded cheese and chiles, then the remaining corn mixture. Bake in the oven for 1 hour, or until a knife inserted in the center comes out clean.

❡ Serve in the casserole.

Left: Tortilla Tamale Casserole; right: Fresh Corn Tamale Casserole

BREAKFASTS AND DRINKS

BREAKFASTS AND DRINKS

EXICAN BREAKFASTS CAN VARY FROM AN EARLY MEAL OF COFFEE AND BREAD, TO A FULL repast, also known as *almuerzo*, which is eaten later in the morning. This sumptuous meal is truly one of the great breakfasts of the world.

❧ It starts with a plate of the many fruits available in Mexico year-round: papaya (pawpaw) with lime, watermelon, cantaloupe (rockmelon), pineapple, bananas, and mangoes; or the rarer tropical fruits such as mamey (mammee), *cherimoya* (custard apple), and *sapodilla*, and a glass of fresh juice made from many of the aforementioned fruits or squeezed oranges or grapefruit.

❧ Next, every region has its own variety of egg or *tortilla* dishes, *tamales*, and *pan dulce* (sweet bread), accompanied by beans, fresh *tortillas*, and *salsas*. While *huevos a la Mexicana* (Mexican scrambled eggs) and *huevos rancheros* (fried eggs on flat *tortillas* with green or red sauce) are available throughout the country, eggs are scrambled with the dried beef known as *machaca* in the north, or with *nopales* (nopal cactus paddles) and a tomato-based sauce in Oaxaca. In Veracruz, eggs may be served swimming in a sauce flavored with beans and *epazote* or tomatoes and cilantro (fresh coriander). *Tortilla* dishes vary from bean-dipped *enfrijoladas*, to *chilaquiles* made with fried *tortilla* strips, green or red

Previous pages: A baker makes his way through the deserted early morning streets of Puebla, the scent of sweet rolls still warm from the oven wafting behind him as he delivers to a neighborhood cafetería.

Opposite: Fairground woman filling a chalupa, a popular masa-based snack.

sauce, and fried onions, sometimes with the addition of shredded chicken, and topped with thick cream and crumbled cheese.

❧ The most traditional hot drink in Mexico is chocolate, which, in pre-Hispanic times, was made with water and often thickened with corn *masa*. It seems to have been served more often as a bitter drink, and seasoned with chile, than sweetened with honey. Today, hot chocolate is made with milk or water or a mixture of both, usually from pressed chocolate tablets flavored with cinnamon, sugar, and sometimes almonds, and is unthickened. The water-based version thickened with corn *masa* is called *champurrado*, and is actually a chocolate *atole*, another traditional hot drink, generally made with corn *tortilla masa*, that may also be drunk plain, flavored with different fruits, or simply with cinnamon. Another version is made with cornstarch (cornflour) as the thickener instead of corn *masa*.

❧ Coffee didn't make its appearance in Mexico until 1790, and then it was principally grown for export. Eventually, however, a taste for the drink took hold here too. It was grown in Chiapas, Veracruz, Tabasco, and Oaxaca, with smaller-scale production elsewhere. The very Mexican and delicious *café de olla*, flavored with *piloncillo* (solid molasses) and cinnamon, is prepared all over the country.

❧ There is a very fine line in Mexico between hot herbal or other infusions drunk for taste and those drunk for medicinal purposes. The most common infusions are chamomile, spearmint, cinnamon, lemongrass, lemon or orange leaves, linden, and rue. These are what is commonly referred to as *tés* (teas) in Mexico rather than the black teas from India, China, or Sri Lanka, which are also available.

TORTILLA DE HUEVO CON SALSA DE CHILE

MEXICAN OMELET WITH CHILE SAUCE

This Mexican omelet, a typical dish from the regions of Puebla and Oaxaca, is presented at the table in the same frying pan in which it is cooked. The sauce can be made from one of a number of dried chiles, such as the pasilla, guajillo, ancho, *or* cascabel. *This recipe, from the fabulous kitchen of Yaya and Alicia Herrera, is delicious served as the focus of a late breakfast.*

⅔ oz (20 g) pasilla, guajillo, ancho, *or* cascabel
   chiles, *seeded and stems discarded*
1 cup (8 fl oz/250 ml) water
½ teaspoon salt, or to taste
2 medium cloves garlic, minced (finely chopped)
¼ cup (2 fl oz/60 ml) vegetable oil
6 eggs, lightly beaten
pinch salt

SERVES 4

❡ Toast the chiles briefly over a flame or in a heated dry frying pan.
❡ Puree the chiles in a blender with the water, salt, and garlic until smooth and set aside.
❡ Heat the oil in a 10-inch (25-cm) non-stick pan. Add the eggs and a pinch of salt. Cook over medium heat, swirling the pan and lifting the edges of the eggs with a spatula so that the uncooked portion runs underneath.
❡ When the bottom is set, quarter the omelet and gently turn each wedge over to finish cooking, approximately 1½ minutes.
❡ Cut the wedges in half again and pour the chile mixture on top. Cook until the sauce begins to bubble, and serve immediately from the pan.

CHILE CON QUESO

CHILE WITH CHEESE

This recipe is from the famous video director, Pedro Torres. Chile con Queso is typically served in Saltillo, Coahuila, as a mid- to late-morning brunch with tamales and Frijoles Refritos (see page 150). It is also delicious rolled into tacos of flour or corn tortillas.

10 oz (315 g) tomatoes, seeded and roughly chopped
2 serrano chiles, stems removed and roughly chopped
3 tablespoons vegetable oil

1 small onion, roughly chopped
½ teaspoon salt, or to taste
6 oz (185 g) queso asadero, Chihuahua, *Monterey Jack,* mozzarella, or any mild melting cheese, sliced

SERVES 6–8

Top: Chile with Cheese; bottom: Mexican Omelet with Chile Sauce

❡ Using the pulse button on a food processor, process the tomatoes and chiles, making certain to leave some texture.

❡ Heat the oil in a flat *cazuela* or a 9-inch (23-cm) frying pan. Sauté the onion over medium heat until translucent. Add the tomato

mixture and salt, and cook until fairly dry, approximately 5 minutes.

❡ Place the sliced cheese over the mixture and lower the heat. Cover and cook for 3 to 4 minutes until the cheese melts.

❡ Serve immediately in the same pan.

HUEVOS ESTILO JALAPA

SCRAMBLED EGGS JALAPA-STYLE

Here are two delicious egg dishes from Mexico City's El Bajio Restaurant, where some of the most extraordinary Veracruz-style breakfasts are served. The Jalapa-style eggs are scrambled and served swimming in tomato sauce in individual earthenware pots. Carmen "Titita" Ramirez Degollado, the restaurant's owner, recommends serving the dish with freshly made hot tortillas and Frijoles de la Olla (see page 150).

For the sauce:
1 clove garlic, peeled
1 onion, coarsely chopped
2 oz (60 g) fresh jalapeño chiles, with stems, seeds, and veins removed
1⅓ lb (615 g) tomatoes, coarsely chopped
2 tablespoons corn or vegetable oil
¼ teaspoon salt, or to taste
1 cup (8 fl oz/250 ml) water
1 small bunch (⅓ oz/10 g) cilantro (fresh coriander) without roots, washed and tied with string
For the eggs:
2 tablespoons corn or vegetable oil
12 eggs, lightly beaten
salt to taste

SERVES 6

❡ For the sauce: Puree the garlic, onion, chiles, and tomatoes in a blender. Heat the oil in a large pot and strain the sauce into the oil. Simmer over medium heat until thickened, approximately 10 minutes. Add the salt and water, and simmer over low heat for another 15 minutes. Add the cilantro, simmer for 5 minutes, then remove and discard the cilantro.
❡ To make the eggs: Heat the oil in a large frying pan and scramble the eggs, seasoning with salt.
❡ Divide the eggs among 6 earthenware pots or deep soup bowls. Fill each with about ½ cup (4 fl oz/125 ml) of sauce and serve immediately.

HUEVOS TIRADOS CALDOSOS

SCRAMBLED EGGS WITH BLACK BEANS, BROTH, AND EPAZOTE

As in the previous recipe, the scrambled eggs are served bathed in a broth in individual pots. In this case, it is a bean broth flavored with epazote, a unique-tasting herb that often accompanies beans in Mexico. The eggs can also be scrambled directly with the beans (without broth) for huevos tirados. Serve with hot tortillas.

For the sauce:
3 medium cloves garlic, peeled
2 small onions, coarsely chopped
1½ cups (12 fl oz/375 ml) Frijoles de la Olla (see page 150), measured with broth
2 cups (16 fl oz/500 ml) water
2 tablespoons corn or vegetable oil
½ teaspoon salt, or to taste
1 oz (30 g) epazote, washed and tied in a bunch, plus 6 leaves, optional (for garnish)
For the eggs:
2 tablespoons corn or vegetable oil
12 eggs, lightly beaten
salt to taste

SERVES 6

❡ For the sauce: Puree the garlic and onions in a blender with the bean broth; use a little of the water, if necessary. Heat the oil in a wide earthenware pot or medium saucepan. Pour the garlic mixture and the beans into the oil and fry over low heat for about 10 minutes, stirring. Season with salt and add the remaining water and the bunch of *epazote*. Bring to a boil, and simmer for 15 to 20 minutes; the sauce should be thickened but still "brothy." Remove and discard the *epazote* before serving.
❡ To make the eggs: Heat the oil in a large frying pan and scramble the eggs, seasoning with salt.
❡ Divide the eggs among 6 individual earthenware pots or deep soup bowls, cover with the sauce, decorate with the *epazote* leaves, if desired, and serve immediately.

EPAZOTE

The pungent, jagged-leafed herb, epazote, has almost as many English-speaking aliases as it has uses in the Mexican household. Also known as goosefoot, wormseed, pigweed, Jerusalem oak and pazote, it is considered a weed in most countries. In Mexico, however, it is essential to many bean dishes for its unique flavor and because it is a carminative, which means it reduces gas. Epazote is also favored by herbalists for its worm-repelling properties, and the leaf is used to expel phlegm and treat asthma. The fruit and oil distilled from it are toxic. It is also available dried, but then the flavor is greatly diminished, and there really is no substitute for the fresh leaves.

Top: Scrambled Eggs with Black Beans, Broth, and Epazote; bottom: Scrambled Eggs Jalapa-style

REQUESÓN REVUELTO A LA MEXICANA

RICOTTA CHEESE SCRAMBLED LIKE MEXICAN EGGS

In this recipe, from Diana Kennedy's book The Art of Mexican Cooking, *ricotta cheese takes the place of scrambled eggs—an excellent alternative for those who wish to avoid them. The ricotta must be well drained, almost dry. If it is not, Diana Kennedy recommends squeezing it gently in a piece of cheesecloth, then spreading it to dry before use. This recipe can be served as a brunch dish and also makes an excellent filling for fried tacos.*

¼ cup (2 fl oz/60 g) safflower oil
1 onion, minced (finely chopped)
4–5 serrano *chiles, or to taste, minced (finely chopped)*
1¼ cups (8 oz/250 g) unpeeled tomatoes, minced (finely chopped)
2½ cups (1¼ lb/600 g) ricotta cheese, firmly packed
½ teaspoon sea salt, or to taste

SERVES 4

❡ Heat the oil in a frying pan and add the onion and chiles. Fry gently without browning for 1 minute. Add the tomatoes and cook over high heat, stirring occasionally, until the mixture is fairly dry, about 4 minutes. Add the ricotta and salt, and mix well. Cook over medium heat for about 4 minutes, until it begins to turn a light golden color and comes away cleanly from the surface of the pan when turned with a spoon.
❡ Serve immediately with corn *tortillas.*

INFLADAS DE FRIJOL

"INFLATED" BEAN TORTILLAS

These infladas *from Carmen Ramirez Degollado of El Bajío Restaurant are made with* tortillas *formed from a mixture of corn* tortilla masa *and refried beans which are then deep-fried until they "inflate". The dish is a specialty of the port of Veracruz, where it is eaten with* café lechero, *or milk coffee. The* infladas *must be eaten immediately.*

5 oz (155 g) Frijoles Refritos *(see page 150); quite dry*
1 lb (500 g) prepared tortilla masa *(see* Tortillas de Maíz *page 55)*
salt, to taste
1 qt (1 l) vegetable oil
red chiles, for garnish

MAKES ABOUT 20

❡ Process the *Frijoles Refritos* in a food processor until they are completely smooth. Place in a bowl with the *tortilla masa* and salt to taste, and process the mixture together with a spoon until the dough is uniform in color and texture. Press the mixture

Left: Ricotta Cheese Scrambled like Mexican Eggs; right: "Inflated" Bean Tortillas

into *tortillas* one at a time (see *Tortillas de Maíz* page 53 for the technique), and fry as follows: Heat the oil in a large pot over high heat. Put one *tortilla* into the pot, spooning it with hot oil to bathe it well, until it inflates. Remove it from the pot and drain on paper towels to remove any excess oil. Repeat with the remaining *tortillas*, one at a time.

¶ Serve immediately with *Salsa Negra* (see page 25) and garnish with chiles, if desired.

ENFRIJOLADAS SANTA CLARA

SANTA CLARA ENFRIJOLADAS

Enfrijoladas *are one of the most widely popular dishes in Mexico. They range from* tortillas *that are simply dipped in a thin bean puree and topped with chopped onion to this adaptation of an elaborate dish from the Fonda Santa Clara Restaurant in Mexico City.*

2 cups (11 oz/340 g) Frijoles de la Olla *(see page 150) plus 1 cup (8 fl oz/250 ml) bean broth*
1 (5 oz/155 g) chorizo *sausage, skinned*
⅓ cup (3 fl oz/90 ml) vegetable oil
8 corn tortillas
2 cups (14 oz/400 g) cooked, shredded chicken
⅓ cup (3 fl oz/90 ml) heavy (double/thickened) cream, optional
⅓ cup (1 oz/30 g) cilantro (fresh coriander), minced (finely chopped)
1 onion, minced (finely chopped)
4 serrano chiles, charred, with seeds and stems removed, and minced (finely chopped)

SERVES 4

❡ Put the beans and broth in a blender and puree until smooth. Remove and set aside.
❡ Coarsely chop the *chorizo* in the blender, then fry in a hot pan without oil to release the fat. Remove, drain on paper towels, and keep warm.
❡ Heat 3 tablespoons of oil in a frying pan and dip each *tortilla* in the oil briefly on each side. In a separate frying pan, heat the remaining oil and fry the bean mixture until all the oil has been absorbed.
❡ Dip each *tortilla* in the bean puree, then place ¼ cup of the chicken and a tablespoon of the bean puree on top. Roll up the *tortilla* and put 2 on each plate. Cover with more bean puree and the cream, if desired. Top with the cilantro, onion, chiles, and *chorizo*, then serve.

Santa Clara Enfrijoladas

CITRUS FRUITS

Although citrus fruits were introduced after the Spanish conquest, they have come to play a major part in the culinary traditions of Mexico.

Limón (Mexican lime): There is nothing, not even chile, more omnipresent on the Mexican table than *limón*, the Mexican lime. Whereas in other countries you would find salt and pepper on the table, in Mexico, you will find salt and a tiny *cazuela* (pot) of cut limes. They accompany a good *trago* (mouthful) of tequila or beer, and are squeezed in soups, on broiled (grilled) meat, or on any *taco*. The juice is drunk as *agua de limón* (lemonade) or in a *margarita,* and is used to marinate fish and shellfish, either before cooking or to be eaten raw as seviche.

Although a sour fruit, the Mexican, or key, lime is sweeter and certainly less acidic than its European or American counterpart. It's smaller and often a more

yellow-green. It is also very different in taste from a yellow lemon, which is only occasionally seen in Mexico as an import. In general, limes seem more adapted to tropical climates and lemons to subtropical or temperate zones.

Naranja (orange): This is second in popularity in Mexico to the lime, and is used virtually exclusively for juice. Any self-respecting Mexican would never serve bottled orange juice: it is always freshly squeezed in satisfyingly large glasses, and that means squeezed at the moment it is ordered, whether on a street stand, in a restaurant, or at someone's house. Although other varieties are available, oranges in Mexico tend to be more green or yellow-orange, even when they are sweet and juicy; this is because in tropical climates, the fruit matures before the skin has changed color. Another

choice for orange lovers in Mexico is to eat them sliced with chile and salt.

Mandarinas (mandarines): Named after their origins in China, where most citrus fruits originated, these are especially popular in Mexico in December at the height of their season. Whether *mandarinas* is translated as tangerines, mandarines, or clementines, in Mexico, whether large or small, they are all called simply *mandarinas.* Baby mandarines are used to fill *piñatas* (balloons filled with sweets) for children's parties and *posadas,* festivities during the nine days before Christmas that recall Joseph and Mary's search for lodging. These are given the special name of *mandarinas piñateras.*

Lima ágria (bitter lime): This is a less common citrus fruit which is used only in the cuisine of Yucatán. The most famous use of the bitter lime is as the main flavoring of the

soup named after it: *sopa de lima,* a chicken-based clear soup with *tortilla* strips and shredded chicken.

Naranja ágria (bitter, or Seville, orange): Even though bitter-orange trees grow elsewhere, they are generally admired for decorative, rather than used for culinary, purposes. This orange is also only used in the cuisine of Yucatán. It is a flavoring for *cochinita pibil* (a pork dish wrapped in banana leaves and baked in the ground) and other dishes, and takes the place of lime in many fresh chile sauces from the Yucatán.

Limón real, or limón dulce (royal, or sweet, lemon): A specialty of Colima on the Pacific coast, this is like a small, white grapefruit in size and color, and has an interesting, slightly sweet flavor; the juice is drunk alone or in an *agua fresca.*

Lima (lime): This is simply a nippled, yellow-green fruit about the size of an American lime. It is not at all acidic, but slightly sweet and somewhat tasteless. It is peeled and eaten rather than squeezed.

Toronjas (grapefruit): These quite wonderful, deep pink-red fruits are available in markets all over Mexico.

1. limón (lemon); 2. naranja (orange); 3. mandarinas (mandarines); 4. lima agria (bitter lime); 5. naranja ágria (bitter, or Seville, orange); 6. limón real/limón dulce (royal, or sweet, lemon); 7. lima (lime); 8. toronjas (grapefruit)

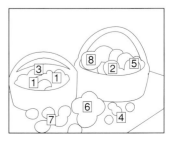

Top: Cheese Biscuits "Tamiahua"; bottom: Peanut Cookies

GALLETAS CON QUESO "QUESADILLAS DE TAMIAHUA"

CHEESE BISCUITS "TAMIAHUA"

This very old recipe is from Guille Lárraga from Tamiahua, Veracruz. The cookies are commonly called bocado *(bite) or* quesadillas *(because they are made of cheese). Dutch cheese, such as the Edam used in this recipe, was very popular in the port cities along the Gulf of Mexico where it arrived on European ships.*

2 cups (8 oz/250 g) all-purpose (plain) flour
3½ oz (100 g) butter
4 egg yolks
2 oz (60 g) lard
3½ oz (100 g) Edam cheese, grated
1 teaspoon salt, or to taste
¼ cup (2 oz/60 g) sugar, optional
cinnamon to taste, optional

MAKES 44 BISCUITS

❡ Preheat the oven to 350°F (180°C/Gas 4).
❡ On a clean surface or in a large bowl, combine the flour and butter with your fingers until it resembles grains of rice. Make a well in the center and add the yolks, lard, cheese, and salt. Combine the ingredients into a dough without kneading.
❡ Divide the dough in half and flatten each portion with the palm of your hand until it is ½ inch (1 cm) thick. Cut circles in the dough with a tequila glass (or a shot glass or a 1¼-inch/3.5-cm cookie cutter). Repress any scraps and cut as well until all the dough is used.
❡ Put the rounds on a cookie sheet (baking tray) and bake for 30 minutes without browning; the surfaces will bubble slightly while cooking. Remove from the pan with a spatula and transfer to a plate.
❡ Sprinkle with the sugar and cinnamon, if desired. Serve warm or at room temperature.

POLVORONES DE CACAHUATE

PEANUT COOKIES

These cookies come from Veracruz, where peanuts are produced. They can be served for breakfast or as a mid-morning snack with coffee, hot chocolate, or atole.

2½ cups (10 oz/315 g) all-purpose (plain) flour
1 teaspoon baking powder
3½ oz (100 g) lard
1 egg
3½ oz (100 g) peanuts, shelled, skinned, toasted, and
  ground to a paste in a food processor
⅔ cup (5 oz/155 g) sugar

MAKES 40 COOKIES

❡ Preheat the oven to 300°F (150°C/Gas 2).
❡ Sift the flour with the baking powder onto a clean surface. Make a well in the center and add the lard and egg. Combine the ingredients with your fingers to make a smooth dough. Add the peanut paste and knead the dough lightly.
❡ Roll the dough into balls about the size of a walnut and put them on a greased cookie sheet (baking tray) 3 inches (7.5 cm) apart. Flatten the balls slightly. Bake for 20 to 25 minutes, or until they turn a light golden brown.
❡ Remove them from the oven and sprinkle generously with the sugar while they are still warm.

Some of the myriad of sweet breads and rolls in Mexico.

SWEET BREADS AND ROLLS

The Spanish introduced wheat to Mexico, along with the techniques for baking rolls and an endless variety of sweet breads. A great deal of commercial baking is still done by hand; while large mixers may knead great quantities of dough, quick hands cut, shape, and glaze it, or maneuver long, thin paddles of *bolillos* (rolls) into the oven. Baking is a ballet of rhythmic, precise movements.

Pan dulce (sweet bread): Mexicans have a pronounced sweet tooth, which is ready to be satisfied by the huge variety of sweet breads sold from wide baskets outside the markets or from bakeries. Trays laden with an assortment are brought home to be enjoyed with morning coffee or evening hot chocolate. Each has its own name: *conchas* (shells); *novias* (brides) are shells with a white, sugar-dough coating; *borregos* (sheep) have a "woolly" covering of grated coconut; *besos* (kisses) are made by folding the dough over so it meets in the middle. These few examples show the touch of humor that is never missing from the details of daily life. The Mexican name for croissants is *cuernitos* (horns), a lively reference to the fact that croissants look like little horns or, perhaps, unfaithful husbands. (When a husband or wife has *cuernitos* it means that his or her partner been unfaithful).

Coyotas: A specialty of the north, these round pastries are made with a sweet puff pastry-like dough and are filled with *piloncillo* (solid molasses).

Churros: These are made from a simple pastry of flour, water, and salt that is squeezed through a tube with ridges to form a long, cylindrical shape. After being deep-fried, they are rolled in sugar and eaten hot for breakfast or in the evening with hot chocolate.

Bolillos: Although traditionally only *tortillas* would accompany a meal, it is now quite common for a basket of *bolillos* to be served. They are crusty, fresh, oblong rolls, twisted to a point at either end and slashed diagonally across the top. The dough is similar to that for making baguettes, so the rolls dry out fast and must be eaten fresh.

Teleras: These rolls are slightly softer and flatter than *bolillos*, with two cuts along the length of the top. For breakfast, they are served as *molletes*, cut in half, topped with beans and cheese, and toasted. Their most common use, however, is for *tortas*, the Mexican sandwich. *Tortas* are a complex affair: they are usually spread with cream and beans, filled with a slice of hot, broiled (grilled) or breaded meat or cheese, and topped with pickled chiles and avocado slices.

FRUITS FOR EATING AND DRINKING

The caption of a Frida Kahlo still-life painting reads: "The bride gets a fright upon seeing the ripe openness of life." Luscious fruits, the sensual quality of watermelon and papaya (pawpaw), a display of bananas, coconuts, and pineapple are what she sees. Peeking out from behind the huge fruits, the diminutive bride rests her frightened gaze on an owl, the symbol of wisdom.

Ripe fruits, all the tastes, smells, and vibrant colors of life, are a daily reality in all parts of Mexico. You cannot avoid life here, it leaps out at you, daring you to enter into its mysteries.

Piña (pineapple): Grown in tropical Mexico, pineapples are served sliced on a fruit

fermented with water and *piloncillo* (solid molasses) to make an alcoholic drink, *tepache*. Further fermented it becomes fairly mellow and makes a mild vinegar.

To prepare pineapple, remove the crown, unless it will be used for decoration, and cut off the bottom. Standing the pineapple upright, slice off the rind from top to bottom, following the curve of the fruit, but cutting deeply enough to remove the eyes. Either slice the flesh crosswise into rounds or lengthwise into sections. Cut out the heart or eat around it. A whole, unpeeled pineapple can be hollowed out and used as a receptacle for pineapple ice or mixed fruits.

Papaya (pawpaw): Perhaps the most common fruit at the breakfast table, papaya (pawpaw) is always eaten with a squeeze of lime, which brings out its taste admirably. Mexican papayas are generally large, 8 inches (20 cm) to more than a foot (30 cm) in length, and their flesh ranges in color from yellow-orange to a deep orange-red. The latter, called *papaya roja* (red papaya), are the most highly valued. It is hard to tell the difference from the outside, although the red papayas tend to be smaller. The fruit seller will know, or will cut out a triangle of fruit to show you. Baby Hawaiian papayas (5 inches/12 cm long) are now available in Mexico, and are prized for their sweetness.

Papaya juice for breakfast, or the less concentrated papaya water for lunch, makes a delicious drink. Papaya juice mixed with orange juice is a favorite combination.

The seeds used to be spread between layers of meat to tenderize it, as papaya produces an enzyme, papain, which breaks down protein.

plate, blended with water and sugar into *agua fresca*, a refreshing drink, or sprinkled with chile and salt and sold from a fruit cart. Even the sliced-off rind is used,

Sandía (watermelon): Watermelon is served at the breakfast table either sliced on a fruit plate or blended to make a juice, seeds strained out, and either with or without sugar and water. In Mexico, it is appreciated not only for its refreshing taste but also for its sheer beauty. It holds a certain fascination for Mexican artists, including Rufino Tamayo, whose painting for the backdrop of the National Auditorium in Mexico City is a vibrant study of watermelon slices.

Melón (cantaloupe): In Mexico, both the flesh and the seeds of cantaloupe (rockmelon) serve as a drink. The flesh is pureed with water and sugar to make the ubiquitous *agua fresca*. The fresh seeds, pureed along with the fruit, add body and flavor to the melon water. They can also be dried, ground, and blended with water and sugar to make an *horchata*. Cantaloupe is very popular as a breakfast fruit, and is also prepared as a dessert cooked with ground almonds and egg yolks.

Fresas (strawberries): Originating in Chile, strawberries grow in temperate climates. Although less common than tropical fruits on the Mexican table, strawberries are eaten fresh for breakfast or dessert, or made into jam.

Sliced, dried strawberries are eaten in certain areas of Mexico as a sweet snack, and crystallized strawberries are a specialty of Irapuato, Guanajuato, one of the areas where they are produced. The strawberries are cooked with sugar and water for an hour and left to sit in the syrup. They are then put out to dry in the sun on a rack for a day and a half, dipped in sugar, and left for another day.

Coco (coconut, green): Whole, green coconuts are a common sight in coastal Mexico, where they are sold by the roadside simply pierced through the top so the liquid can be drunk through a straw. At this immature stage, the coconut "milk" is plentiful, while the flesh is still very gelatinous. As the coconut ripens, much of its liquid will be absorbed into the flesh, which hardens into a solid, white layer (see Coconut, brown, in "Fruits and Desserts").

Many other fruits excellent for eating and drinking are available in Mexico (see also "Fruits and Desserts" and "Chiles and Cactus").

1. piña (pineapple); 2. papaya (pawpaw); 3. sandía (watermelon); 4. melón (canteloupe); 5. fresas (strawberries); 6. coco (coconut, green); 7. watermelon "water"; 8. melon "water"

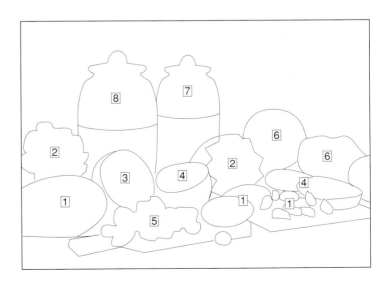

REFRESCO DE ZAPOTE NEGRO Y MANDARINAS

BLACK ZAPOTE AND TANGERINE DRINK

Black zapote, with its unusual black pulp, is a tropical fruit harvested in the winter. Mexicans traditionally combine this fruit with orange juice and sherry to make a seasonal dessert, but these can be substituted for tangerine juice for a tasty breakfast beverage, an idea from Patricia Quintana. This drink is best served very cold so leave it in the refrigerator for at least 3 hours before serving, but don't add ice, which would dilute it.

2 large (1 lb/500 g) black zapotes, halved and pulp removed
4 cups (1 qt/1 l) tangerine juice
⅓ cup (3 oz/90 g) brown sugar, or to taste

MAKES 6 CUPS (1½ qt/1½ l)

❡ Place the black *zapote* pulp in a large strainer (sieve) over a bowl and press the pulp through with a large wooden spoon.
❡ Put the pulp in a pitcher, add the juice and sugar, and stir until dissolved.
❡ Serve thoroughly chilled.

AGUA DE PEPINO

CUCUMBER DRINK

This recipe can be used as a prototype for all aguas frescas. Here it is made with cucumber as the main ingredient, but any number of fruits could be substituted for the cucumber, including watermelon, canteloupe (rockmelon), papaya (pawpaw), strawberry, or mango. Adjust the sugar and lime according to your taste, and the amount of water you add according to how strong you like the flavor.

1 large cucumber, peeled and cut into large pieces
2 cups (16 fl oz/500 ml) water
1 cup (8 fl oz/250 ml) ice
3 tablespoons (1½ oz/45 g) sugar, or to taste
juice of ¼ lemon or ½ lime, or to taste

MAKES 1 qt (1 l)

❡ Place the cucumber in a blender, and puree with all of the remaining ingredients until completely smooth.
❡ Serve immediately, garnished with cucumber and lime.

Top: Black Zapote and Tangerine Drink; right: Cucumber Drink

HOT AND COLD DRINKS

Té limón (lemongrass tea):
This is one of the most common teas in Mexico. It is made from a grass that has nothing to do with the citrus family but has a very lemony flavor, hence the name lemongrass. In Thai cuisine, lemongrass is used bulb and all to flavor soups and curries, but in Mexico, just the stalks are sold, tied in bundles, and they are used only as an infusion to be drunk hot.

Flor de jamaica (hibiscus flowers): This is used to make a refreshing and popular drink called *agua de jamaica*, and is produced in only one of the thirty-two states of Mexico, Guerrero. Farmers dry the flowers in the sun before sending them to market. The flowers should be pliable rather than brittle and their color a rich crimson.

Agua de jamaica (hibiscus water): To make *agua de jamaica*, add the hibiscus flowers to boiling water for 5 minutes, then set aside for about 15 minutes before straining. Add cold water and sugar to taste. Drink cold.

Tamarindo (tamarind): This is the seedpod of a large tree that grows on Mexico's Pacific coast. A hard, brown exterior protects the sticky, acidic pulp inside. For *agua de tamarindo* (tamarind water), the pulp and seeds are boiled in water for 5 minutes, then pushed through a sieve to strain out the seeds. More sugar and water are added to taste and the liquid is chilled. Tamarind is also used for making sweets in the shape of soft, round balls, which may be sweet, or flavored with salt and chile.

Chía: These are tiny, almost metallic-looking seeds that are covered with a gelatinous layer when rehydrated in water, and are very beneficial to the digestion. Traditionally they are added to *agua de limón* (lemonade) which is always made with the Mexican lime. Soak ½ cup (about 3½ oz/ 100 g) in a cup (8 fl oz/ 250 ml) of cold water for at least half an hour, then stir to separate them. Add this to 4 cups (1 qt/1 l) of *agua de limón* (lemonade) or so and stir before serving.

Horchata: This is a technique of Spanish origin for making a refreshing drink with ground seeds, nuts, or grains mixed with sugar and water. In Mexico, it is commonly made with melon seeds or dry rice, sometimes with the delicious addition of ground almonds. It is an especially popular drink in the Yucatán Peninsula.

Manzanilla (chamomile tea): The small white-and-yellow flowers are sold fresh in Mexico, and the infusion is made with the stems as well as the flowers. It is often drunk as a cure for stomach ailments or simply as a relaxing tea before going to bed.

Cacao (cocoa): Toasted and ground, these beans are the basic ingredients for making chocolate, one of Mexico's most important contributions to the gastronomic world. In pre-Columbian Mexico, chocolate was highly appreciated and was always present on Emperor Montezuma's table. It was drunk mixed with water, sometimes sweetened, and sometimes flavored with chile.

Cacao is grown in Chiapas and Oaxaca, where it is ground, usually mixed with sugar, cinnamon, and almonds, and pressed into tablets which gives Mexican chocolate its distinctive flavor. Hot chocolate is now commonly made with milk, although in certain regions, the Aztec tradition of making it with water is still customary. In either case, a chocolate moulinet is used to whip up a froth while heating it.

Granos de café (coffee beans): Even though coffee beans were originally cultivated in North Africa, the American continents now grow some of the best coffee in the world. Of the types grown in Mexico, the variety called *Coatepec*, named after a small village in Veracruz, is the most popular for export. Both Veracruz and Chiapas are coffee-producing areas. In the port of Veracruz, the custom is to pour a rich, concentrated coffee "syrup" into your cup simultaneously with hot milk. The most popular way of drinking coffee, though (other than instant coffee, which has taken a firm hold in Mexico), is *Café de Olla*, which is sweetened and flavored with cinnamon. Its name comes from the round, earthenware pot, or *olla*, it is brewed in; it is served in cups of a similar shape.

Hierba buena (spearmint): *Hierba buena* and *menta* (peppermint) are used for making tea, especially the former, which is much more common in Mexico and has a milder flavor. Peppermint has smaller, dark green leaves, and the stems are purplish.

1. té limón (lemongrass tea); 2. flor de jamaica (hibiscus flowers); 3. agua de jamaica (hibiscus water); 4. tamarindo (tamarind); 5. chía; 6. melon seeds; 7. manzanilla (chamomile tea); 8. cacao (cocoa); 9. chocolate tablets; 10. hot chocolate; 11. granos de café (coffee beans); 12. hierba buena (spearmint)

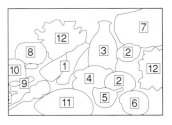

CAFÉ DE OLLA

MEXICAN COFFEE

The name of this coffee is derived from the Mexican clay pot in which it is prepared. The piloncillo and cinnamon give it a flavor different from any other. Café de Olla is served in the morning, or on cold evenings after a traditional Mexican supper such as tamales or pozole. In rural Mexico, it is traditionally served during a period of mourning, sometimes laced with a dash of hard liquor.

4 cups (1 qt/1 l) water
½ cup (3½ oz/100 g) piloncillo, in chunks, or light molasses
2-inch (5-cm) cinnamon stick
½ cup (2 oz/60 g) roasted coffee, medium grind

MAKES 4 CUPS

¶ Boil the water in a clay or enamel pot with the *piloncillo* and cinnamon. Once the *piloncillo* has dissolved, reduce the heat and add the coffee. Cover and simmer for 5 minutes. Remove from the heat and strain the coffee into another clay or enamel pot. Serve hot in little earthenware cups, ½ cup (4 fl oz/125 ml) per person. The coffee can be reheated, but do not boil it.

¶ This recipe makes a light coffee. For a sweeter, spicier version, add 1 teaspoon of aniseed and 2 or 3 whole cloves. A little brandy may also be added before serving.

AGUA FRESCA DE TÉ LIMÓN

LEMONGRASS DRINK

Although lemongrass tea, with its beautiful topaz color, is usually drunk hot, here it is served as a refreshing iced tea.

1 bundle lemongrass stalks (2½ oz/75 g), washed
5 cups (1¼ qt/1.25 l) water
¼ cup (1½ oz/50 g) sugar, or to taste

MAKES 4 CUPS (1 qt/1 l)

¶ Place the lemongrass in a saucepan with 3 cups (24 fl oz/750 ml) of the water. Cover and simmer gently over medium heat for 5 to 8 minutes or until the liquid is aromatic and yellow-green in color. Remove from the heat, add the sugar, and stir until dissolved. Cool, and strain into a glass pitcher. Add the remaining 2 cups (16 fl oz/500 ml) of water.
¶ Chill until very cold. If you add ice, serve immediately to avoid diluting the flavor.

Left: Mexican Coffee; right: Lemongrass Drink

Front: Hot Chocolate; back: Corn Masa Atole

CHAMPURRADO

HOT CHOCOLATE

Champurrado, *which has been popular since Aztec times, is a hot drink made with tortilla masa, water, and chocolate. The sugar and cinnamon are later additions, the spice having been introduced from Ceylon by the Spanish. Oaxacan chocolate, which is pressed with sugar, ground almonds, and cinnamon, is usually used, but you can obtain a similar flavor simply by adding a little ground almond to semisweet or bittersweet chocolate. Champurrado is traditionally served in little olli-tas de barro, or glazed clay cups. It can be made ahead of time and reheated, and it will keep for up to 3 days in the refrigerator. This recipe is from Carmen Ramirez Degollago.*

9 cups (2¼ qt/2.25 l) water
½ cup (4 oz/125 g) sugar
2 tablespoons cinnamon
9 oz (280 g) Oaxacan chocolate, or semisweet (cooking) chocolate, or bittersweet (dark) chocolate
7 oz (210 g) prepared corn tortilla masa (see page 55)

MAKES 8 LARGE OR 16 SMALL CUPS

¶ Place 2 cups (16 fl oz/500 ml) of water in a blender and puree with all of the remaining ingredients until smooth.
¶ Pour the mixture into a glazed clay pot or medium saucepan with the remaining water. Cook over low heat, stirring constantly with a *molinillo* or wire whisk until thickened, about 30 minutes.
¶ Serve immediately or, if preparing in advance, allow to cool, then refrigerate.

ATOLE DE MASA DE MAÍZ

CORN MASA ATOLE

Corn atole is a drink that has existed in Mexico since pre-Hispanic times. It is easy to prepare, high in carbohydrates, and consumed primarily by rural Mexicans in regions where corn is grown. Atole gives a feeling of fullness and is usually drunk on cold mornings or evenings. It is generally sweetened with sugar or chunks of piloncillo (molasses), although residents of southeastern Puebla prefer alternating a sip of atole with a bite of a piece of piloncillo.

3⅓ oz (100 g) prepared corn tortilla masa (see page 55)
2½ cups (20 fl oz/625 ml) water

MAKES 3 SERVINGS

❡ Dissolve the *masa* in a bowl filled with the water, using your hands to break up the dough until no lumps remain.
❡ Cook the mixture in a small clay or enameled pot over low heat, stirring constantly until thick, about 10 minutes. Serve immediately.

ATOLE DE MAICENA CON FRESAS

STRAWBERRY-FLAVORED ATOLE WITH CORNSTARCH

Cornstarch (cornflour), rather than tortilla masa, is another way of thickening atole. This drink is a breakfast favorite, accompanied by tamales or sweet bread. It can also be made with pineapple or guavas, but puree the fruit with a little of the water and strain before adding it to the pot.

10 oz (315 g) strawberries, cleaned and hulled
⅓ cup (2½ oz/75 g) sugar, or to taste
3 cups (24 fl oz/750 ml) water
3 tablespoons cornstarch (cornflour), dissolved in
   ¼ cup (2 fl oz/60 ml) water
1 cup (8 fl oz/250 ml) milk
sugar to taste

SERVES 6

❡ Put the strawberries in a bowl, add the sugar, and set aside for 15 minutes.
❡ Meanwhile, bring the water to a boil in a pot and add the cornstarch mixture. Boil for 10 minutes, stirring occasionally. Add the milk and boil for 5 minutes. Puree the strawberry mixture in a blender and add it to the pot. Boil for 3 minutes. Add more sugar to taste and serve hot.

ATOLE DE PIÑA

PINEAPPLE ATOLE

In this recipe from La Cocina Veracruzana, *the traditional atole is flavored with cooked fruit. The pineapple could be replaced with guavas, pears, or peaches.*

1 cup (8 oz/250 g) corn tortilla masa (see Tortillas de
   Maíz page 55 and halve quantities)
2 qt (2 l) water
2 cups (16 fl oz/500 ml) fresh pineapple, chopped
3 cups (21 oz/600 g) sugar

MAKES 5 qt (5 l)

❡ Dissolve the *masa* in 2 cups (16 fl oz/500 ml) of water and strain out any lumps. Puree the pineapple with the remaining water and the sugar in batches in a blender. Pour into a large saucepan and cook over medium heat, stirring constantly, for 15 minutes. Add the *masa* mixture and cook, stirring regularly, for 20 to 25 minutes.
❡ For a variation, you can substitute milk for half of the water. In this case, you can puree the pineapple with the water and cook the fruit as above. Add the milk with the sugar before adding the masa and proceed as indicated.

Front: Strawberry-flavored Atole with Cornstarch; back: Pineapple Atole

SOUPS

S O U P S

SOUP IS AN INDISPENSABLE PART OF A MEXICAN'S MAIN MEAL, WHICH IS GENERALLY SERVED AROUND TWO OR three in the afternoon. As a matter of fact, two soups are usually served: the *sopa aguada*, or liquid soup (soup as we know it), starts the meal, followed by a *sopa seca*, or dry soup, which is a rice or pasta dish.

❡ Among the liquid soups, some of the most common are a simple *caldo de pollo*, or chicken stock, usually with rice and chicken pieces floating in it; *sopa de fideos*, or vermicelli soup; and *tortilla* soup. The latter two are made with a tomato and chicken stock base. *Tortilla* soup, also known as Aztec soup, is a great way to use up stale *tortillas*. They are cut into thin strips, fried, then added to the soup just before it is served, accompanied by fried pieces of *pasilla* chile and cubes of fresh cheese.

❡ Similar to *tortilla* soup is *sopa de miga* (breadcrumb soup). Chicken stock is simmered with several fried garlic cloves, and then poured over a piece of bread and seasoned with the pungent herb *epazote* and dried *cascabel* chiles. The result is famous as a cure for a *cruda* (hangover)!

❡ Another favorite is bean soup, preferably black bean. The boiled beans are blended with their cooking liquid and the mixture is fried with tomato and diced onion. This soup may also be seasoned with

Previous pages: Pots steaming with promise at a market stall. Soups are an integral part of the Mexican table, sometimes forming a meal on their own.

Opposite: Scrutinizing the day's selection as she has done for decades, this Mexican woman lets the best of the season dictate the vegetable content of her homemade caldo pollo *or chicken broth.*

epazote and whole, dried chiles. Just before serving, pieces of fried *tortilla* and strips of avocado are added.

❡ Wild and cultivated mushrooms, especially the smaller varieties (*señoritas* and *clavitos*), are much used for stock-based soups in the colder regions of the central plateau, around Toluca, where they grow.

❡ Dried yellow fava (broad) beans *(habas)* are cooked until they fall apart for a soup flavored with cilantro (fresh coriander) or mint and served with powdered oregano and a little olive oil. *Sopa juliana* consists of several shredded vegetables cooked together in a flavored stock.

❡ Spanish-style *pucheros* (also called *cocidos*) are often encountered on the Mexican table. These are a kind of beef casserole with vegetables such as carrots, zucchini (courgettes), potatoes, *chayotes* (vegetable pears/chokoes), pieces of corn on the cob, string beans, and cabbage. An old Mexican custom, seldom used today, is to eat the *puchero* in three stages: first, the stock, to which is added chopped onion, green *serrano* chiles, avocado, and a few drops of lime juice; then, the still-hot vegetables dressed with olive oil and a little more lime juice; and, finally, the boiled beef with a piquant sauce and *tortillas*.

❡ Very similar to *pucheros* are the very Mexican *moles de olla*, which can be made with beef, pork, or chicken, or mountain kid (*guazmole* and *mole de caderas* from Puebla); the stock is flavored with dried chiles.

❡ Finally, cream soups are frequently served in Mexico. Although these really belong to the realm of international cuisine, they are often prepared in Mexico with distinctively national flavors: for example, cream of squash blossom soup and cream of *chile poblano*, both of which may also include fresh corn kernels.

CALDO DE POLLO

CHICKEN STOCK

This is a light chicken stock that serves as a base for soups, sauces, and casseroles. While some people make a stronger stock by adding more vegetables and chicken backs and feet, many prefer it like this, so that the stock remains a subtle backdrop to the flavors of the soup or sauce to which it is added. You can save the meat from the wings for tacos *(if you have the patience to remove it).*

8 cups (2 qt/2 l) water
1 onion, stuck with 2 cloves
4 cloves garlic, unpeeled
½ teaspoon black peppercorns
2 allspice berries
3 teaspoons salt, or to taste
2 lb (1 kg) chicken wings

Chicken Broth with Rice

MAKES 6 CUPS (1½ qt/ 1.5 l)

❡ Put all but the last ingredient in a large pot and bring to a boil. Add the chicken wings and return to a boil. Skim the foam from the surface, lower the heat, and simmer for 1 hour.

❡ Strain the stock, discarding the solids, and allow to cool before refrigerating.

❡ Once the fat solidifies, remove it from the top and discard. The stock can also be frozen.

CALDO DE POLLO, ARROZ, Y CAMARONES

CHICKEN BROTH WITH RICE AND SHRIMP

This version of the ever-popular chicken broth with rice originated in Huitzuco, Guerrero, and is from Silvia Figueroa de Llamas. The accompanying ingredients are what contribute to the flavors of the soup, especially the shrimp (prawns), and each person can suit his or her own taste by adding a medley of flavors.

7 cups (1¾ qt/1.75 l) chicken stock
½ cup (3 oz/90 g) rice, well rinsed
1 teaspoon salt, optional
½ cup (4 fl oz/125 ml) olive oil
4 tablespoons chopped cilantro (fresh coriander)
4 tablespoons minced (finely chopped) serrano chiles
½ cup (4 oz/125 g) minced (finely chopped) tomatoes
8 medium shrimp (prawns), cooked and minced (finely chopped)
1 lime or lemon, cut into sixths

SERVES 6

❡ Bring the stock to a boil in a large saucepan and cook the rice for 15 to 20 minutes until it "flowers." (To let the rice flower, or *florear*, means to boil it until the grains open and break apart.) Add salt if desired.

❡ To serve, set out the olive oil on the table and put each of the remaining ingredients in separate bowls. Ladle the soup into serving bowls and let each person add the other ingredients to taste, squeezing in a few drops of lime juice just before eating.

FIDEOS
(Noodles or Pasta)

Pasta in Mexico is served either in a sopa aguada (liquid soup, or soup as we know it), or as a sopa seca, or dry soup, which is what would generally be called a pasta or rice dish.

Sopa seca is a simple tomato broth cooked with the pasta or rice until it is dry, and served before the main course. In either case, the pasta or rice is always fried first until golden, sometimes with onion and garlic, the excess oil drained off, and then the broth ingredients added and simmered with the pasta or rice until it is tender.

Although dry soup is usually made with very fine, folded vermicelli, pasta for liquid soups comes in every conceivable shape, from letters and stars, to municiones (ammunition or little round balls) or pepitas de melón (melon seeds).

Top: Chicken Broth with Avocado and Tortillas; bottom: Mushroom and Cascabel Chile Soup

CALDO DE POLLO CON AGUACATE Y TORTILLAS

CHICKEN BROTH WITH AVOCADO AND TORTILLAS

This light soup from Sarah Wiseman is just one of many variations of stock-based soups eaten in Mexico. Here, to complement the delicate flavors of the avocado, cilantro (fresh coriander), and chile, the fried tortilla *strips must be very thin. As is often the case with Mexican soups, a little lime juice is used to accentuate the different flavors.*

½ cup (4 fl oz/125 ml) vegetable oil
6 tortillas, *cut into thin strips*
8 cups (2 qt/2 l) chicken stock
1 half chicken breast, cooked and shredded
1 serrano chile, *seeds removed and chopped*
squeeze of lime juice
1 teaspoon salt, or to taste
1 large avocado, peeled, pitted, and sliced or cubed
2 tablespoons cilantro (fresh coriander), roughly chopped

SERVES 8

❡ Heat the oil in a frying pan and fry the *tortilla* strips until crisp. Drain on paper towels.
❡ Heat the stock with the chicken, chile, lime juice, and salt.
❡ Put the avocado and *tortilla* strips in separate bowls to pass around at the table, and serve the hot broth, sprinkled with the cilantro.

SOPA DE HONGOS Y CHILE CASCABEL

MUSHROOM AND CASCABEL CHILE SOUP

Mild-flavored cultivated mushrooms get a zesty boost from the other ingredients in this treasured recipe from the Ahumada Russek family.

1½ lb (750 g) cultivated mushrooms, cleaned and sliced
1½ teaspoons salt, or to taste
1 lb (500 g) tomatoes, roasted on a comal or cast-iron griddle
1 thick slice onion, toasted on a comal or cast-iron griddle
1 clove garlic, toasted on a comal or cast-iron griddle
2 cascabel chiles; 1 toasted and seeded, the other whole

1 tablespoon vegetable oil
1 tablespoon (½ oz/15 g) butter
4 cups (1 qt/1 l) chicken stock

SERVES 6

❡ Put the mushrooms and salt in a saucepan with just enough boiling water to cover. Cook over high heat for 2 to 3 minutes until tender and drain.
❡ Put the tomatoes, onion, garlic, the seeded chile, and half the mushrooms in a blender and puree until smooth.
❡ Heat the oil and butter in a casserole dish and strain the tomato mixture into the pan. Simmer for 3 to 4 minutes. Add the stock, the remaining mushrooms, and the whole chile. Add more salt if necessary. Raise the heat and boil for a few minutes. Serve immediately.

The cazuela stall in the marketplace entices tourists as well as local cooks.

CAZUELAS

These fired and glazed earthenware pots and casseroles are the traditional cooking ware of Mexico. Different shapes and sizes lend themselves to their different purposes. Bean pots are tall and straight-sided, narrowing at the mouth to minimize evaporation. The voluptuous, round *ollas*, for making, among other things, hot chocolate, allow room for frothing the chocolate with a wooden *moulinet*, while the narrow mouth prevents splashing. These are also used for hot punches and *café de olla* ("pot coffee"), and the shape helps these hot drinks maintain their heat.

Unglazed pots of this shape are not used for cooking, but keep drinking water marvelously cool. Wider, open casseroles with high or low, sloping sides are for making *moles* and sauces, casseroles, or just about any dish. The wide bottoms are good for first frying the ingredients, while the high sides can accommodate the volume of the finished dish. This same shape is mirrored in the tiniest dishes for serving salt or lime pieces at the table, in slightly larger ones for table sauces or other ingredients, and so on up to the huge *cazuelas* capable of holding enough *mole* to serve dozens of people.

The beauty of these casseroles is that the same dish can be used for cooking and serving. To prepare them for cooking, one method is to rub them all over with garlic, outside and in, especially on the bottom. Then fill the casseroles with water, bring it to a boil, reduce heat to a simmer, and cook until almost completely evaporated. Do this every time you want to use the casserole. Alternatively, a little oil may be added to the water instead of rubbing the pots with garlic. Pots used for drinks or liquids do not need to be cured first.

SOPA DE CALABAZA DE CASTILLA

PUMPKIN SOUP

Winter nights on the altiplano, or high plateau, can get quite chilly and are warmed by this simple, milk-based soup.

1½ lb (750 g) pumpkin, seeded and cut into large cubes
1 teaspoon salt, or to taste
3 cups (24 fl oz/750 ml) milk
3 tablespoons (1½ oz/45 g) butter
1 tablespoon grated onion
¼ cup (2 oz/60 g) cooked rice
freshly ground black pepper

SERVES 6

❡ Place the pumpkin in a large saucepan with water to cover. Add the salt, and cook until tender. Drain, discarding the water. Scrape the flesh off the skin and place in a blender. Add the milk and puree.

❡ Melt the butter in the same saucepan and sauté the onion over medium heat until translucent. Add the pumpkin mixture and the rice.

❡ Season with plenty of pepper and cook over low heat for 15 minutes, stirring occasionally. Serve.

❡ The soup can be prepared up to 2 hours in advance and reheated just before serving.

SOPA DE AVENA

OATMEAL SOUP

This is a very old recipe that has come back into popularity today because of the renewed interest in whole cereal grains for their nutritional value and source of necessary fiber.

4 tablespoons (2 oz/60 g) butter
½ cup (2 oz/60 g) rolled oats
3½ oz (100 g) tomatoes, peeled, seeded, and chopped
2 tablespoons chopped onion
1 small clove garlic, peeled
3 cups (24 fl oz/750 ml) chicken stock
1 teaspoon salt, or to taste
freshly ground black pepper to taste

SERVES 4

❡ In a medium saucepan over low heat, melt the butter, add the oats, and stir constantly for approximately 2 to 3 minutes.

❡ Puree the tomatoes, onion, and garlic in a blender and add them to the oats. Stir for 2 to 3 minutes. Add the stock, salt, and pepper. Cover and cook over low heat for 20 minutes.

SOPA DE PLATANO MACHO

PLANTAIN SOUP

When I was first served this soup by Celia Chavez de Garcia Terrés, I couldn't figure out what gave it its wonderful taste—even though there is almost nothing added to the flavor of the main ingredient. Perhaps that is simply because plantains are usually fried in Mexico and it is unusual to find them in a soup.

Left: Pumpkin Soup; center: Oatmeal Soup; right: Plantain Soup

2 tablespoons (1 oz/30 g) butter
1½ tablespoons chopped leek
1 large barely ripe plantain, about 8 oz (250 g) or
   2 bananas, peeled and sliced
5 cups (1¼ qt/1.25 l) chicken stock
salt and pepper to taste

SERVES 6

❡ Melt the butter in a pot over medium heat and sauté the leek until translucent.

❡ Put the plantain slices in the pot and sauté gently on both sides without browning, turning occasionally for about 10 minutes or until cooked. Place the leek, plantains, and 2 cups (16 fl oz/500 ml) of stock in a blender and puree until smooth.

❡ Return the mixture to the pot, add the remaining stock, and season to taste. Bring to a boil and cook for 5 minutes. If the soup is too thick, you may need to thin it with more stock.

❡ Serve sprinkled with black pepper, if desired.

CALDO DE QUESO

CHEESE BROTH

This soup is typical of the state of Sonora, its simplicity being characteristic of the austerity of the region. The cheese is so stringy that sometimes scissors are needed to cut the strands as the soup is being served. You can vary the recipe by adding strips of poblano chiles.

8 oz (250 g) potatoes, cut into ¼-inch (6-mm) cubes and rinsed
2 tablespoons vegetable oil
2 tablespoons minced (finely chopped) onion
9 oz (280 g) tomatoes, chopped
1 teaspoon salt, or to taste
pinch baking soda (bicarbonate of soda)
1 cup (8 fl oz/250 ml) hot water
3 cups (24 fl oz/750 ml) milk
8 oz (250 g) Chihuahua, Oaxaca, mozzarella, or other stringy cheese, shredded
12 dried piquín chiles, or 1 teaspoon red pepper flakes

SERVES 6

❡ Place the potatoes in a small pan and add salted water to cover. Boil until the potatoes are cooked but still firm, approximately 15 minutes. Drain and set aside.
❡ Heat the oil in a medium saucepan over low heat and sauté the onions until just translucent.
❡ Puree the tomatoes in a blender until smooth and strain into the saucepan over the onions. Add the salt, baking soda, potatoes, and water. Scald the milk separately and add it to the tomato mixture. Simmer for 2 to 3 minutes until all the ingredients are heated through.
❡ Place the cheese in a soup tureen and pour in the hot soup, stirring until the cheese has melted. Pass the chiles so that each person may add 2 to his or her bowl and crush them with a spoon, or sprinkle the chile flakes in each bowl, before adding the soup. A small amount may also be strewn over the soup's surface for garnish, if desired.

SOPA DE ELOTE, CALABACITAS Y CILANTRO

CORN, ZUCCHINI AND CILANTRO SOUP

In this simple home-style soup, all of the ingredients complement each other deliciously. The recipe is courtesy of Chata Von Bertrab.

2 tablespoons vegetable oil
kernels from 3 ears corn
1 tablespoon minced (finely chopped) onion
6 cups (1½ qt/1.5 l) chicken stock
3 zucchini (courgettes), cut into ⅓-inch (8-mm) cubes, or coarsely grated
6 tablespoons minced (finely chopped) cilantro (fresh coriander)
salt and black pepper to taste
8 tablespoons (4 oz/125 g) queso fresco, farmer's cheese, or mild feta, cut into ½-inch (1-cm) cubes

SERVES 6

❡ Heat the oil in a medium saucepan over medium heat. Add the corn kernels and cook, stirring occasionally, for 6 to 8 minutes. Add the onion and sauté until translucent.
❡ Add 2 cups (16 fl oz/500 ml) of the stock and cook until the corn is tender. Add the remaining stock, zucchini, cilantro, and salt and pepper. Bring to a boil and simmer, just long enough to barely cook the zucchini.
❡ Serve, allowing guests to help themselves to the cheese passed in a separate bowl.

SOPA DE CAMARÓN Y CEBOLLA

SHRIMP AND ONION SOUP

This soup combines both French and Mexican elements. As in French onion soup, the onions are gently sautéed in butter until very tender, but here the shrimp (prawns) and chipotle chiles are the main flavorings, and chicken and shrimp stock are used instead of beef stock. This recipe is from the Fournier family.

4 cups (1 qt/1 l) water
¼ onion
2 cloves garlic, unpeeled
½ bay leaf
1 sprig fresh thyme or 1 pinch dried
1 teaspoon salt, or to taste
2 lb (1 kg) shrimp (prawns), unpeeled
3 tablespoons (1½ oz/45 g) butter
3 onions, halved and finely sliced
1 tablespoon all-purpose (plain) flour
2 cups (16 fl oz/500 ml) chicken stock
1 or 2 canned chipotle chiles

SERVES 6–8

❡ Boil the water in a medium saucepan with the ¼ onion, garlic, bay leaf, thyme, and salt. Add the shrimp and cook for 3 minutes. Drain, reserving the stock, and peel the shrimp.

¶ Melt the butter in a large saucepan over low heat and sauté the sliced onions for about 25 minutes until tender, stirring occasionally. Add the flour and stir, to prevent burning, for 2 to 3 minutes. Pour the reserved shrimp stock and the chicken stock into the pan.

¶ Add the shrimp and chiles and simmer for 3 minutes. Serve.

¶ If you prefer a less spicy flavor, add the chiles just before serving.

Top left: Cheese Broth; bottom left: Corn, Zucchini, and Cilantro Soup; right: Shrimp and Onion Soup

SOPA DE CHILE ANCHO Y REQUESÓN

ANCHO CHILE AND RICOTTA SOUP

This is a red chile sauce made into a delicious soup with the addition of chicken and ricotta. It is unusual to have dried chiles as the main ingredient in a soup, but it works wonderfully in this recipe from the Otero Arvide family.

2 oz (60 g) ancho chiles, toasted on a comal or griddle, stems removed, and soaked in warm water until soft
8 oz (250 g) tomatoes, charred on a comal or griddle
1 (½-inch/1-cm) thick slice onion, lightly charred
1 clove garlic, lightly charred, then peeled
4 cups (1 qt/1 l) chicken stock
2 tablespoons vegetable oil
2 tablespoons (1 oz/30 g) butter
7 oz (220 g) ricotta cheese
2 tablespoons coarsely chopped cilantro (fresh coriander)

MAKES 5 CUPS (1¼ qt/1.25 l)

❡ Put the chiles, tomato, onion, garlic, and 2 cups (16 fl oz/500 ml) of stock in a blender and puree until smooth.
❡ Heat the oil and melt the butter in a medium casserole. Strain the chile mixture into the pan and cook for 5 minutes, stirring occasionally. Blend the remaining stock and the ricotta in a blender until smooth. Add the mixture and salt to taste to the pan, and cook over medium heat until hot. Serve, sprinkled with the cilantro.

SOPA FRIA DE ELOTE CON HUEVA DE LISA

COLD CORN SOUP WITH FISH ROE

This recipe from Arturo and Lila Lomeli is a modern creation but uses only ingredients traditional to Mexico.

kernels from 4 ears fresh corn
4 cups (1 qt/1 l) chicken stock
1 onion, coarsely chopped
1 bay leaf
pinch of thyme and oregano
3 gray mullet roe or any other hard roe, well washed
pinch nutmeg
1 cup (8 fl oz/250 ml) heavy (double/thickened) cream
1 large poblano chile, roasted, peeled, deveined, seeded, and cut into strips, for garnish

SERVES 8

❡ Put the corn kernels and stock in a pot and cook for 10 minutes or until tender. In another pot, cover the onion, herbs, and roe with boiling water and cook for 7 minutes. Drain, discarding the water and herbs. Peel the fish roe, discarding the skin, and then break up the roe with a fork.
❡ Put the corn and stock in a blender with the onion and roughly blend. Pour the mixture back into the pot and add the nutmeg, cream, and roe. Simmer for a few minutes to blend the flavors.
❡ Refrigerate until cold. Serve garnished with chile.

Left: Ancho Chile and Ricotta Soup; right: Cold Corn Soup with Fish Roe

Whether stuffed, deep-fried, or as an ingredient in a soup, squash blossoms are a ubiquitous commodity in Mexico.

SQUASH BLOSSOMS

Squash blossoms are sold in great bunches of several dozen for just a few pesos in Mexico. These delicate flowers are brought to market early in the morning, their fresh blooms wide open and shining yellow-orange in the sunlight. But in a matter of hours, exposed to the heat, the cut flowers will wilt and sweat, so they must be bought and used quickly, or stored in the refrigerator, which will prolong their life slightly.

As much a part of daily food as the vegetable they come from, the flowers form the stuffing for *quesadillas*, crêpes, chicken breasts, fish, or chiles, sautéed with a little onion and, perhaps, *epazote* or chile; or they can be made into soup combined with *poblano* chile strips and corn kernels—for which they have a natural affinity—zucchini (courgettes), or even fresh and wild mushrooms.

Squash blossoms are different from zucchini flowers which have been used in Italy for centuries and which are quite popular today in our homes and restaurants. However, in a pinch, one can be substituted for the other.

Different cooks have different views as to what parts of the flower to leave in and what to take out. While all agree that the stigma (the pollen-laden center) and the points of the green calyx (around the base of the flower) should be removed, some remove the entire calyx, while others prefer to leave part of it for the crunch and the added volume it provides. An inch or two (3 or 5 cm) of the edible stems may be included, but they should first be stripped of their slightly prickly skin, rather like stringing stalks of celery.

Stuffing squash blossoms to deep-fry or steam has only recently become popular in Mexico, as has breading or batter-frying them. Their higher price in other parts of the world has led to squash blossoms receiving this individual attention.

While the most predominant growing area in Mexico is in the central plateau, squash, along with beans, often forms a part of the *milpa*, or corn patch. This is a technique of growing mixed crops together not only for their food value, but also because they replenish the soil with complementary elements, enriching the earth's productivity. It is a technique long employed by the pre-Columbian civilizations.

HUATAPE DE CAMARÓN

SHRIMP AND SPINACH SOUP

Thickening soups with tortilla masa, which adds an interesting flavor, is a common practice in central Mexico and Veracruz. There are many variations of this soup from southern Tamaulipas and northern Veracruz: some are made with tomatoes or ancho chiles, others are fried with lard instead of olive oil; and others still have eggs broken into them to cook in the broth. This version of the soup was created by Guille de Lárraga.

8 cups (2 qt/2 l) water
3 cloves garlic, unpeeled
2 thick slices onion
1 teaspoon salt plus salt to taste
2 lb (1 kg) unpeeled shrimp (prawns), rinsed
½ teaspoon peppercorns
¼ teaspoon cumin seeds
1 tablespoon plus 2 teaspoons olive oil
3½ oz (100 g) spinach leaves, washed and stemmed
1 sprig epazote, optional
3½ oz (100 g) tortilla masa (see Tortillas de Maiz page 53) or mix ⅓ cup (1 oz/30 g) masa harina (tortilla flour) with about ¼ cup (2 fl oz/60 ml) warm water to form a soft dough

SERVES 8

❡ In a large saucepan, bring the water to a boil with 1 garlic clove, 1 slice of onion, and 1 teaspoon of salt. Add the shrimp and boil for 3 minutes or until the shrimp turn pink. Strain off the liquid and reserve. Discard the garlic and onion. Peel the shrimp and set aside.
❡ Heat a small frying pan and toast the peppercorns and cumin seeds. Remove and place in a blender. In the same pan, char the remaining garlic cloves and onion on both sides. Remove, peel the garlic, and place the garlic and onion in a blender with ¼ cup (2 fl oz/60 ml) of the reserved liquid. Blend until smooth.
❡ Heat 1 tablespoon of oil in a large pot over medium heat. Add the pureed mixture and cook for about 4 minutes. Meanwhile, quickly puree the spinach leaves with all but ¼ cup (2 fl oz/ 60 ml) of the reserved liquid in the blender. Add the spinach mixture to the pot along with the *epazote* and the *tortilla masa* dissolved with the remaining ¼ cup (2 fl oz/60 ml) of liquid. Add salt to taste and cook, stirring occasionally, over low heat for 20 minutes.
❡ Add the shrimp and cook until heated through.
❡ Serve with the remaining 2 teaspoons of oil dribbled over the top.

SOPA DE PESCADO Y MARISCOS

FISH AND SHELLFISH SOUP

This rich soup from the Veracruz coast can be served as an appetizer or as a meal in itself. The masa harina is used as a thickener and also gives the soup a distinctive flavor. If it is not available, you can just omit it; the stock will be slightly thinner but this Mexican interpretation of cioppino will be just as delicious.

2 lb (1 kg) red snapper (sea bass or red emperor), cleaned and scaled, with the head and bones reserved
1 sprig fresh thyme
1 sprig fresh oregano
1½ teaspoons salt, or to taste
6 cups (1½ qt /1.5 l) water
8 oz (250 g) small shrimp (prawns), unpeeled
4 dried cascabel chiles or large guajillo chiles, 3 with seeds and stems removed and 1 whole
1 lb (500 g) tomatoes, peeled, seeded, and roughly chopped
⅓ cup (3 fl oz/90 ml) olive oil
1 small onion, grated
1 large clove garlic, minced (finely chopped)
1 lb (500 g) squid, cleaned, with tentacles removed and cut into ¼-inch (½-cm) rings
2 tablespoons masa harina (tortilla flour) blended with ½ cup (4 fl oz/125 ml) cold water
1 small bay leaf

SERVES 8

❡ Remove the fillets from the fish, skin, and cut into 2-inch (5-cm) pieces. Set aside.
❡ Put the fish head and bones, the thyme, oregano, salt, and water into a large saucepan and cook over medium heat for 15 minutes. Add the shrimp and cook for 3 minutes. Remove the shrimp and peel. Strain the stock and reserve.
❡ Soak the 3 seeded chiles in hot water for about 10 minutes to soften. Drain, discard the liquid, and puree the chiles in a blender with ½ cup (4 fl oz/125 ml) of the reserved stock until smooth. Add the tomatoes and continue to blend until smooth.
❡ Heat the oil in a large saucepan over medium heat. Add the onion and garlic and cook for approximately 5 minutes until translucent. Add the tomato mixture and cook, stirring occasionally, until the oil rises to the surface, approximately 10 to 15 minutes.
❡ Add the remaining fish stock, the fish pieces, squid, and shrimp. Bring the mixture to a simmer.
❡ Add the *masa harina* mixture, bay leaf, and the whole chile. Simmer over low heat, stirring occasionally, for 20 minutes. Serve.

Front left: Shrimp and Spinach Soup; back left: Fish and Shellfish Soup; right: Oyster Soup with Chipotle Chiles

SOPA DE OSTIÓN CON CHIPOTLE

OYSTER SOUP WITH CHIPOTLE CHILES

Whole toasted chiles are often added to clear soups but here the chipotles are fried, rather than toasted, to soften them In this recipe by Alicia Almada de Rodriguez, stock granules are used to avoid adding further liquid.

1 cup (8 fl oz/250 ml) oil, for deep-frying
6 large, whole dried chipotle chiles
6 tablespoons chopped parsley
2 tablespoons vegetable oil
2 onions, chopped
2 lb (1 kg) whole tomatoes, broiled (grilled) and chopped to make 2¾ cups (22 fl oz/685 ml)
6 jars shucked oysters and reserved liquid; about 3 cups (24 fl oz/750 ml) oysters and 8 cups (2 qt/2 l) liquid

2 tablespoons Worcestershire sauce
2 tablespoons Bovril or concentrated beef juices
2½ tablespoons chicken stock granules

SERVES 6

❡ In a small frying pan heat enough oil to deep-fry the chiles until soft. Drain and put 1 in each soup bowl. Sprinkle with the parsley.

❡ Heat the 2 tablespoons of oil in a large pot and sauté the onion until translucent. Add the tomatoes and cook over medium heat for 20 minutes.

❡ Add the oyster liquid, Worcestershire sauce, Bovril, and chicken granules and cook over low heat for 20 minutes.

❡ Place the oysters with water in a small saucepan and bring just to a boil over high heat. Drain, discarding any liquid, and add them to the pot.

❡ To serve, ladle the soup into the bowls already containing the chiles and parsley.

CHILES AND CACTUS

CHILES AND CACTUS

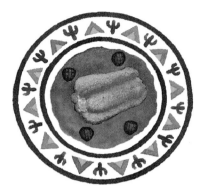

MEXICAN CUISINE IS BASICALLY A HYBRID, INCORPORATING CHILES AND CACTUSES AS TWO of its outstanding native ingredients.

❡ Although the American and, specifically, Mexican origin of chile is beyond doubt, the use of chiles has spread to practically every continent today. From the fiery Chinese dishes of the Sichuan (Szechwan) region and the equally pungent Indian and Sri Lankan curries, to mild Hungarian paprika and Spanish *pimentón*—both made from dried chiles—all are varieties originating from the Mexican chile or capsicum group of plants.

❡ When the Europeans first explored America, it was Christopher Columbus himself who carried the first chile seeds back to the Old World and, ever since, travelers to the New World have done the same. There were two routes for chiles on their way to Europe and Asia, both controlled by the Spaniards and Portuguese. One, across the Pacific, started from Acapulco or El Callao in Peru via the *Nao de China* (Portuguese-controlled galleons) and went directly to China and the Philippines. The other, across the Atlantic from America and principally from Mexico, had the Iberian Peninsula as its first stop. From there, the travels of the chile plants continued at the hands of Venetian, Turkish, and Greek traders.

Previous pages: Ancho chiles for sale at the market. This wide chile is the dried form of the poblano chile, and is commonly used as a base for sauces.

Opposite: The flat-jointed paddles of the prickly pear or nopal *cactus are prized for food, as are their juice-packed fruits. However, they are covered in fine, sharp thorns and require extreme caution when handling.*

❡ By the time Hernán Cortés conquered the Aztec Empire, between 1519 and 1521, the taste for some of the chiles, whose seeds had arrived almost thirty years earlier with Columbus, had begun to spread throughout Spain.

❡ Originating from Mexican seed and, to a much lesser degree, from others of South America, more than 200 types of chile pepper are consumed in the world today. Their cultivation is widespread, as the plant flourishes in tropical heat as well as in temperate climates, even those with sharply marked seasonal differences.

❡ Cactuses, ancient native plants of Mexico, serve as an abundant source of food and drink. The *nopal*, or prickly pear cactus, produces both fruit—*tunas*—and vegetable in the form of its edible paddles. The maguey, or century plant, is the source of *aguamiel*, or honey water, as its sap is known, which, when fermented, becomes *pulque*, the traditional Aztec drink. In some water-poor villages, babies are weaned on *aguamiel*. Maguey arms, or *pencas*, have a thin skin called *mixiote*, which acts much like a flavorful parchment (baking paper) to wrap packages of food for steaming, while the arms themselves line pits in the ground for steam-baking *barbacoa* (see page 186). The maguey worm breeds at the heart of the succulent, and is a great Mexican delicacy when fried and crunchy. The nonculinary contributions of the maguey are the tips and fibers, which are traditionally used as needles and thread for sewing.

❡ Other varieties of the century plant include the *agave tequilera*, or blue agave (*agave tequilana*), and the *agave mezcalera*. These are famous for the alcohols fermented and distilled from their juices, known, respectively, as tequila and mescal.

CHILES ANCHOS RELLENOS DE FRIJOLES

ANCHO CHILES STUFFED WITH BEANS

Almost any medium to large chile can be stuffed, whether it's fresh or dried. This dish is made with ancho chiles, which are mild and pleasantly sweet. Fillings are equally varied—meat, fish, seafood, vegetables, cheese, or, as in this case, beans, can all be used.

3 cups (24 fl oz/750 ml) water
¼ cup (2 fl oz/60 ml) plus 1 teaspoon mild white or
    cider vinegar
1 bay leaf
1 sprig fresh thyme
1 sprig fresh marjoram
6 ancho chiles (4–5 inches/10–12 cm long), slit
    lengthwise with stems intact, seeded, and deveined
1½ cups (12 oz/375 g) Frijoles Refritos (see page 150)
¼ cup (2 fl oz/60 ml) oil
1 onion, halved and sliced
salt and pepper to taste
½ teaspoon oregano, or to taste
½ cup (4 oz/125 g) queso fresco, queso añejo, or feta
    cheese, crumbled

SERVES 6

❡ Preheat the oven to 350°F (180°C/Gas 4).
❡ In a medium saucepan, bring the water to a boil with ¼ cup of the vinegar, the bay leaf, thyme, and marjoram. Turn off the heat, add the chiles, and soak for 15 minutes.
❡ Drain the chiles, discarding the liquid.
❡ Stuff the chiles with the *Frijoles Refritos* and place them in an ovenproof dish that is large enough to hold all of them in a single layer.
❡ In a small saucepan, heat the oil over a medium heat. Add the onion, and salt and pepper to taste; then cook until translucent.
❡ Add the remaining teaspoon of vinegar and the oregano. Cook for 1 minute and pour over the chiles.
❡ Bake the chiles in the oven for 15 to 20 minutes. Remove and allow to cool.
❡ Sprinkle with the cheese and serve at room temperature.

CHILES EN ESCABECHE
Pickled Chiles
The most frequently pickled chile is the jalapeño. To pickle them, the chiles are sautéed gently with a variety of seasonings, including thyme, bay leaves, oregano, and peppercorns, as well as slices of garlic, onion, and carrots. Then, they are covered with vinegar and a dash of sugar to cut the acidity, and kept in a cool, dark place or under refrigeration for several days to develop the flavor. Pickled chiles, canned or in bottles, are also available commercially, both in Mexico and elsewhere. Some recipes included in this book call for both the chiles and their pickling vinegar.

CHILES POBLANOS RELLENOS DE QUESO Y ENVUELTOS EN PASTA HOJALDRADA

CHEESE-STUFFED POBLANO CHILES IN PASTRY

This is a variation on traditional stuffed chiles, which are usually dipped in a simple egg batter and deep-fried. They are rather more filling too, and one per person makes a generous appetizer or light lunch.

8 poblano or other mild chiles, about 7 inches (18 cm)
    long, roasted (see box page 114)
1 lb (500 g) Chihuahua, Monterey Jack, or other mild
    white Cheddar cheese, shredded
1 lb (500 g) ready-made puff pastry
1 egg, lightly beaten

SERVES 8

❡ Preheat the oven to 400°F (200°C/Gas 6).
❡ Stuff the chiles with the cheese and close the seam by overlapping the sides slightly.
❡ Roll out the pastry to a thickness of about ⅛ inch (3 mm). Place a chile, seam-side down, onto the pastry and cut around it with a sharp knife, allowing enough pastry to completely wrap the chile.
❡ Wrap the chile, sealing the pastry edges with water. Repeat with the remaining chiles. Place the pastries on a greased cookie sheet (baking tray), seam-side down, and allow to rest for approximately 30 minutes.
❡ Brush the pastry with the egg and bake for 20 minutes. Reduce the heat to 350°F (180°C/Gas 4) and bake for another 10 minutes or until the pastry is golden brown.
❡ Serve with a bowl of either *Salsa Cruda de Guadalajara* (see page 22) or *Salsa de Jitomate* (see page 24).

Front: Ancho Chiles Stuffed with Beans; back: Cheese-stuffed Poblano Chiles in Pastry

Poblano Chiles Stuffed with Shrimp, Apples, and Almonds

CHILE NORESTE

POBLANO CHILES STUFFED WITH SHRIMP, APPLES, AND ALMONDS

This unusual recipe for stuffed poblano chiles makes a change from the traditional ingredient combinations. The many different flavors combine quite successfully, making this recipe a favorite among gourmets in search of new ideas. This recipe is from Roberto Santibañez of La Circunstancia Restaurant in Mexico City.

For the chiles:
1 lb (500 g) small shrimp (prawns), cooked and diced
2 golden delicious or other apples, peeled, cored, and cut into ¼-inch (0.5-cm) cubes
½ cup (2 oz/60 g) blanched almonds, coarsely chopped and toasted in the oven until golden
½ cup (4 fl oz/125 ml) homemade mayonnaise
6 large poblano chiles, roasted (see box page 114)
For the vinaigrette:
1 cup (8 fl oz/250 ml) olive oil
⅓ cup (2½ fl oz/75 ml) raspberry vinegar
1 small piece cooked beet (beetroot), the size of ¼ lime
6 fresh raspberries
salt and pepper to taste

SERVES 6

❡ To make the filling: Mix the shrimp, apples, almonds, and mayonnaise together in a bowl.
❡ Stuff the chiles with the filling and close the slit, overlapping slightly.
❡ Blend the vinaigrette ingredients in a blender until emulsified and smooth. You may need to add a little water.
❡ To serve, cover the bottom of 6 salad plates with the vinaigrette and put a chile in the center of each plate, slit side down. Serve at room temperature.

PREPARING JALAPEÑO CHILES FOR STUFFING
Make a T-shaped cut in each chile, so that it can be stuffed after it is cooked. The top of the "T" is a horizontal cut about ½ inch (1 cm) below the stem. Make a perpendicular cut to the tip of the chile to complete the "T." Put the chiles in a medium saucepan with water to cover and a pinch of salt. Cook over high heat for 20 minutes, or until the chiles are tender and change to an olive green color. Remove them from the pan and drain on paper towels; use a small spoon to remove the seeds. Once these chiles are prepared, they may be stuffed with any of a number of fillings including Zaragalla de Cazón (see page 210) or Atún Tipo Bacalao (see page 206).

Dried Chiles

Mexicans consume almost 15 lb (7.5 kg) of fresh chiles and nearly 2 lb (1 kg) of dried chiles per person annually, the world's highest average. This predilection goes beyond the limits of home and restaurant: every day of the year, and in every city and town of the country, vendors pushing carts offer fresh fruits and vegetables dressed with lime juice, salt, and ground *piquín* chile, a tiny pod scarcely ¼ inch (5 mm) long, dried, powdered, and very, very hot. Flour *chicharrones* (small, fried and puffed snacks) and pork *chicharrones* (fried pork skin) are also eaten on the street with a hot sauce that combines several dried chiles.

One of the dried chiles in greatest demand is the *chipotle*, either pickled in vinegar, canned in a tomato-based sauce (*chipotles adobados*), or stuffed. *Chipotles* are made from fresh *jalapeño* peppers, and the Aztec root of their name reveals the secret of their preparation: *chilli poctli*, or smoked chile. The chiles are partially dried in the sun and then put in a kind of smoking oven to complete the process. A favored type of these is *chipotles mecos*, made from a variety of *jalapeño* that is slightly larger and has cork-like creases that help absorb the smoked flavor. *Chipotle* is an essential ingredient for certain dishes, such as meat balls in tomato sauce, and *pambazos*, a type of crusty bun filled with diced potatoes and *chorizo* (Mexican sausage), and as a table condiment. The pickled and sauced varieties are available canned.

Dried *chipotles* stuffed with cheese are a delicacy of Puebla. They are fried in egg batter like stuffed *poblano* chiles. Because of their heat, they are first soaked in several changes of water and finally in a mixture of water and *piloncillo* (light molasses).

The chiles *mora* and *morita* are progressively smaller varieties of *jalapeños*, and are also slightly smoked when dried.

Many fresh chiles in Mexico undergo a name change in their dried state. Fresh *poblano* chiles become *ancho* chiles or *mulato* chiles when dried, the difference depending on the slight variation in the type of *poblano* chile that has been dried. When held up to the light, the *ancho* chiles, which are more commonly found in Mexico, have a marked red reflection, while the *mulatos* are blackish.

Further name changes occur according to place. In the North, *anchos* are called *chiles colorados* (red chiles), and in Chihuahua, they may be called *chiles de la tierra* (chiles of the earth).

Ancho chiles are as popular as the fresh *poblanos* for stuffing. They are not usually very hot (although removing the veins is a good idea) and taste agreeably sweet. They are commonly stuffed with either cheese or a *picadillo*, a chopped-meat mixture that contains dried fruits and nuts.

Pasilla chiles are a fairly mild dried chile. When fresh, they are the *chile chilaca*, similar to the American Anaheim. Dried, these long, thin chiles look black. Like *anchos* and *mulatos*, they are often combined in *Mole Poblano* (see page 168); they also make an excellent chile sauce on their own, and are fried in rings or strips as a crunchy and tasty accompaniment to one of Mexico's most famous soups—*sopa azteca*, or *tortilla* soup.

Next to *piquín* chiles, dried *arbol* chiles may be the hottest, and are added to sauces when just plain heat is required. They keep the same name, fresh or dried. They are an average of 2 inches (5 cm) long, very narrow, and are a smooth-skinned bright red.

Chiltepines, from the North, are about as small as *chile piquín*, and the two names are often used interchangeably. However, *chiltepines* are round rather than slightly oblong. *Canica* chiles are also round but slightly larger than *chiltepines*—about the size of a marble.

Cascabel chiles have the shape of a round bell and are filled with loose seeds that rattle, hence, the name, which means rattle. They are about 1 inch (2.5 cm) in diameter and are cultivated in the Bajío.

Guajillo chiles, cultivated largely to the north of the center of Mexico, come in a large and very mild variety (*guajillo grande*), as well as a smaller, medium-hot one (*guajillo chico*). Both are smooth-skinned, dark red in color, and elongated. The larger ones measure about 5 inches (12 cm) long and are proportionally fatter than the smaller ones, which are about 3 to 4 inches (8 to 10 cm) long. The large ones give a wonderful flavor to sauces without making them too hot. They are also used in a method of preparing shrimp (prawn) or fish *al ajíllo* (*ají* is the name given to chiles in most of Latin America) where sliced garlic and sliced *guajillo* chiles are sautéed in olive or vegetable oil before the seafood is added.

As in the case of fresh chiles, many dried varieties are available only in certain areas, where special sauces and dishes are created from them. This is nowhere more true than in Oaxaca, where the variety of special red (*costeños*), black, and "yellow" (*chilhuacles*) chiles, to mention a few, form the basis of Oaxaca's famous seven *moles*.

1. ancho; 2. mulato; 3. pasilla;
4. guajillo grande; 5. guajillo chico; 6. piquín; 7. morita;
8. chipotle; 9. cascabel; 10. arbol;
11. mora; 12. canica; 13. costeño

CHILES ANCHOS RELLENOS DE CHARRALITOS

*ANCHO CHILES STUFFED WITH SMALL
DRIED FISH*

Ancho *chiles are the dried version of* poblano *chiles, and
are almost as popular for stuffing. Here they are filled with*
charralitos, *tiny dried minnows, which are only about
1 inch (2.5 cm) long. The* charralitos *are reconstituted
and sautéed in olive oil with shallots and almonds. José
Luis Cortez and the* charral *(dried fish) vendor at the San
Juan Market in Mexico City created this recipe.*

6 *ancho chiles*
½ *lb (250 g)* charralitos *or any very small (1 inch/
2.5 cm long) dried fish*
½ *cup (4 fl oz/125 ml) olive oil*
1 *large shallot, chopped*
3½ *oz (100 g) almonds, slivered*
½ *teaspoon salt, or to taste*

Front: Ancho Chiles Stuffed with Small Dried Fish; back: Poblano Chiles Stuffed with Cheese

1 cup (8 fl oz/250 ml) heavy (double/thickened) cream
3½ oz (100 g) Oaxaca or mozzarella cheese, shredded

SERVES 6

❡ Soak the chiles in cold water for 20 minutes to soften and drain. Make a slit lengthwise and carefully remove the seeds and veins. Soak the *charralitos* in warm water for 5 minutes and drain.
❡ Preheat the oven to 350°F (180°C/Gas 4).
❡ In a large frying pan, heat the oil and sauté the shallot over medium heat until soft. Add the

charralitos, almonds, and salt, and sauté for 5 to 10 minutes until golden and crispy.
❡ Stuff the chiles with the *charralitos* mixture and place them in an ovenproof serving dish greased with olive oil. Spoon over the cream and sprinkle on the cheese. Bake for approximately 5 minutes, or until the cheese has melted.
❡ Serve by itself as an appetizer, or as a main course with white rice.

CHILES POBLANOS RELLENOS DE QUESO

POBLANO CHILES STUFFED WITH CHEESE

Cheese is the most traditional of chile stuffings. Here the tomato sauce flavored with carrots, vinegar, and sugar combines well with the poblano *chiles and melted cheese to make this one of Mexico's favorite dishes. This recipe is a variation on the classic dish from* Frida's Fiestas *by Lupe Rivera.*

For the sauce:
3 tablespoons olive oil
1 onion, minced (finely chopped)
2 carrots, peeled and thinly sliced
10 tomatoes, roasted, peeled, seeded, and chopped
½ cup (4 fl oz/125 ml) white or cider vinegar
3 tablespoons (1½ oz/45 g) sugar
2 tablespoons oregano
For the chiles:
16 poblano *chiles, toasted, skinned, and deveined*
14 oz (400 g) queso fresco, *farmer's cheese, or mild feta, crumbled*
flour, for dusting
5 eggs, separated
½ cup (4 fl oz/125 ml) vegetable oil

SERVES 8

❡ To make the sauce: Heat the oil in a saucepan and sauté the onion until translucent along with the carrots. Add the tomatoes, vinegar, and sugar, and simmer for approximately 10 minutes. Stir in the oregano, season to taste with salt and pepper and cook for a further 10 minutes, or until the tomatoes have cooked down.
❡ For the chiles: Stuff the chiles with the cheese and close, overlapping the sides slightly. Dust with flour.
❡ Beat the egg whites until stiff. Beat the yolks with a pinch of salt and fold together with the egg whites to make a batter. Dip the stuffed chiles in the batter and fry in very hot oil until golden. Drain on paper towels to remove any excess oil.
❡ Place the chiles in a serving dish and pour the tomato sauce over the top; serve.

FRESH CHILES

The word *chile* has its origin in Nahuatl, the Aztec language, and Mexico is one of the world's largest producers and consumers of them. The great variety of fresh chiles in Mexico varies from region to region and greatly influences local cuisines.

In the Southeast, especially the Yucatán, the fiery *habanero* chile reigns in local table sauces, often seasoned with bitter orange juice and large-leaved oregano. Also from the Southeast is the Mayan named *x-cat-ik* chile, used to flavor prepared meat or fish dishes. In Oaxaca, *güeros*, or "blonde" chiles, and *chiles de agua* ("water" chiles) are regional favorites. The first, as their name would imply, are light yellow in color, like the *x-cat-ik*, but a little longer, while the *chiles de agua* are light green and as large as *poblano* chiles but more tapered.

In the North, fresh *piquín* chiles—tiny, round balls that are *very* hot—are used, while in the rest of the country, these are better known in their dried form. The flavorful, long, thin, black-green *chilaca* chiles are most common in the center of the country, while the *jalapeños* (also known as *cuaresmeños* in Veracruz and as *huauchinangos* in Oaxaca) are a favorite of the Veracruz coast. These are also found and used in the rest of Mexico and are the most commonly pickled chile. *Jalapeños* are widely used chopped in sauces and are even stuffed, though small in size.

Manzano chiles are similar in shape and color range to *habaneros* (orange, yellow, green, and in this case, red, too), but they are slightly larger—about 2 inches (5 cm) long—and, being bell-shaped, almost as wide. Another distinguishing feature is that their skin is thicker and smoother than that of *habaneros*, which gives the impression of being almost translucent, and they are not quite as hot.

The most typical chiles available all over Mexico are the large, dark green *poblanos* and the small *serrano* chiles. The size of *poblano* chiles—5 to 6 inches (12 to 15 cm) long—renders them excellent for stuffing, but they are also greatly used cut into *rajas*, or strips, which are sautéed with onion and mixed with cream for a *taco* filling. They combine excellently with corn kernels and cheese, as well as many other ingredients. However they are used, the chiles are first roasted to peel and cook them, and the seeds are removed. As with all chiles, removing the inside veins, which contain some of the heat-producing chemical, makes the chiles milder. Pureed, these roasted chiles make an excellent sauce, called simply *salsa de chile poblano*. It is usually served with chicken.

Poblano chiles are becoming increasingly available in many parts of the world. If substitution is necessary, choose a chile large enough to stuff and with a skin that's thick enough to blister and peel. The long, green chile and the Anaheim found in the United States are good examples. Substituting with sweet green bell peppers (capsicums) destroys the subtle piquancy of the dish.

Serranos are narrow, green chiles from 1 to 2 inches (3 to 5 cm) long. They are often chopped with their seeds, making them very piquant, although removing the seeds first will make them milder. These are added to fresh table sauces, Mexican scrambled eggs (with onion and tomato), *guacamole*, and an endless number of other fresh or cooked dishes. They are also a favorite blistered whole on a flat *comal* (cast-iron griddle) or broiler (grill) to accompany broiled poultry or meat.

Fresh green or red *arbol* chiles, grown in Jalisco, Nayarit, Aguascalientes, and Zacatecas, to the north of the center, are similar to *serranos* but are narrower, more pointed, and hotter still.

1. poblano; 2. jalapeño; 3. chilaca; 4. arbol; 5. x-cat-ik; 6. serrano; 7. habanero; 8. güero; 9. manzano

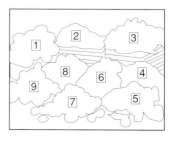

TARTA DE QUESO EN CHILE POBLANO

CHEESE TART WITH A POBLANO CHILE CRUST

This Mexican version of a quiche takes advantage of the affinity between cheese and poblano chiles. Since the chiles take the place of a pastry crust, the dish is also lighter than a traditional cheese tart.

1 tablespoon (½ oz/15 g) butter
8–10 large poblano chiles, roasted (see box page 114)
½ cup (4 fl oz/125 ml) heavy (double/thickened) cream
1½ tablespoons shredded onion
1 clove garlic, minced (finely chopped)
½ teaspoon salt
3½ oz (100 g) Chihuahua, Monterey Jack, or any mild white Cheddar cheese, shredded
5 eggs, beaten

SERVES 6–8

❡ Preheat the oven to 350°F (180°C/Gas 4).
❡ Butter a 9-inch (23-cm) pie plate. Halve the chiles lengthwise, stem to tip, then completely line the sides and bottom of the dish with them, placing the wider stem ends toward the outside edge of the plate and overlapping the pieces slightly. Cut any remaining chiles into wide strips and use to fill any spaces in the "crust" so the filling won't leak.
❡ In a bowl, mix together the cream, onion, garlic, salt, and cheese. Add the eggs, mix to combine, and pour over the chile crust.
❡ Cover the outside edge of the chile crust with a strip of aluminum foil. Bake for approximately 40 minutes, or until firm and lightly browned.
❡ Remove from the oven and cut off any burned edges with scissors. Slice, and serve hot or at room temperature.

Cheese Tart with a Poblano Chile Crust

CHILES EN NOGADA

STUFFED CHILES IN FRESH WALNUT SAUCE

This is one of Mexico's most famous and beautiful dishes; it even shares the colors of the Mexican flag. Originally from Puebla, it is customarily prepared in July and August, when the best poblano chiles, walnuts, and pomegranates are in season. Though it is becoming popular to substitute pecans and blanched almonds, only fresh walnuts achieve the creamy texture and lightly sweet flavor of the original recipe. You can also make a casserole version of this dish by baking the ground (minced) meat between the top and bottom layers of chile strips, heating it through in the oven, then topping with walnut sauce, parsley, and pomegranate seeds before serving.

For the sauce:
2 cups (16 fl oz/500 ml) milk
2 oz (60 ml) panela *or farmer's cheese, diced*
1¼ cups (5½ oz/170 g) fresh walnuts, shelled; or 1 cup (4½ oz/ 140 g) pecans and ¼ cup (1 oz/30 g) blanched almonds
¼ teaspoon cinnamon
pinch nutmeg
1 teaspoon salt, or to taste
½ teaspoon sugar, or to taste
For the chiles:
2 lb (1 kg) pork, cut into 1-inch (2.5-cm) cubes
½ onion, cut in half
3 cloves garlic, minced (finely chopped)
2 teaspoons salt plus ½ tablespoon salt, or to taste
1 cup (8 fl oz/250 ml) vegetable oil
2½ lb (1.25 kg) tomatoes with skins, seeded and chopped into ½-inch (1-cm) cubes
2 onions, minced (finely chopped)
1½ tablespoons minced garlic
1 (1½-inch/4-cm) piece of cinnamon stick
pinch ground cloves
1 plantain, or underripe banana (3½ oz/100 g), peeled and cut into ¼-inch (0.5-cm) cubes
1 firm peach, skinned, pitted, and cut into ¼-inch (0.5-cm) cubes
⅓ cup (2½ oz/75 g) acitrón (crystallized biznaga cactus) or candied orange peel, cut into ¼-inch (0.5-cm) cubes
⅓ cup (2½ oz/70 g) raisins
⅓ cup (2½ oz/70 g) almonds, blanched and slivered
⅓ cup (2½ oz/70 g) pine nuts
1 large sprig parsley
12 poblano chiles, roasted (see box) and deveined
flat-leafed (continental or Italian) parsley, for garnish
seeds of 1 large pomegranate, for garnish

SERVES 12

¶ To make the sauce: Blend all the ingredients in a blender until very smooth. Set aside.

¶ For the chiles: Put the meat in a saucepan with enough water to cover and cook over medium heat.
¶ Add the onion, garlic, and 2 teaspoons of salt. Cook for 1 hour, or until the meat is tender, skimming any foam from the surface with a large spoon and discarding. Drain the meat, reserving ½ cup (4 fl oz/125 ml) of cooking liquid.
¶ Heat the oil in a large saucepan over medium heat and add the next 12 ingredients and the remaining salt, along with the pork. Cook over medium heat for 15 to 20 minutes, stirring occasionally to prevent sticking (the meat will begin to fall apart). The meat should be slightly moist. If it becomes dry, add some of the reserved cooking liquid. Remove the cinnamon stick and the parsley sprig.
¶ Stuff each chile with the pork mixture and place them on serving plates. Pour the sauce over the chiles, avoiding the bases and stems, if possible.
¶ Garnish with the parsley leaves and pomegranate seeds. Serve at room temperature.

ROASTING POBLANO CHILES AND CHILE STRIPS

Char the chiles on all sides over an open flame or under the broiler (grill). Seal immediately in a plastic bag for 10 minutes and allow to sweat. Wearing rubber gloves, peel the chiles under running water, being careful not to tear them and keeping the stems intact. For roasted poblano chiles for stuffing leave the chiles whole. Vertically slit along one side, or slice a piece off the stem end, and seed. For a milder flavor, also remove the veins; they are somewhat stringy and can generally just be pulled off, or you can use scissors to cut them out, leaving the chile intact. The whole chiles are now ready for stuffing.
For chile strips: Remove the stems and the thick knobs under them. Lay the chiles flat and cut them lengthwise into ¼-inch (0.5-cm) strips; the strips can be frozen in a plastic bag. An alternate method, used in many restaurants to prepare large quantities of chiles, is to heat oil in a deep fryer until smoking. Submerge the chiles, several at a time, for 30 seconds or less, until the skin bubbles and turns white. Drain, shaking the fryer basket, or place them on paper towels. Sprinkle immediately with salt and peel when cool enough to handle under a light stream of running water. Poblano chiles are often used whole and stuffed as in Chile Noreste (see page 107), Chiles Poblanos Rellenos de Queso (see page 111), and Pescado Centli (see page 206). They can also be used sliced into strips or rajas. For a simple taco filling, the strips can be added to sautéed onion and heavy (double/thickened) cream.

Stuffed Chiles in Fresh Walnut Sauce

RAJAS DE CHILE MANZANO CON JUGO DE LIMON

MANZANO CHILES IN LIME JUICE

One of the hottest chiles is the manzano, *which is strong yel-low in color and has black seeds. Its very distinctive flavor is complemented by the other ingredients in this relish. It is served on the table so diners can help themselves.*

5 (5-oz/150-g) manzano *chiles*
1 *small onion, halved and sliced*
4 *tablespoons (2 fl oz/60 ml) lime juice*
¼ *teaspoon crushed dried oregano*
½ *teaspoon salt*

MAKES ¾ CUP (6 oz/185 g)

❡ Roast the chiles over an open flame or under a broiler (grill), turning to char on each side. Seal immediately in a plastic bag for 10 minutes and allow to sweat.
❡ Wearing rubber gloves, cut the chiles in half vertically. Peel and seed them under running water until all or most of the skin is removed. Place the chiles on a cutting board, remove the stems, and cut lengthwise into ¼-inch (0.5-cm) strips.
❡ Place the chiles and all the other ingredients in a small glass bowl to macerate, preferably overnight.
❡ Serve as a relish on the table to accompany *tortilla* and *taco* dishes.

NOPALITOS

PRICKLY PEAR PADDLES OR NOPAL PADDLES

This is the typical way of preparing nopales *for many different dishes including salads, soups, and scrambled eggs.* Nopales *can be prepared at home, or purchased year-round freshly cooked in the markets. They can also be bought, already cooked, in jars.*

9 oz (250 g) nopales *or prickly pears, edges and spines sliced off with a sharp knife*
1 *teaspoon salt*

MAKES 3 CUPS (12 oz/750 g)

❡ Cut the *nopales* into ½-inch (1-cm) cubes. Put them into a pot of boiling water to cover with the salt for about 45 minutes, or until tender. They will change to an olive-green color when cooked. Drain and rinse under cold water until all the sticky liquid is removed.
❡ An alternate method to prepare *nopales* is to make about 6 cuts lengthwise from the tip halfway to the base. Spread a little minced (finely chopped) garlic on both sides of the paddles and sprinkle with salt to taste. Grill them on a hot *comal* or cast-iron griddle with a little oil. Flip them once with a metal spatula until cooked on both sides. The *nopales* should be slightly burned to give them more flavor.

Top: Manzano Chiles in Lime Juice; bottom: Prickly Pear Paddles or Nopal Paddles

CACTUS AND SUCCULENTS

Tequila and mescal are made from different varieties of blue *agave,* or century plant. While tequila is fermented and distilled directly from the juices of the plant, mescal goes through a smoking process, which gives it its particularly strong flavor.

Mescal is produced largely in the state of Oaxaca, and usually has a worm in the bottle to identify it. The heart of the tequila producing region is Tequila, Jalisco. It is sold either *blanco,* or unaged, which is referred to as silver tequila in English; or *reposado* or *añejo,* aged for different periods in wooden barrels. Many of the best varieties made in small quantities are never sold outside of the region, let alone exported overseas. Tequila aficionados have to go to the source to taste these special varieties.

Pulque, the fermented juice of a different variety of maguey, is drunk either straight (it has about the same alcoholic content as beer) or *curado,* blended with fresh fruit. The latter is preferred by those who are not too keen on its rather sour taste.

Mixiote is a thin skin peeled off the arms, or *pencas,* of the maguey and used to make flavorful packages of stewed mutton or goat, also called *mixiote.* It is sold in ivory-colored folded sheets resembling parchment (baking paper), which should still be pliable.

Prickly pear, or *nopal,* cactuses abound in central Mexico. The appearance of their thin, oblong paddles, or joints, one coming out of another and growing outward and upward, is quite distinct from that of the maguey cactus, whose great arms, thick at the heart, taper out to a point in all directions.

The paddles are an edible vegetable, called *nopalitos,* and the smaller ones are the most tender. Their prickles are removed by running a knife (or a machete, the great knife indispensable for working the fields) flat against the paddle and along the edge, while leaving as much of the green skin as possible. They are then either boiled (see page 116) in small pieces for salads, soups, or eggs, or broiled (grilled) with a brushing of oil. *Nopalitos* produce a slimy liquid that can be removed by running the boiled vegetable immediately under cold water.

The prickly pear cactus has been a source of food since Aztec times not only for its nutritious paddles, but also for the fruit it bears, called *tuna.* More or less the size and shape of kiwifruit (Chinese gooseberry), these are usually either green or a vibrant magenta. The thick skin can be peeled back with the fingers after slitting along one side. This is made easier if the top and bottom ends are sliced off first—but beware of the minuscule thorns. The fruit contains a lot of edible seeds—though they are swallowed, not chewed—and the fruit is very refreshing. *Tuna* is excellent as an *agua fresca*—"fresh water" mixed with water and sugar—and as a *nieve,* or sherbet (sorbet). In either case, the fruit is pureed, then strained, and the seeds discarded.

Xoconostles are a variety of *tuna* from a different species of *nopal* cactus, and are acid rather than sweet. They are used to flavor sauces and casseroles, or *moles de olla.* They are slightly smaller than the sweet *tunas,* and their skin is a mottled light green and pink. When cut open, the seeds are concentrated in the center instead of dispersed throughout the flesh.

Cabuches are small cactus buds from the desert areas of San Luis Potosí. Fresh ones are not available outside the growing area, but canned ones can be found. They have a subtle, almost artichoke-like flavor and make an interesting addition to salads.

Pitahaya, another cactus fruit, is probably one of the most exotic fruits in appearance. Standing about 6 inches (15 cm) high, it is a bright pinkish magenta with bright green protrusions. The inside of the fruit is either white with thousands of tiny, black seeds or the same bright magenta as the outside. It is eaten raw with a spoon directly from its halved shell. The flavor tends to be rather bland, although it seems to be more prominent if the fruit is chilled first.

1. tequila; 2. mescal; 3. pulque; 4. mixiote; 5. prickly pear paddles with thorns; 6. prickly pear paddles, thorns removed; 7. green tuna (prickly pear fruit); 8. red tuna (prickly pear fruit); 9. xoconostles (sour prickly pear fruit); 10. cabuches; 11. pitahaya; 12. maguey arms

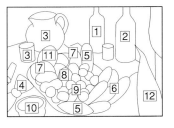

Vegetables, Beans, and Pulses

VEGETABLES, BEANS, AND PULSES

IT WAS A SURPRISE TO THE SPANISH CONQUERORS TO FIND MANY FRUITS AND VEGETABLES IN MEXICO THAT were similar to those of Europe, as well as many other plants hitherto unknown to them. Mexico is blessed with an astounding range and quantity of fruits and vegetables. It has tropical, subtropical, temperate, desert, and even cold, mountainous regions within its borders, which favors the cultivation of a wide variety of plants. In addition, the majority of Mexico has no real winter, allowing most vegetables to be available year-round.

¶ Although technically fruits, tomatoes or green *tomatillos* are the base for many sauces (always used separately for red or green sauces), and red tomatoes are also eaten in salads. Onions and garlic are always present, chopped in raw dishes or sautéed as the flavor base for a dish. Shredded lettuce adds crunch to corn-dough snacks and the pork and hominy stew, *pozole*. Zucchini (courgettes) are a favorite vegetable sautéed with onion, tomato, and cilantro (fresh coriander). Carrots, along with potatoes and peas, are added to rice or to flavor stock.

¶ Avocados (a fruit that's used like a vegetable) lend their rich flavor and oily texture to *tortas* (Mexican sandwiches made with rolls), *tacos*, soups, and sauces. *Chayote* (vegetable pear/choko) and chunks of corn on the cob are added to brothy stews called *mole de olla*.

Previous pages: Mexico's marketplaces provide a palette for the colorful spectrum of people and fresh produce.

Opposite: A wide variety of wild mushrooms is available in the markets of the central highlands during the rainy season which runs from July until October.

¶ As we have seen, the basic trinity of the Mexican diet is corn, beans, and chiles. Beans are the main source of protein for a majority of the people and are generally eaten at every meal. Because beans are a daily food, they are prepared in a number of ways to create variety. The simplest, *Frijoles de la Olla* (see page 150), consists of boiling the beans with a piece of onion and plenty of water so that there is a slightly thick broth when the beans are cooked. In Mexico City, where the altitude is more than 7,000 feet (2,000 meters), a pressure cooker is commonly used to cook the beans—without it, they may take many hours. In some areas, such as the Yucatán, Chiapas, and Tabasco, it is the custom to boil beans with a piece of pork, preferably from the head.

¶ Mexicans also like to eat beans that have been boiled until there is relatively little broth left, the beans and broth then being fried in lard but left whole. When beans are fried and mashed to form a dry bean paste, they are known as *Frijoles Refritos* or refried beans (see page 150). These are used for many *antojitos* and as an accompaniment to breakfast or lunch.

¶ The most typical pulses consumed in Mexico are lentils, dried green peas, chickpeas, and *habas*, a yellow fava (broad) bean—all of which are a base for soups.

¶ Rice is the essential *sopa seca* ("dry soup") for most Mexican meals. It is typically served before the main course, although it's becoming more common in Mexico to serve it with the main dish, especially *moles*. A favorite presentation is *Arroz a la Mexicana* (see page 148), a red rice dish fried with fresh tomatoes cooked with pieces of potato, carrot, and peas. White rice is usually seasoned with garlic and onion and sometimes topped with slices of fried plantain.

PURÉ DE MEMBRILLO

QUINCE PUREE

This is a variation of a very old recipe from Berta Legaspi de Arroyo's family. This dish is delicious served as an accompaniment to broiled (grilled) beef, chicken, or pork.

2 lb (1 kg) quinces, peeled and cored
2 tablespoons brown sugar
salt, to taste
2 tablespoons minced (finely chopped) leek or shallot
¼ cup (2 oz/60 g) melted butter
freshly ground black pepper, to taste
6 tablespoons heavy (double/thickened) cream

SERVES 6

❡ Put the quinces, 1 tablespoon of the sugar, and a pinch of salt in a saucepan with water to cover. Cook over high heat for 45 minutes, or until the quinces are soft; drain. Process in a food processor until smooth.
❡ Sauté the leek in the butter until translucent. Add the quinces, the remaining sugar, and salt and pepper. Simmer for 2 to 3 minutes, stirring well.
❡ Top each serving with a tablespoon of cream.

MOUSSE DE CILANTRO

CILANTRO MOUSSE

Roberto Santibañez, chef of La Circunstancia Restaurant in Mexico City, serves this as a complement to Camarones con Cuitlacoche *(see page 198). It is also delicious eaten with crackers as an hors d'oeuvre.*

1 bunch cilantro (fresh coriander), de-stemmed and chopped
1 cup (8 fl oz/250 ml) milk
1 cup (8 fl oz/250 ml) homemade mayonnaise
6 oz (185 g) cream cheese
1½ envelopes (⅓ oz/10 g) gelatin, dissolved in ½ cup
(4 fl oz/125 ml) water

SERVES 6–8

❡ Blanch the cilantro twice for a few seconds in 2 separate pots of boiling salted water. Rinse and blend with all the remaining ingredients in a food processor or blender until smooth. Pour into individual molds and refrigerate until set.
❡ Serve alone with *totopos* (fried *tortilla* triangles) as an hors d'oeuvre, or as an accompaniment to *Camarones con Cuitlacoche.*

Top: Quince Puree; bottom: Cilantro Mousse

casseroles and broths. Its pronounced anise-like flavor goes particularly well with fish, which may have a strip of *hoja santa* wrapped around it before being gently sautéed. It is also paired with meat or chicken, as in the Veracruz specialties *tlatonile* and *mole de acuyo*. In pre-Hispanic times, it was even used to enhance the flavor and aroma of chocolate drinks.

Perejil (flat-leafed/ Italian/continental parsley): Although curly parsley is sometimes found in Mexico, it is the flat-leafed (Italian or continental) variety which is seen in the marketplaces. Although not nearly as commonly used as cilantro, parsley is sometimes added to soups and rice dishes. A sprig is often placed on top of steaming rice to subtly flavor it, and parsley is pureed with cilantro to make *arroz verde* green. It is, however, much more common to see it as a decoration on anything from market displays to buffets or served dishes than as a common ingredient in Mexican cooking.

BEYOND CILANTRO

Herbs in Mexico are sold in very large bunches for a few pesos. To buy them, you generally ask for a bunch, a peso's, or half a peso's worth.

Cilantro (fresh coriander): Probably the single most ubiquitous herb in Mexican cooking, the tender stems and leaves of cilantro are used to flavor everything from green sauces, *guacamole*, and chicken stock, to cooked squash, seafood cocktails, and green sausage. A tiny bowl of it often sits on the table to be sprinkled in *tacos* or soups.

Hierbas de olor (bay leaves, thyme, and marjoram): Fresh or dried, these herbs are commonly used to flavor stocks, sauces, casseroles, and *picadillos* (chopped meat mixtures). Bay leaves in Mexico are much milder and smaller than the variety commonly used in the US and Europe, which is why many

recipes in this book call for half a bay leaf.

Orégano (oregano): There is a range of oregano, the largest and strongest of which is that used in the Yucatán. Oregano is always sold dried, although the fresh marjoram in the herb mixture *hierbas de olor* is actually a variety of oregano. Oregano's use is widespread: sausages; some fresh, pickled chile sauces; meat dishes (especially goat or pork); and pickled seafood.

Epazote (wormseed): This is one of the most unusual-tasting herbs in the Mexican repertoire. It is strong-smelling and highly complementary to black beans and wild mushrooms. In Puebla, *mole de epazote* is a brothy, red, goat's meat casserole flavored with *epazote*. Red or green *epazote* is used interchangeably; it varies in strength, so be sure it smells

strong when you buy it. Seeds are now available from many mail-order companies, and it grows very easily.

Papaloquelite: This aromatic and unusual herb varies from region to region. The word *quelite* comes from the Nahuatl *quilitl*, which refers to any edible herb or leafy vegetable. *Papaloquelite* is a very strong-tasting herb with large, soft, round leaves. In Puebla, it is used to flavor sandwiches made of tender, cooked mutton known as *semitas* (after the type of bread roll used).

Pipicha: Another unusual herb, this has long, thin leaves reminiscent of tarragon, but with a completely different, rather pungent, taste. It is often stewed with pork.

Hoja santa/acuyo (holy leaf): This has large, spade-shaped leaves up to 8 inches (20 cm) wide and is often used as a *tamal* wrapping or to flavor

*1. cilantro (fresh coriander);
2. hierbas de olor (thyme, marjoram, and bay leaves);
3. perejil (flat-leafed/Italian/continental parsley); 4. red epazote; 5. green epazote; 6. hoja santa/acuyo; 7. papaloquelite; 8. pipicha; 9. orégano (oregano); 10. Yucatecan oregano*

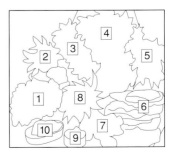

MOUSSE DE AGUACATE Y ESPINACAS CON VINAGRETA DE AVELLANAS

AVOCADO AND SPINACH MOUSSE WITH HAZELNUT VINAIGRETTE

The addition of spinach, watercress, parsley, and cilantro (fresh coriander) in this recipe from Patricia Quintana turns an ordinary avocado mousse into something very special.

For the mousse:
6 large ripe avocados, peeled and pitted
1 cup (8 fl oz/250 ml) thick yogurt
1 cup (8 oz/250 g) ricotta cheese, drained
1 medium onion, shredded and squeezed
1½ cups (1½ oz/45 g) spinach leaves, washed and soaked in water with a pinch of salt for 5 minutes
½ cup (½ oz/15 g) watercress, washed and soaked in water with a pinch of salt for 5 minutes
½ cup (½ oz/15 g) parsley or cilantro (fresh coriander) sprigs, washed
⅓ cup (2½ fl oz/75 ml) lime or lemon juice
½ cup (4 fl oz/125 ml) corn oil
2 small zucchini (courgettes), coarsely chopped
3 cloves garlic, peeled
salt and pepper, to taste

4 envelopes (1 oz/30 g) plain gelatin, soaked in ¾ cup (6 fl oz/185 ml) cold water
For the vinaigrette:
⅓ cup (2½ fl oz/75 ml) lime or lemon juice
2 small cloves garlic, minced (finely chopped)
¾ tablespoon coarse salt, or to taste
1 teaspoon freshly ground black pepper
¾ cup (6 fl oz/185 ml) olive oil
1 cup (8 fl oz/250 ml) corn oil
1 cup (4 oz/125 g) hazelnuts, roasted, shelled, and chopped
watercress or parsley, for garnish

SERVES 12

❡ To make the mousse: Put the first 12 ingredients in a blender and blend until smooth.
❡ Heat the gelatin gently, just to dissolve. Add to the avocado mixture and season with more salt and pepper. Pour into a lightly oiled mold and refrigerate for 3 hours.
❡ For the vinaigrette: Put the lime juice, garlic, salt, and pepper in a large bowl. Add the oils in a thin stream while beating with a wire whisk. Add the hazelnuts and allow to stand for 2 hours.
❡ Unmold the mousse on a serving platter and garnish with watercress or parsley. Serve the vinaigrette in a sauce bowl and accompany with toasted rye bread.

The texture and appearance varies greatly among avocados.

AVOCADOS

The name avocado comes from the Nahuatl *auácatl*, meaning testicle. The sexual reference doesn't end there: research doctor Francisco Hernandez reported in 1575 that avocados were not only agreeable to the taste and quite nutritious, but also that they "excited the sexual appetite and augmented the semen." The English name, avocado pear, is an unwitting double reference to shape.

What we know today as *guacamole* is a derivation from the Aztec *auacamulli*, which referred to the avocado mashed with chile that was sold in markets in Cortés's time. When not mashed into a *guacamole* or added to a green sauce, avocados are sliced to add to *tacos*, rice, or seafood cocktails. On its own, avocado makes a wonderful *taco* filling, and it complements the toasty flavor of a fresh, hot *tortilla* like nothing else. Avocado soup is a more recent addition to Mexican cuisine. Hot, stuffed avocado halves are a contemporary invention, but the delectability of hot avocado is well known from the tradition of adding pieces of avocado to a hot broth or soup as it is served.

There are several varieties of avocado in Mexico: The most common year-round and arguably the best is the Haas, about 4 inches (10 cm) long with either a green or black bumpy skin; the *criollo*, with its edible, thin, purple skin, is a delicacy to be enjoyed when available. It is often the only variety found locally in country villages, whereas the Haas is distributed largely through commercial production. The *fuerte*, or *aguacali*, is slightly larger, while the largest *pajua* can be longer than 6 inches (15 cm) but has a rather watery taste.

The leaf of the avocado tree is used extensively to flavor casseroles and *moles* and as a wrapping for small *tamales*. The leaves are used fresh and sometimes toasted, and have a rather anise-like flavor.

Top: Avocado and Spinach Mousse with Hazelnut Vinaigrette; bottom: Stuffed Avocados with Corn Fungus

AGUACATE RELLENO CON CUITLACOCHE

STUFFED AVOCADOS WITH CORN FUNGUS

In this recipe from Shelton Wiseman, the velvety richness of the hot avocado complements the unusual flavor of the cuitlacoche *(corn fungus).*

For the filling:
4 tablespoons (2 fl oz/60 ml) vegetable oil
½ onion, chopped
1 clove garlic, chopped
1 lb (500 g) fresh cuitlacoche *(corn fungus), cleaned of corn silk and coarsely chopped, or 16 oz/500 g canned* cuitlacoche, *drained*
1 poblano chile, roasted, peeled, seeded, and chopped
1 sprig epazote, chopped, optional
salt, to taste
For the sauce:
2 tablespoons vegetable oil
½ onion, chopped
1 large or 2 small poblano chiles, roasted, peeled, seeded, and chopped
1 cup (8 oz/250 ml) heavy (double/thickened) cream

salt and pepper, to taste
3 ripe avocados, preferably Haas, peeled, pitted, and halved

SERVES 6 AS AN APPETIZER

❡ To make the filling: Heat the oil in a large frying pan and sauté the onion and garlic until translucent. Add all the remaining filling ingredients and cook for approximately 15 minutes over medium heat, or until the *cuitlacoche* is tender. (If using canned *cuitlacoche*, cook for 5 minutes.) The recipe can be made in advance to this point and reheated before serving.

❡ To make the sauce: Heat the oil in a medium frying pan and sauté the onion until translucent. Add the chile and stir for 2 minutes. Add the cream, heat through, and season with salt and pepper. Pour the mixture into a blender and blend until smooth. The sauce should be thick enough to coat the back of a wooden spoon so thin with a little milk or stock if required. Reheat before serving.

❡ Heat a large saucepan half full with water to just below boiling point. Drop the avocados into the water for about a minute to heat through. Remove carefully. Cover the bottom of 6 plates with the chile sauce and put an avocado half on each, cut-side up. Fill with the *cuitlacoche* mixture and serve.

PÂTÉ DE CUITLACOCHE CON SALSA DE CILANTRO

CORN FUNGUS PÂTÉ WITH CILANTRO SAUCE

Although cuitlacoche *(corn fungus) is traditionally cooked as a filling for* tacos *or* quesadillas, *here it is the main ingredient in a contemporary pâté that is served with cilantro (fresh coriander) sauce.*

1 tablespoon vegetable oil
1 tablespoon (½ oz/15 g) butter
½ onion, minced (finely chopped)
1½ lb (750 g) fresh cuitlacoche (corn fungus), cleaned
    of corn silk and chopped (or canned and drained)
3 poblano chiles, roasted, peeled, deveined, and cut into strips
salt, to taste
½ teaspoon granulated chicken stock or 1 bouillon
    cube, crushed
2 envelopes (½ oz/15 g) gelatin
½ cup (4 fl oz/120 ml) chicken stock
1 cup (8 fl oz/250 ml) heavy (double/thickened) cream
6½ oz (200 g) cream cheese
For the sauce:
1 bunch cilantro (fresh coriander), stems removed
1 serrano chile, stem removed
3 spinach leaves
6 tomatillos
1 teaspoon salt, or to taste
½ teaspoon granulated chicken stock or 1 bouillon
    cube, crushed
1 cup (8 fl oz/250 ml) heavy (double/thickened) cream,
    for serving
cilantro (fresh coriander) or parsley, for garnish

SERVES 8

❧ Heat the oil and butter in a pan and sauté the onion until translucent. Add the *cuitlacoche* and cook for approximately 10 to 15 minutes. (Its appearance will not change much.) Add the chiles, and season with salt and granulated chicken stock.

❧ Soften the gelatin in the fresh chicken stock in a small saucepan for 5 minutes. Put the saucepan over a low heat for 1 minute to dissolve the gelatin, stirring constantly.

❧ Combine the *cuitlacoche* mixture, the cream, and the cream cheese in a food processor and process until smooth. Add the gelatin and process again until thoroughly combined.

❧ Pour the mixture into a 1-qt (1-l) terrine mold or 8 individual molds. Refrigerate for at least 3 hours until set.

❧ To make the sauce: Process the first 6 ingredients in a food processor until smooth.

❧ To serve, unmold the pâté and put a slice or individual mold on each plate. Surround with the sauce, garnish with the cream and cilantro or parsley, and serve with melba toast.

ENSALADA DE ALUBIAS, PIMIENTOS, Y EJOTES

NAVY BEAN, RED PEPPER, AND GREEN BEAN SALAD

If you want to try a different kind of salad, this one is ideal. Serve it as an appetizer or as an accompaniment to meat or poultry.

1 cup (5½ oz/170 g) canned large navy (haricot) beans,
    drained and rinsed
5 oz (155 g) green beans, cleaned, boiled in water with a
    pinch of salt until just tender, and cut into 1½-inch
    (4-cm) long slivers
½ medium red bell pepper (capsicum), seeded and cut
    into 1½-inch (4-cm) long slivers
1 tablespoon chopped onion
1 tablespoon minced (finely chopped) flat-leafed (Italian
    or continental) parsley
For the dressing:
2 tablespoons olive oil
1 tablespoon light white or cider vinegar
½ teaspoon salt, or to taste
freshly ground black pepper

SERVES 6

❧ Put the navy beans, green beans, red bell pepper, onion, and parsley in a salad bowl or large shallow dish and toss well.

❧ For the dressing: Combine all the remaining ingredients in a small bowl and whisk thoroughly. Pour over the salad and toss to mix.

❧ Serve immediately.

GUAJES

These flat, bright green beans are approximately ½ inch (1 cm) long and can be eaten raw as a snack, or are sometimes used to flavor a soul-satisfying casserole from the state of Morelos, and a well-known *kid* (baby goat) casserole from Puebla called guazmole. *The beans are native to Mexico, where their indigenous name is* oaxi *or* uaxiquivitl.

Front: Corn Fungus Pâté with Cilantro Sauce; back: Navy Bean, Red Pepper, and Green Bean Salad

ENSALADA DE LECHUGAS CON JÍCAMA Y MANGO

MIXED SALAD WITH JÍCAMA AND MANGO

This salad from José Galindo uses both Mexican ingredients and foreign elements, such as the red oak leaf and Boston (butterhead) lettuces. The result is surprisingly delectable.

2 heads each red oak leaf and Boston (butterhead) lettuce, washed and torn
1 red onion, halved and finely sliced
2 firm mangoes, peeled and cut into ¾-inch (2-cm) cubes
1 jícama, peeled, and cut in ¼- x 2-inch (0.5- x 5-cm) strips, or substitute water chestnuts
2 avocados, pitted, peeled, and sliced
For the vinaigrette:
⅓ cup (3 fl oz/90 ml) cider vinegar
2 cloves garlic, peeled
2 shallots, peeled and chopped
1 cup (1 oz/30 g) chopped flat-leafed (Italian/continental) parsley
1 cup (1 oz/30 g) chopped cilantro (fresh coriander)
1 tablespoon honey
1 teaspoon salt, or to taste
½ teaspoon black pepper
1 pinch ground cloves
½ cup (4 fl oz/125 ml) vegetable oil
½ cup (4 fl oz/125 ml) olive oil

SERVES 12

❡ Place the lettuce leaves, onion, mangoes, and *jícama* in a salad bowl.
❡ To make the vinaigrette: Place all of the ingredients in a blender and blend until completely smooth.
❡ Pour the vinaigrette over the salad and toss. Garnish with the avocados slices, and serve immediately.

LETTUCES

Although many varieties of lettuce are now cultivated in Mexico, the traditional varieties are the long-leafed romaine (cos), called orejoná *("big ears"), and a round, green, crisp head lettuce, called* romanita. *This is somewhere between a Boston (butterhead) lettuce and an iceberg. The crispiness of these lettuces is perfect for their most typical use, which is to shred, or julienne, them to add a fresh crunch to* antojitos, tacos, *and the pork and hominy stew* pozole. *Lettuce can also used for salads with tomato and onion, but salads in Mexico are usually made with cooked vegetables rather than raw lettuce.*

ENSALADA DE BERROS Y CILANTRO

WATERCRESS AND CILANTRO SALAD

This salad, which is a delicious accompaniment to meat or fish, was taught to Manena Almada by a bricklayer who uses it as a taco filling. The savory combination of the salad's fresh ingredients with tortillas is delightful.

Left: Mixed Salad with Jícama and Mango; right: Watercress and Cilantro Salad

¼ cup (1½ oz/45 g) scallions (spring onions), white
  part only, sliced
3 cups (2½ oz/75 g) watercress, washed and stems
  removed
2 cups (⅔ oz/20 g) cilantro (fresh coriander), washed and
  lightly packed
2 serrano chiles, chopped

¼ teaspoon salt, or to taste
2 tablespoons lime or lemon juice

SERVES 6

¶ Separate the scallions into rings. Put the first 4
ingredients into a salad bowl and toss to mix well.
Add the salt and lime juice, and toss again. Serve.

UNUSUAL VEGETABLES

There are so many unusual vegetables in Mexico that it would be hard to make an exhaustive list. The following are some of the most popular.

Romeritos: This herb-like vegetable gets its name from its visual similarity to rosemary (*romero* in Spanish). The leaves are longer and softer than rosemary's and the taste is rather bland, like a slightly seaweedy spinach. Its principal use is in the dish called *revoltijo* (but often referred to as *romeritos*), a fricassee-like specialty served during Christmas and Lent. There, it plays a background role to a rich *mole* (mixture) with dried shrimp (prawn) patties. *Romeritos* should be washed thoroughly to remove any dirt before being cooked in boiling water until tender.

Verdolagas (purslane): This is a slightly acidic green vegetable, abundant during the rainy season. Both the spongy green leaves and the tender stems are eaten, having first been boiled until tender, then added to a pan of onion and garlic sautéed with green or red tomatoes and a little *serrrano* chile. It combines wonderfully with the acidity of the tomatoes or *tomatillos*, and is often later cooked with the stock and meat of leftover pork roast or casserole for a satisfying and popular dish. Alternatively, the sautéed purslane can be used to dress fried eggs or fill a *taco*, perhaps combined with cooked potato cubes or cheese to balance its acidity. Although it is more common to cook them, the tender leaves can also be added to salads.

Guauzontles/huauzontles: This is a branch-like green vegetable with tender buds. Traditionally, the vegetable is "stuffed" with cheese, with pieces of cheese placed between the bud-laden branches, dipped and fried in an egg batter (the same as for *chiles rellenos*), and served in a tomato broth. They are delicious, but to eat them, you either have to pull the tender buds off the branch with your teeth or scrape them off with a knife and fork. If you are lucky, they will be served to you by a dedicated cook who has removed the tender parts.

Chayote (vegetable pear/choko): In Mexico there are at least three varieties of this member of the squash family: prickly and green, smooth-skinned in shades of green, and the smaller white one. Although many consider the large, spiny green *chayote* to have the best taste, it is still a bland, mild flavor somewhat similar to cooked cucumber. *Chayote* cries out for some assistance from chiles or herbs—a common addition throughout Mexico and the Caribbean. The neutral flavor of *chayote* lends itself to many styles of cooking: It can be peeled, cut into chunks or strips, then boiled or fried before being combined with other ingredients, or boiled whole, with the pulp used in fritters or pureed for soup. Another style of preparation is cutting the vegetable in half, removing the seed, and stuffing the boat-shaped container with different fillings. In this case, the pulp is usually combined with cheese and other seasonings and baked as a vegetable or an appetizer. In some areas, as in Tabasco, the stuffing is sweet and served as a dessert. The abundant, entwining vines of the evergreen *chayote* plant are easily grown in warm, moist climates. The tender seed and the roots (see *chinchayote*) can also be eaten.

Chinchayote/chayotextle (chayote root): This long root is white inside with a thin, light brown skin. While the storekeeper may not like it, the best way you can test the freshness of the *chayote* root is to scratch it with your fingernail: it should prick easily and exude a milky substance. It is boiled until tender, then peeled and sliced. In Veracruz, it may be added to a pork casserole, while a specialty of Guadalajara is to fry it sliced in the same egg batter that is used for *chiles rellenos*. It is served with *Salsa Cruda de Guadalajara* (see page 22), a tomato-based sauce that contains no chile.

Jícama: This root vegetable is becoming increasingly popular outside Mexico. It is always eaten raw, usually cut in sticks or thick slices with just a sprinkling of lime juice and chile powder. It is sold prepared in this way from fruit carts, or served as a tidbit before a meal. Its delightful crunch makes a wonderful addition to salads. Because of its similarity in texture to water chestnuts, many Chinese cooks in Mexico use it as a substitute. Likewise, if *jícama* is unavailable, substitute water chestnuts, daikon, turnip, or even celeriac. *Jícamas* vary in size from 2 to 6 inches (5 to 15 cm) in diameter. Remove the skin, which ranges from thin and white to a thicker, dusty, light brown, with a vegetable peeler. To test for freshness, you should be able to scratch a bit away easily with a fingernail.

Chaya: This favored vegetable in the Yucatán gets its name from the Maya word *chay*. This leafy vegetable grows from Tabasco to the Yucatán, and is very common in their cuisines, especially in *tamales* like the popular banana leaf-wrapped *dzotoblchay* of the Yucatán, where it is chopped and added to the *masa*. In Tabasco, a smaller version is made, which is sometimes wrapped in the *chaya* leaf itself, that ranges in size from 4 to 8 inches (10 to 20 cm). Both of these are served with a light tomato sauce, unusual because *tamales* in the rest of the Republic are not served with sauce, and the Tabascan one is sprinkled with the dry and acidic *Chiapas* cheese. The leaves have a firm texture like that of Swiss chard (spring greens/silverbeet), which could be used as a substitute. The five-pointed leaves range in size from about 4 to 8 inches (10 to 20 cm). They may be boiled and added to a meat or seafood dish, pureed into a soup, or used as a filling for crêpes. There are two kinds of *chaya*: *chaya mansa* (gentle *chaya*), which has smooth leaves and is the type you will usually find in the market; and *chaya brava* (fierce *chaya*), which has furry prickles on the leaves that can cause a rash when the leaves are raw but are harmless when cooked.

1. *romeritos*; 2. *verdolagas (purslane)*; 3. *guauzontles/ huauzontles*; 4. *spiny green chayote (vegetable pear/choko)*; 5. *white chayote (vegetable pear/choko)*; 6. *green chayote (vegetable pear/choko)*; 7. *chinchayote/chayotextle (chayote root)*; 8. *jícama*; 9. *chaya*

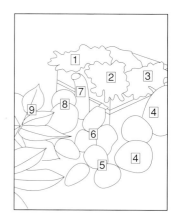

GUISADO DE GARBANZOS Y PIMIENTOS EN JITOMATE

CHICKPEAS AND GREEN BELL PEPPERS WITH TOMATOES

Of Middle-Eastern origin, chickpeas, or garbanzos, were introduced into Mexico by the Spanish. The combination of chickpeas, peppers, and tomatoes is, however, distinctly Spanish in character, even though the latter two ingredients originated in Mexico (sweet bell peppers evolved from the original capsicum of Mexico). Chickpeas are sold dried or canned in Mexico. Either way, the skins should be removed by covering the cooked chickpeas with cold water and rubbing them to loosen the skins, which are hard to digest and ruin the texture of a dish. This vegetable melange can be eaten alone as an appetizer or teamed with Arroz Blanco (see page 148) as an accompaniment to meat or chicken.

2 green bell peppers (capsicums)
2 tablespoons olive oil
2 cloves garlic, minced (finely chopped)
12 oz (375 g) tomatoes, peeled, seeded, and minced
    (finely chopped)
1½ teaspoons salt, or to taste
freshly ground black pepper, to taste
1 can (16 oz/500 g) chickpeas, drained and skins removed
1 small bay leaf
1 small sprig fresh thyme or pinch dried thyme

SERVES 6

❦ Quarter the peppers, discard the stems and seeds, and remove the skin with a vegetable peeler. Cut the peppers into ¼-inch (0.5-cm) strips.
❦ Heat the oil in a large saucepan over medium heat, then sauté the garlic until soft but not brown. Add the tomatoes, salt, and pepper.
❦ Cover and cook for approximately 5 minutes, or until slightly thickened.
❦ Add the chickpeas, peppers, bay leaf, and thyme. Cook for a further 5 minutes and serve.

ENSALADA DE CEBOLLITAS DE CAMBRAY

SCALLION SALAD

With the little scallions (spring onions) looking like tiny translucent balloons, this salad is as beautiful to look at as it is good to eat. Cooking the onions makes their flavor more gentle, and the vinaigrette adds a touch of sweetness.

The avocado brings both a different color and a contrasting rich, meaty texture to this interesting salad.

1 lb (500 g) scallions (spring onions), about 1½ inches
    (3 cm) in diameter, washed, and stems and root
    ends discarded
For the vinaigrette:
2 tablespoons white or cider vinegar
½ teaspoon Dijon mustard
½ teaspoon honey
4 tablespoons (2 fl oz/60 ml) olive oil
salt and white pepper, to taste
1 avocado, cut into thin wedges

SERVES 8

❦ Place the scallions in a large saucepan and cover with water. Bring to a boil, cover, and cook over high heat for approximately 10 to 15 minutes, or until tender. Drain and dry on paper towels.
❦ Carefully remove the outer layers of the scallions by pressing between your fingers to "pop" out the inner bulbs. There will be 5 or 6 layers per onion.
❦ For the vinaigrette: Whisk the vinegar, mustard, honey, oil, and salt and pepper to taste, until thoroughly blended.
❦ Place the scallions in a salad bowl.
❦ Toss the vinaigrette with the onions just before serving. Garnish with the avocado.

VINEGARS AND OILS

The two vinegars most commonly used in Mexico are white vinegar and cider vinegar. White vinegar is usually made from cane alcohol, although a white-wine vinegar is also available. Red vinegar is never called for in traditional Mexican dishes; however, the growing international sections of supermarkets and specialty stores stock a variety of other options. While much of Mexico's varied cuisine uses lime juice instead of vinegar for acidity, vinegar is used in salads and escabeches—pickled foods from chiles to pig's trotters to shrimp (prawns). Fruit vinegars, especially those made from pineapple, are often prepared at home, and a lot of apple vinegar is used in the northern states. Mexican recipes seem to call for larger portions of vinegar than most other recipes; you may like to adjust the amounts down somewhat. Corn and safflower are the most prevalent vegetable oils used for cooking in Mexico today, and have replaced lard in many dishes in these cholesterol-conscious times. Olive oil is used where there is a Spanish influence in the cuisine, notably in Veracruz, the landing port of the Spanish conquistadors and subsequent traders.

Top: Chickpeas and Green Bell Peppers with Tomatoes; bottom: Scallion Salad

ENSALADA MEXICANA

MEXICAN SALAD

Toasted sesame seeds and browned almonds are common additions to Mexican food. These, along with the fried tortilla squares and pasilla chiles makes this salad a very typical Mexican dish.

Left: Mexican Salad; right: Bean Salad

3 cups (2½ oz/75 g) fresh spinach leaves, torn into ½-inch (1-cm) strips
1 teaspoon plus 1 tablespoon vegetable oil
¼ cup (1 oz/30 g) blanched almonds
2 (6-inch/15-cm) tortillas, cut into ½-inch (1-cm) squares
1 pasilla chile
For the dressing:
1 tablespoon light white or cider vinegar

1 tablespoon shredded onion
salt and freshly ground black pepper, to taste
3 tablespoons vegetable oil
2 cups (1 lb/500 g) queso fresco, panela, or farmer's
cheese, cut into ½-inch (1-cm) cubes
¾ oz (20 g) sesame seeds, toasted

SERVES 4

❧ Put the cleaned and well-dried spinach in a salad bowl.

❧ Heat 1 teaspoon of the oil in a small frying pan and gently fry the almonds for approximately 2 to 3 minutes over a very low flame, or until they just start to turn golden-brown. Remove the almonds and set aside.

❧ Add the remaining oil to the pan and, over a high flame, quickly fry the *tortilla* squares until they are crisp. Be careful not to burn them. Remove, drain on paper towels to remove any excess oil, and set aside.

❧ Fry the chile in the oil. Remove, drain on paper towels, and slice into ¼-inch (0.5-cm) rings, discarding the seeds. Set aside.

❧ To make the dressing: Combine the vinegar, onion, salt, and pepper in a bowl. Add the oil, little by little, whisking constantly to blend.

❧ Add the toasted almonds, *tortilla* squares, cheese cubes, and chile to the salad bowl containing the spinach. Pour on the dressing and toss gently until well mixed.

❧ Sprinkle with the sesame seeds and serve.

ENSALADA DE FRIJOL

BEAN SALAD

In the state of Sonora, this salad is eaten during the hot season. It is one of the rare instances in Mexico where cooked pulses are used in a salad.

⅓ tablespoon minced (finely chopped) scallion
(spring onion)
2 tablespoons light or cider vinegar
1½ cups (12 oz/375 g) cooked pinto (borlotti) beans plus
3 tablespoons bean broth (see Frijoles de la Olla
page 150), at room temperature
4 teaspoons dried oregano, or to taste
½ teaspoon salt, or to taste
⅓ cup (3 fl oz/90 ml) olive oil

SERVES 4

❧ Marinate the scallion in the vinegar for 10 minutes, stirring occasionally.

❧ Meanwhile, toss the beans, bean broth, oregano, and salt together gently in a serving bowl. Add the vinegar and chopped scallion, salt, and oil, then gently mix them all together until thoroughly blended. Taste for seasoning, adding more salt, if desired.

❧ Serve at room temperature. You can either serve immediately or allow to sit for 2 hours to wed the flavors.

MEDICINAL AND SPIRITUAL HERBS

The ancient practice of using herbs, bark, and seeds for medicinal purposes in Mexico is very much a living science. In fact, just about everything we eat or drink has medicinal properties, which can be put to appropriate use by those who understand them. Neither is medicine limited to the physical body: for spiritual cures, whether for oneself or a loved one, or for a physical space, such as a house or room, special purifying ceremonies are performed.

The herbs in a typical *limpia* (spiritual body cure) include rosemary, basil, fennel, parsley, rue, pirul, and a few red and white flowers. (Pirul leaves are from the tree that produces the berries we know as pink peppercorns.) It is interesting to note that many of these herbs are familiar to us as seasonings for food but are not commonly used for culinary purposes in Mexico, with the exception of parsley. Others, such as fennel, are also used medicinally as a tea. However, basil is apparently used in one traditional dish: In Campeche, it is used to flavor a dish called *pibepollo,* that state's version of the Yucatecan *mucbilpollo.*

Star anise can be bought at the pharmacy or at the medicinal herb stall of a Mexican market. Mothers boil it with water to add to their baby's bottle to cure stomach aches. Lettuce leaves boiled in water are added to a baby's bath to help the baby sleep well. An infusion of basil is a remedy for headaches; rue relieves gas; the barks, *contrahierba* and the stronger *palo santo,* are infused into teas for calming nerves; lemon leaves act as a calmant and a digestive; cinnamon tea combats diarrhoea; *epazote,* widely used in Mexican cooking, helps combat parasites; and so on—the list is endless.

The medicinal herb stalls of a good Mexican market may have a line of people waiting to buy the items recommended by their doctor, or to ask the advice of the stall holder about a simple ailment. The most famous and largest market dedicated almost entirely to selling these herbs, bark, strange medicines, and even animals is the Sonora market in downtown Mexico City.

An unlimited array of herbs is drunk as infusions, often for their medicinal properties, while still others are used in spiritual purification—for example, being brushed over a person's body or burnt as incense to cleanse a physical space.

1. pirul; 2. basil; 3. ruda (rue);
4. parsley; 5. hinojo (fennel);
6. lemon leaves; 7. rosemary;
8. star anise; 9. contrahierba;
10. palo santo; 11. lettuce

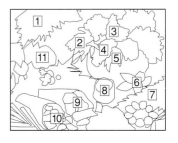

FLORES DE CALABAZA EMPANIZADAS Y FRITAS

FRIED SQUASH BLOSSOMS

In Mexico, squash blossoms (resembling those of a pumpkin more than a zucchini) are very popular in soups, casseroles, and quesadillas. They are also delicious simply coated in a tempura batter and fried. Zucchini flowers can be substituted as they're more readily available.

12 (2 oz/60 g) squash (pumpkin) or zucchini blossoms
1 egg, beaten
5 tablespoons fine breadcrumbs
4 tablespoons (2 fl oz/60 ml) vegetable oil
parsley for garnish, optional

MAKES 12

❡ Clean the squash blossoms, removing the stems, if desired, and the small green spikes at the base. Press the hard bulbs to flatten, then separate and extend the petals until the flower shape is visible.

❡ Dip the flowers in the egg, then in the breadcrumbs. Heat the oil in a frying pan over medium heat and fry 6 flowers at a time until crisp and golden; change the oil if necessary between batches. Drain on paper towels.

❡ Serve, garnished with chopped parsley, if desired.

Fried Squash Blossoms

TORTITAS DE CILANTRO O PEREJIL

CILANTRO OR PARSLEY PATTIES

These herb fritters are equally delicious with cilantro (fresh coriander) or parsley. They can be served for brunch, as an appetizer, or, as they were served by Diana Salvat de Campillo, as a main course with Arroz Blanco (see page 148).

3 cups (24 fl oz/750 ml) water
4 (10 oz/315 g) tomatillos
1 serrano *chile*, or to taste
2 tablespoons vegetable oil
½ onion, chopped
1 clove garlic, minced (finely chopped)
½ teaspoon salt, or to taste
For the patties:
2 eggs, separated
½ tablespoon all-purpose (plain) flour
1 cup (1 oz/30 g) chopped cilantro (fresh coriander) or
   parsley leaves with some stems
½ teaspoon salt, or to taste
4 tablespoons (2 fl oz/60 ml) vegetable oil

MAKES 6 PATTIES

❧ Put the water in a small casserole and boil the *tomatillos* and chile over high heat until soft. Drain, then blend with 2 tablespoons of water in a blender until smooth.

❧ Heat the oil in a casserole over medium heat and sauté the onion and garlic. Add the *tomatillo* mixture and salt, and simmer for 5 minutes, stirring occasionally. Remove from the heat and set aside.

❧ To make the patties: Whip the egg whites with an electric beater until firm but not dry. In a separate bowl, beat the yolks with a fork. Add the flour, cilantro or parsley, and salt, and mix well. Fold the whites into the mixture.

❧ Heat the oil in a frying pan over medium heat and drop in a few heaping spoonfuls of the patty mixture. Fry for 1 minute on each side. Drain the patties, then place in the casserole with the *tomatillo* sauce. Reheat and serve.

TORTITAS DE VERDURAS SIN FREIR

OIL-FREE VEGETABLE PATTIES

Fried patties, or fritters, are very popular in Mexico, but these are unusual in that they are not "fried" in oil. Serve with any spicy cooked tomato or tomatillo sauce.

1 (8-oz/250-g) potato, peeled and shredded
1 (5-oz/155-g) carrot, peeled and shredded
⅓ cup (2 oz/60 g) scallions (spring onions), very
   finely sliced
1 small poblano *chile* (2 oz/60 g), toasted, peeled, seeded,
   and cut into 1¼-inch (3-cm) strips
2 small eggs
2 tablespoons all-purpose (plain) flour
¼ teaspoon salt, or to taste
freshly ground black pepper, to taste

MAKES 12 PATTIES

❧ Press the potato, carrot, scallions, and chile with paper towels to remove any excess moisture. Place the eggs in a bowl and beat lightly. Mix in the flour, salt, and pepper, then add the vegetables. Blend until well-mixed with quite a thick consistency.

❧ Heat a *comal* or cast-iron griddle and drop on 1 heaping tablespoon of batter per patty. Press down with the back of the spoon to make circles 2½ inches (6 cm) in diameter. Cook for 2 minutes on each side.

❧ Serve either as an appetizer with any tomato or *tomatillo* sauce, or on their own, as a vegetable with the main meal.

Top: Cilantro or Parsley Patties; bottom: Oil-free Vegetable Patties

ONIONS AND OTHER POPULAR VEGETABLES

The yellow, or Spanish, onion does not exist in Mexico; rather, it is the large, white, thin-skinned onion found throughout the country that is used in all Mexican cooking (in this book's recipes, this is what "onion" refers to). White onions are especially good when used raw in sauces, where their taste is fresh and crunchy. They are less sweet than yellow onions (which caramelize better), and influence the overall taste of a dish. The average size varies from 4 to 12 ounces (110 to 350 g), although

they can weigh up to 1 lb (500 g) each. Red onions are used raw in salads and sometimes fresh in sauces or pickles.

New onions (green onions) vary in size from as small as ½ inch (1 cm) in diameter to about 1½ inches (4 cm). The bulb is round rather than flat like scallions (spring onions), and they are always sold with their green stems intact. They are delicious charred on a broiler (grill) and eaten whole, green stem and all, with a squeeze of lime juice, or they may be added raw to salads.

Carrots, potatoes, string beans, and Swiss chard (spring greens/silverbeet) are among the many vegetables typically found in Mexican markets that we are all familiar with. Potatoes are generally waxy and thin-skinned rather than starchy. Both red and white potatoes and the small "new" potato varieties are commonly available.

Small, long, or round zucchini (courgettes), another favorite vegetable, are delicious sautéed with onion, tomato, and cilantro (fresh coriander); and

garlic, a much-favored seasoning, is found in both white and pink varieties.

1. Swiss chard (spring greens/silverbeet); 2. potatoes; 3. carrots; 4. green beans; 5. round zucchini (courgette); 6. white onions; 7. garlic; 8. red onions; 9. new onions

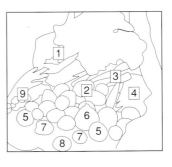

TORTA DE ZANAHORIA

CARROT TORTE

This recipe is from Patricia Quintana's book, Puebla, Cocina de Los Angeles. *With her usual innovative flair, Patricia makes madeleines with this mixture and serves them as a garnish to the main course. This recipe makes about 55 madeleines.*

3 cups (24 fl oz/750 ml) water
1 teaspoon salt, or to taste
1 teaspoon sugar, or to taste
2 lb (1 kg) carrots, peeled
½ cup (4 fl oz/125 ml) milk
1 cup (8 oz/250 g) butter
1¾ cups (12 oz/375 g) sugar
8 eggs, separated
2 cups (9 oz/280 g) rice flour
1½ teaspoons baking powder

Left: Carrot Torte; right: Potatoes with Oregano

¼ teaspoon plus pinch salt
parsley, for garnish

SERVES 8–10

❡ Preheat the oven to 350°F (180°C/Gas 4). Grease and flour a 8–9½-inch (20–24-cm) ring mold.

❡ Put the water, salt, and sugar in a saucepan. Add the carrots and cook for 25 minutes over medium heat. Let cool a little. Drain, reserving the liquid, and then puree in a blender with the milk and a little of the cooking liquid, if necessary to make a smoother puree.

❡ Cream the butter with an electric mixer for 8 minutes, or until fluffy. Continue to beat while gradually adding the sugar, to make a smooth paste.

❡ Add the egg yolks one at a time, beating continuously until all of the ingredients are thoroughly blended.

❡ Sift the flour 3 times with the baking powder and ¼ teaspoon of salt. Alternately beat the carrot puree and flour into the butter-yolk mixture.

❡ In a separate bowl, beat the egg whites and the pinch of salt with an electric mixer or wire whisk until stiff but not dry. Fold them into the batter. Pour the batter into the mold and bake for 45 minutes, or until a cake tester inserted into the center comes out clean.

❡ Let the cake cool slightly. Turn the mold over and tap the bottom to release the cake on a plate. Garnish the center with parsley sprigs and serve as an accompaniment to meat or chicken.

PAPAS CON OREGANO

POTATOES WITH OREGANO

Oregano is used as a seasoning all over Mexico, almost always as a dried herb. Along with the garlic, it gives a great flavor to these potatoes which are crispy on the outside and soft in the middle.

1 lb (500 g) potatoes, unpeeled
4 tablespoons (2 fl oz/60 ml) vegetable oil
3 cloves garlic, peeled and minced (finely chopped)
½ teaspoon salt, or to taste
1 tablespoon dried oregano, crushed

SERVES 4

❡ Put the potatoes in a medium pot and add salted water to cover. Simmer over medium heat until cooked but still firm. Drain and peel. Let cool for 5 minutes, then cut into ½-inch (1-cm) slices.

❡ Heat the oil and garlic in a large frying pan over medium heat. Add the potatoes and salt before the garlic begins to brown. Fry the potatoes on both sides until golden. Add the oregano and continue to fry for another minute, to combine the flavors.

❡ Serve as an accompaniment to *Cecina Flameada* (see page 182), pork chops, or broiled (grilled) beef.

❡ Any leftover potatoes can be reheated in a frying pan over low heat.

TORTITAS DE PAPA

POTATO PATTIES

These potato patties are typical fare in economical restaurants, or fonditas, *where they are usually served as an appetizer with a cooked tomato or* tomatillo *sauce, or with* Salsa Cruda de Guadalajara *(see page 22). When accompanying a main course, they would be served without a sauce.*

1 lb (500 g) potatoes, unpeeled
4 egg yolks
¼ cup (1 oz /30 g) shredded añejo cheese, or dry feta
¾ teaspoon salt, or to taste
½ cup (4 fl oz/125 ml) vegetable oil

MAKES 8 PATTIES

❡ Place the potatoes in a pan with enough salted water to cover. Cook until tender but still firm. Drain, peel, and mash the potatoes, then cool slightly. Add the egg yolks, cheese, and salt, and mix well.

❡ Form round 2½-inch (7-cm) patties. Heat the oil in a small frying pan over medium heat and cook 2 or 3 patties at a time for about 2 minutes per side, or until golden. Drain on paper towels to remove any excess oil, and serve.

❡ The patties can also be reheated in a slow oven or on top of the stove in a non-stick pan.

CAMOTE DE LA CALLE

STREET VENDOR'S YAMS

On the streets of Mexico City from June to September, a peculiar steam whistle in the late afternoon announces the arrival of the street vendors with their hot roasted yams and plantains. The yams are split down the middle, sweetened with condensed milk, and sold in brown paper.

4 (11-oz/345-g) yams or sweet potatoes
vegetable oil for coating

MAKES 4

❡ Wash the yams well, dry, coat with the oil, and wrap in aluminum foil. Heat a *comal* or cast-iron griddle over low heat and roast the yams, covering them with a metal baking pan. Cook for 1 hour, turning every 15 minutes until the yams are soft. The skin will be slightly burned.

❡ The yams can be served with butter, like a baked potato, and eaten skin and all.

Left: Potato Patties; right: Street Vendor's Yams

TORTITAS DE AVENA

OATMEAL FRITTERS

These fried tortitas are served with a light tomato sauce. The acidity of the tomato balances the fat from the frying. They can also be served with a fruit puree instead of the tomato sauce. This recipe is from María Eugenia Valdés Villarreal.

1 cup (3½ oz/100 g) rolled oats
2 small onions, minced (finely chopped)
5 tablespoons chopped parsley
4 eggs, lightly beaten
½ teaspoon salt, or to taste
For the sauce:
4 tablespoons (2 fl oz/60 ml) vegetable oil
1 lb (500 g) tomatoes, quartered and seeded

Left: Oatmeal Fritters: right: Rice with Lentils

1 onion, minced (finely chopped)
½ bay leaf
½ sprig fresh thyme
1 sprig fresh parsley

MAKES 10 FRITTERS

❧ In a bowl, mix the oats, onions, parsley, eggs, and salt thoroughly. Let rest for 5 minutes.

❧ For the sauce: Heat 2 tablespoons of the oil in a medium frying pan. Blend the tomato and onion in a blender and strain on top of the hot oil. Add the herbs and cook over high heat until the fat rises to the surface, about 8 minutes. Remove the herbs and set the pan aside.

❧ Heat the remaining 2 tablespoons of oil in a separate medium frying pan. Put 1 rounded tablespoon of the oat mixture at a time into the pan and flatten with a spatula. Cook, turning once, over medium heat until golden.

❧ Place the fritters in the tomato sauce and cook over very low heat for approximately 10 minutes, turning once. Serve.

ARROZ Y LENTEJAS

RICE WITH LENTILS

This recipe emerged from the large Lebanese community in Mexico. Since both lentils and rice are loved in Mexico, the dish was readily adopted and is generally served in the tradition of a sopa seca *(dry soup), as an appetizer.*

½ cup (3½ oz/100 g) lentils
2½ cups (20 fl oz/625 ml) water
1 slice onion plus 4 onions, halved and finely sliced
¾ teaspoon plus ½ teaspoon salt, or to taste
1 cup (8 oz/250 ml) vegetable oil
½ cup (3½ oz/100 g) rice, rinsed until the water runs clear and drained thoroughly

SERVES 4

❧ Bring the lentils to a boil with the water, onion slice, and ¾ teaspoon of the salt. Cover and simmer over low heat for about 20 minutes, or until tender. Drain, reserving 1½ cups (12 fl oz/350 ml) of the cooking liquid, adding water if necessary.

❧ In a large frying pan, heat the oil and add the onions. Cook over medium heat, stirring as needed, until golden, about 25 minutes. Remove and drain the onions, but reserve the oil in the pan. (This can be done up to 2 hours ahead.)

❧ Reheat the oil and add the rice. Cook, stirring, over medium heat for about 5 minutes, or until it makes a crackling sound. Drain.

❧ Put the cooked rice, lentils, ½ teaspoon of salt, and reserved liquid in a large saucepan. Bring to a boil, cover and cook over low heat for 25 to 30 minutes without removing the lid.

❧ A minute or two before it's finished, stir in the fried onions, reserving some, if desired, to strew over the top.

Beans, Rice, and Pulses

There are more than sixty varieties of beans in Mexico, and ten of these are commonly used. People of the coastal state of Veracruz, as well as those of the Yucatán Peninsula—areas where the Caribbean influence has been the strongest—prefer different types of black beans. In many of the northern states, the lighter-colored varieties are in demand, while the dwellers of the central part of the country eat both kinds, particularly in Oaxaca, which borders on Veracruz.

The most common varieties of lighter-colored beans are pinto, *bayo, flor de mayo,* and Peruvian. Pinto, or spotted, beans are pinkish brown and speckled; *bayo,* or bay, beans are a uniform light brown; *flor de mayo* (May flower) are a brighter red than pintos, often a little smaller, but also speckled; and Peruvian beans are light yellow. All of these are used pretty much interchangeably.

As we have seen, both *Frijoles de la Olla* (see page 150) and *Frijoles Refritos* (see page 150) are common accompaniments to breakfast and lunch plates. Refried beans are also spread on *tostadas* or *sopes* as a base for these tasty snacks, upon which other ingredients are sprinkled or piled. Eggs scrambled with beans are called *frijoles con huevo* (beans with egg), giving beans the upper hand. Refried beans may be stuffed into the delicious dried *ancho* chiles, covered with egg batter, and fried or marinated and served in a vinegar-based *escabeche,* which is rather like a vinaigrette with the addition of onions, carrots, aromatic herbs, and garlic.

In Puebla, there are larger, kidney-shaped beans called *ayocotes.* These are usually dark purple but are also sold in mixed bins of large white, tan, brown, and purple beans. They are delicious served whole: the beans and broth are fried with caramelized onion and bay leaves briefly to season them and to reduce the broth.

Habas, the large, yellow fava (broad) beans cultivated principally in the center of the country, are pureed into a paste and folded into *tlacoyos* (see page 45).

The various types of pulses popular in Mexico are more often than not used in soups (see "Soups" for more information about them). Chickpeas as well as rice are traditionally added to the casserole in a *barbacoa* (pit barbecue), where they cook in the drippings from the meat. In the markets of Mexico City, little plastic packages for the quick preparation of soups, made up daily, contain pre-soaked chickpeas (garbanzos) and raw, chopped vegetables, including cabbage, carrots, *chayote* (vegetable pear/choko), spinach (English spinach), potatoes, and green peas.

Lentils, like chickpeas, are of Arab origin. They are highly appreciated in Mexico in soups and stewed with pork. A typical and interesting way of cooking them is with pineapple. They also appear here for *Arroz y Lentejas* (see page 145), one of Mexico's many rice dishes.

The cultivation of rice originated in Asia, and, according to some scholars, began to be widely cultivated in Spain by the Moors in the eighth century, although it is said to have been introduced to Europe more than 1,000 years earlier by Alexander the Great. The grain was introduced into Mexico after the conquest, and is now largely cultivated in Veracruz, Morelos, and Sinaloa.

Whether white rice or the popular red rice, *Arroz a la Mexicana* (see page 148), the grains are prepared in the following fashion. They are soaked in warm water for a half hour, then rinsed and allowed to dry. This gets rid of any excess starch and allows the rice to cook more evenly. A substantial amount of oil—about ½ inch (1 cm) deep—is then heated in a wide pan, and the grains are fried until lightly colored. The excess oil is then poured out of the pan before the water or chicken stock, for white rice, or freshly pureed tomatoes, for red rice, is added along with salt. A little of the liquid is usually blended with some raw garlic and onion, then stirred into the rice for extra flavor. White rice may have a few drops of lime juice added to it when the stock is added to "bleach" it again, along with a sprig of parsley for flavor. Chopped vegetables, including carrots and peas, are added to cooked red rice.

A green rice is also prepared: it is colored and flavored with cilantro (fresh coriander), parsley, and roasted *poblano* chiles that have been pureed with the water. To this, strips of *poblano* chiles may also be added. Some households create the nation's flag to celebrate Mexican independence (September 15 and 16) by putting all three colored rice dishes side by side.

In Veracruz, historically Mexico's main port from the conquest until recent times (today Tampico is a commercially more important port), the Spanish style of cooking is very evident. Like the typically Spanish *paellas* (seafood cooked with rice), this coastal state boasts many rice dishes containing anything from fresh or dried shrimp (prawns), fish, river shrimp, or crayfish, to squid.

On the sweeter side, rice pudding is made with milk and flavored with sticks of cinnamon. The sweet and refreshing drink *horchata* is made with ground rice mixed with water, sometimes with the elegant and tasty addition of ground almonds.

1. Peruvian beans; 2. dried peas; 3. black beans; 4. flor de mayo; 5. white rice; 6. ayocotes; 7. habas (fava/broad beans); 8. chickpeas (garbanzos); 9. pinto beans; 10. lentejas (lentils); 11. bayo beans

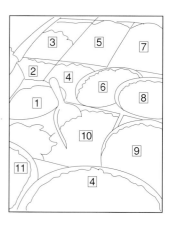

Front: Mexican Rice; back: White Rice

ARROZ A LA MEXICANA

MEXICAN RICE

This is delicious as an appetizer topped with slices of fried plantain, hard-boiled egg, and avocado. It also is a good accompaniment to a mole.

¾ cup (6 fl oz/185 ml) vegetable oil
1 cup (5 oz/155 g) white rice, rinsed and drained
2 tomatoes (6 oz/185 g), chopped
1 small onion, chopped
1 clove garlic, peeled
2½ cups (20 fl oz/625 ml) water or chicken stock
1 teaspoon salt, or to taste
2 jalapeño chiles, chopped
1 sprig parsley

SERVES 4–6

❡ Heat the oil in a medium saucepan until hot. Add the rice, stirring constantly, until slightly browned, or, as old Mexican cooks like to say, it sounds like tissue paper being crushed. Strain the rice and return it to the saucepan.
❡ Combine the tomatoes, onion, and garlic in a blender until smooth. Pour the mixture over the rice and cook over medium heat, stirring with a wooden spatula, for about 5 minutes. Add the water and salt, stir, then put the chiles and parsley on top. Lower the heat, cover, and simmer for approximately 25 minutes or until the

rice is tender but firm.
❡ For a popular variation to this recipe, add ⅓ cup (1 oz/30 g) each cubed potatoes, carrots, and peas with the water.

ARROZ BLANCO

WHITE RICE

White rice is most commonly served by itself as an appetizer, although these days it is often served to accompany fish or seafood as part of the main course.

2 cups (12 oz/375 g) white rice
1 cup (8 fl oz/250 ml) vegetable oil
1 clove garlic, minced (finely chopped)
4 cups (1 qt/1 l) boiling water
2 teaspoons salt, or to taste
1 serrano, chilaca, or jalapeño chile
1 sprig parsley

SERVES 4–6

❡ Put the rice in a strainer and rinse under cold water. Drain, soak in a bowl of warm water for 10 minutes, then drain well.
❡ Heat the oil in a saucepan until very hot and add the rice. Fry until translucent, stirring constantly with a wooden spatula. Strain to remove the oil and return the rice to the saucepan.
❡ Add the garlic, water, and salt and stir lightly. Raise the heat and add the chile and parsley. When the water returns to a boil, cover and reduce the heat. Simmer, undisturbed, for approximately 30 minutes or until the water is absorbed and the rice is cooked.

BANDERA TRICOLOR

To make the tricolored rice dish that's served on Mexican Independence Day because it looks like the country's three-colored flag, make Arroz a la Mexicana and set aside. Double the quantities given for Arroz Blanco, and prepare it through to the rice-frying step. Then divide the rice in half, continue with the preceding recipe, and finish the Arroz Blanco. While it's simmering, cook and puree a stalk of celery, a poblano chile, and 2 tablespoons of cilantro (fresh coriander), then stir into the remaining cup of fried rice containing the garlic. Add the remaining 2 cups of boiling water and proceed as with Arroz Blanco. Reheat the two finished rices, and arrange them —green, white, red—in three vertical stripes on a rectangular dish.

MUSHROOMS

In the pine forests around Toluca (the capital of Mexico state), edible, wild mushrooms of innumerable varieties abound. During the rainy season (June to October), many women of the region rise early to collect the mushrooms before making the trek to local markets. They display their goods in neat piles on bright plastic sheets. The most sought-after kinds find their way to the San Juan market in Mexico City, where restaurants and other interested buyers snap them up. Some of the most colorful varieties, though, such as *santigüeros* (red mushrooms), *canarios* (yellow mushrooms), and *hongos azules* (blue mushrooms),

never make it beyond the local markets. Their merits remain the secret of the locals or the few aficionados prepared to make the trip to find them.

Setas (cèpes) and *morillas* (morels) are as appreciated in Mexico as they are in other countries. Both types are sold fresh or dried. The latter brings the highest price at US$10 to US$20 dollars a pound fresh, or more than ten times that much dried. The Mexican *duraznillo* is the same as the chanterelle. *Señoritas* (young women) and *clavitos* (little nails) are smaller varieties that are often left whole for stock-based soups.

Many of the names given

to the different types of mushroom carry amusing cultural references. For example, *el negro*, a black mushroom, also has the name *el gachupín*, a derogatory name for the Spanish. An orange mushroom is called *enchilada*, after the color of dried chiles, while *escobetas* are little brushes or brooms.

The two principal ways of cooking wild mushrooms in Mexico are in soups or sautéed as a filling for *tacos*, *tlacoyos*, or other *antojitos*. Either way, they are usually sautéed with onion, garlic, chile, and *epazote*, an herb whose earthy pungency makes it a natural addition to the flavor of wild mushrooms.

The cultivated mushrooms

available in Mexico—regular and oyster mushrooms—are prepared the same way as wild mushrooms.

1. señoritas (young women); 2. setas (cèpes); 3. clavitos (little nails); 4. escobetas (little brushes or brooms); 5. morillas (morels); 6. enchilados (chile-colored); 7. el negro, el gachupín (black/ trompette des morts); 8. santigueros (red); 9. canarios (yellow)

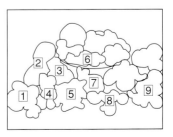

FRIJOLES CON TEQUILA

BEANS WITH TEQUILA

Traditionally frijoles borrachos *(drunken beans) are made with beer and pieces of pork and bacon. In this recipe from Juan Manuel Vivanco from Monterrey, Nuevo León, tequila is used instead of beer, and the pork has been omitted. The tequila is added twice during the last stage of cooking and again just before serving, to intensify the flavor.*

1 lb (500 g) pinto, borlotti, or pink beans, cleaned
10 cups (2½ qt/2.5 l) water
3 tablespoons lard
1 tablespoon salt plus salt to taste
1 small sprig epazote, *optional*
1 medium onion, chopped
1½ cups (12 oz/375 g) tomatoes, seeded, and chopped
4 serrano chiles, *2 whole and 2 chopped*
½ cup (4 fl oz/125 ml) tequila
2 tablespoons chopped cilantro (fresh coriander) leaves

SERVES 8–10

❡ In a large covered pot, simmer the beans with the water and 1 tablespoon of lard for about 2 hours until soft; add 1 tablespoon of salt and the *epazote* after the first hour. Drain the beans, reserving 1 cup (8 fl oz/250 ml) of the broth.
❡ Heat the remaining 2 tablespoons of lard in a *cazuela* or large pot over high heat until it starts to smoke. Add the onion, tomatoes, chiles, and a little salt to taste. Cook until the fat rises to the surface and the vegetables are soft, about 10 minutes. Add the beans and cook for 5 minutes, stirring constantly. Add the reserved broth and half the tequila. Continue cooking until almost all the liquid has evaporated.
❡ When ready to serve, remove from the heat, add the remaining tequila, and sprinkle the cilantro over the top.

FRIJOLES DE LA OLLA

BEANS IN THEIR BROTH

Frijoles de la Olla, *which is made with either* pinto *(borlotti) or black beans, depending on the region, is the most common way of preparing beans in Mexico. They accompany everything from eggs for breakfast to enchiladas for lunch; they can be eaten with a spoon or scooped up with a tortilla. When fried, they become* Frijoles Refritos. *In Mexico City, beans are usually made in a pressure cooker because the altitude of 8,000 feet (2600 meters) makes*

their cooking time very lengthy. Although many cooks can't break the habit of soaking the beans, it is really an unnecessary step. In this recipe, the almost-burnt onion added at the end intensifies the flavor of the beans.

2 cups (12 oz/375 g) pinto (borlotti) or black beans
7 cups (1¾ qt/1.75 l) water
¼ onion, in 1 piece plus 1 thick slice onion
¾ teaspoon salt, or to taste
3 tablespoons vegetable oil

SERVES 8 (5 CUPS COOKED BEANS)

❡ If using a pressure cooker, place the beans, water, the ¼ onion, and salt in the pot, and cook until tender, following the manufacturer's instructions. If using a pot, cook the beans with water and onion over low heat until tender, adding the salt toward the end (otherwise the beans will remain tough).
❡ When the beans are just about cooked, heat the oil in a very small frying pan over high heat. Add the onion slice and fry till almost black on each side. Add to the beans and cook for 10 minutes. Remove both onion pieces before serving.

FRIJOLES REFRITOS

REFRIED BEANS

As popular as Frijoles de la Olla *as an accompaniment to any meal, refried beans also lend themselves to being spread on anything from* tostadas *to* tortas *to add an extra dimension of flavor. They can be formed into a roll and decorated with lettuce leaves, crumbled cheese, and* totopos, *and served on a platter as an hors d'oeuvre.*

⅓ cup (2½ fl oz/75 ml) vegetable oil
1 tablespoon onion, minced (finely chopped)
2 cups (16 oz/500 g) Frijoles de la Olla, *without broth*
2 oz (60 g) queso añejo or dry feta cheese, crumbled
totopos, about 16 triangles (see box page 38)
lettuce leaves, optional

SERVES 4

❡ Heat the oil in a frying pan and fry the onion until translucent. Add the beans and fry over medium heat, mashing them with a potato masher until you have a textured puree.
❡ Continue to cook, stirring constantly, until the beans have absorbed all the oil and dried to a thick paste that pulls away from the pan. Shake the pan in a forward motion, pushing the bean paste toward the far edge of the pan, to roll into a log shape.
❡ Turn the beans onto a serving platter and serve with the cheese, *totopos,* and lettuce leaves.

Front: Beans with Tequila; back left: Beans in their Broth; back right; Refried Beans

Left: Black Beans with "Mountains of Things"; right: Vegetable Casserole in Uncooked Chile Sauce

FRIJOLES NEGROS CON MONTONES DE COSAS

BLACK BEANS WITH "MOUNTAINS OF THINGS"

This dish comes from the novelist Jorge López Páez who often serves this tasty casserole for lunch. Here the beans are served as a main course, accompanied by many different condiments that each diner can add to taste.

1½ lb (750 g) pork spareribs, cut to ¾-inch (2-cm) lengths
1 teaspoon salt, or to taste
¼ onion, chopped
1 clove garlic
juice of 2 small oranges

2 cups (16 oz/500 g) cooked black beans plus 1½ cups (12 fl oz/375 ml) bean broth (use the recipe for Frijoles de la Olla *on page 150 making it with black beans rather than pinto beans in this instance)*
For the toppings:
3 medium tomatoes chopped
1 medium onion, chopped
6 tablespoons chopped cilantro (fresh coriander)
7 oz (220 g) queso fresco *or farmer's cheese, cut into ½-inch (1-cm) cubes*
2 medium avocados, peeled, pitted, and cut into ½-inch (1-cm) cubes
3 tablespoons chopped fresh arbol, jalapeño, *or* serrano *chiles*
3½ oz (100 g) crumbled chicharrón (pork rind)

ADOBO CRUDO

VEGETABLE CASSEROLE IN UNCOOKED CHILE SAUCE

Adobo *is a chile-based sauce usually used for marinating or cooking meat, or sometimes fish. Here the sauce is actually never cooked (hence the name* adobo crudo*) and is served on cooked vegetables. This recipe is from the writer and novelist Jorge López Páez from Huatuzco, Veracruz, where the refreshing dish, served at room temperature, is eaten during the hottest months of the year.*

6 oz (185 g) green beans, strings removed and cut in half
13 oz (375 g) chayote (vegetable pear/choko), peeled, cut
   in half to remove core, and cut into ⅛-inch (3-mm) slices
14 oz (440 g) fresh peas, shelled
14 oz (440 g) potatoes, peeled and sliced
For the *tortitas de zanahoria* (carrot fritters):
10 oz (315 g) carrots, peeled and sliced
1 egg
1 tablespoon queso añejo *or dry feta cheese, shredded*
¼ teaspoon salt, or to taste
½ cup (2½ oz/75 g) all-purpose (plain) flour
½ cup (4 fl oz/125 ml) vegetable oil
For the chile sauce:
2½ oz (75 g) ancho *chiles, stems removed, seeded,*
   deveined, toasted briefly over direct flame, and soaked
1½ cups (12 fl oz/375 ml) water
½ tablespoon cider vinegar
pinch ground cumin
salt, to taste
3½ oz (100 g) queso añejo *or dry feta cheese, crumbled*
1 onion halved and sliced

SERVES 10

❡ Cook the green beans, *chayote,* peas, and potatoes separately in boiling, salted water until tender.
❡ To make the fritters: Puree the carrots in a blender with the egg, cheese, and salt. Remove to a bowl and mix in the flour. Using your hands, form 10 flattish, round fritters with the mixture and fry in the oil over high heat for approximately 2 minutes on each side. Drain on paper towels.
❡ Place the chiles in a blender with the water, vinegar, cumin, and salt, and then blend until very smooth.
❡ In an oiled serving dish approximately 10 x 6 x 2 inches (25 x 15 x 5 cm), layer the potatoes, *chayote,* green beans, carrot fritters, and peas. Cover with half the chile sauce, repeat the layers, and finish with the remaining sauce.
❡ Garnish with the cheese and onion, and serve.

1½ lb (750 g) bacon, fried, drained, and crumbled
5 cups (4 oz/125 g) finely shredded lettuce

SERVES 6

❡ Place the ribs in a pot and add water to cover. Add the salt, onion, and garlic and boil over medium heat. When the ribs are soft and the water is almost completely evaporated, add the orange juice and let evaporate. Set aside but keep hot.
❡ Reheat the beans with the broth in an earthenware casserole that they can also be served in. When heated, add the ribs.
❡ Meanwhile, put the first 8 toppings in individual bowls. Allow each person to fill his or her bowl first with beans and then with a choice of toppings and a handful of lettuce.

MEAT, POULTRY, AND GAME

MEAT, POULTRY, AND GAME

BEFORE THE ARRIVAL OF THE SPANISH CONQUERERS, THE INDIAN CULTURES HAD A DIET BASED ON VEGETABLES, fish, insects, and meat. Although much of the meat they consumed was wild, including venison, rabbit, armadillo, boar, dove, duck, quail, snake, and iguana, they had domesticated the turkey, native to Mexico, and a type of dog called *itzcuintles*. These dogs, known as the Mexican hairless, still exist today, but are prized as pets rather than eaten.

❡ There is much conjecture but very little real knowledge about pre-Hispanic food preparation. Pit barbecuing, steaming, boiling, and direct fire broiling (grilling) were the principal methods used. The technique of wrapping food in leaves, whether in the form of *tamales* or pit barbecuing, is pre-Hispanic, but the *moles, tamales, pibils,* and *barbacoas* of today are a result of the *mestizaje*, or gradual combining of the Old and New World techniques and ingredients.

❡ The Spanish brought with them the domesticated animals common in Europe: pigs, sheep, goats, cattle, and chickens. The pig was not only significant as a new source of protein, but its introduction also heralded a transformation in cooking methods. It was the first available large-scale source of fat and has been the basis for frying foods ever since.

❡ The sheep found excellent pasturage in the central

Previous pages: Before the arrival of the conquistadors, most meat consumed by the Indian cultures was wild. The Spanish introduced domesticated animals, which opened the door on the gamut of fried foods Mexicans have been enjoying ever since.

Opposite: An Indian woman feeds corn to her flock in a mountain village in the state of Veracruz.

plateau, while the goats were able to exist on the drier shrub lands. Sheep or goat is most often used in *barbacoas* but is also popular roasted on a spit.

❡ Cattle ranches abound principally in the northern states of Sonora, Chihuahua, Nuevo León, and Tamaulipas, where vast, open grazing lands are plentiful. All qualities and cuts of beef are enjoyed in Mexico, from the elegant and expensive fillet to the lower priced, thinly cut minute steaks (*bisteces*).

❡ Variety meats (offal) are also very popular, both for their flavor and low price, making them an affordable meat for poorer people. Stomach, tripe, and spine marrow (*medula*) are all prepared in rich soups, while cooked marrow from the shin bone is excellent lightly salted as a *taco* filling. Fried beef liver with onions or steamed cow's head are a common sight in streetside *taco* stands. The more elegant cold dish of cooked beef tongue, pig's feet, and chicken, known as *fiambre*, is served with a herbed vinaigrette and garnished with cooked carrots and potatoes.

❡ Undoubtedly, the preferred meat in Mexico is pork, but chicken is consumed in the highest volume. Both of these are adapted to all local cuisines, from the *pibils* of the Yucatán to the *moles* and *pipiánes* of Oaxaca and Puebla. Like the *barbacoas* of the center, *pibils* are earthen pit ovens: the meat is wrapped in banana leaves and is seasoned with *achiote* (annatto) seed paste. These meats are also shredded and added to many *masa* snacks and *tamales*. Pork is the most common meat used for stuffing chiles, in the form of *picadillos*, where the meat is chopped with a mixture of nuts and dried fruits. It is also made into sausages, which began as a Spanish tradition but ended up in the distinctly Mexican form of *chorizo* and *longaniza*.

ENSALADA DE POLLO, BERROS, Y RAJAS DE CHILE POBLANO

CHICKEN, WATERCRESS, AND POBLANO CHILE SALAD

In this unique chicken salad from Feodora Rozenzweig, the watercress and almonds work together to bring out the flavor of the chicken. The poblano *strips and fried onions add a Mexican touch.*

8 chicken thighs, skinned
½ onion
2 cloves garlic
1 bay leaf
1 sprig thyme
1 sprig marjoram
½ teaspoon salt, or to taste
3½ oz (100 g) watercress, stems removed
½ cup (4 fl oz/125 ml) light mayonnaise
1 cup (8 fl oz/250 ml) yogurt
2 teaspoons lime or lemon juice
3½ oz (100 g) blanched almonds
1½ tablespoons vegetable oil
2 medium onions, halved and sliced
3 poblano chiles, seeded, deveined, and cut into
    ⅓- x ⅔-inch (1- x 2-cm) strips
pinch of salt

SERVES 8

❡ Put the chicken in a large pot with water to cover. Add the half onion, garlic, herbs, and salt. Boil for 20 minutes, or until the meat is tender. Strain and reserve the broth. Bone and chop the chicken into chunks and place in a salad bowl.
❡ Place the watercress, mayonnaise, yogurt, lime juice, almonds, and reserved broth in a blender and puree until smooth, then pour over the chicken.
❡ Heat the oil in a frying pan over medium heat and sauté the onions until translucent. Add the chiles and the pinch of salt, and fry for another 2 minutes. Remove from the heat, cool, and spoon around the chicken salad.

ENCHILADAS TAPATIAS

TAPATIA-STYLE ENCHILADAS

Enhanced by the sweet taste of ancho *chiles, this* enchilada *from* Frida's Fiestas *demonstrates the tradition of dipping the* tortilla *first in hot oil when used with a cooked sauce.*

For the sauce:
8–10 ancho *chiles, roasted, deveined, and stems removed*
2 tablespoons vegetable oil
1 small onion, chopped
2 small cloves garlic, minced (finely chopped)
salt and pepper, to taste
For the enchiladas:
½ cup (4 fl oz/125 ml) vegetable oil
24 small (3-inch/7.5-cm) tortillas
3 half chicken breasts, skinned, boned, cooked,
    and shredded

1 cup (8 fl oz/250 ml) sour cream, or to taste
8 oz (250 g) añejo *cheese or dry feta, crumbled*

SERVES 8

❡ To make the sauce: Soak the chiles in warm water to cover for 10 minutes. Process in a food processor with enough of the soaking liquid to make a thin puree, then strain.

❡ Heat the oil in a medium saucepan and sauté the onion and garlic until translucent. Add the chile puree and the salt and pepper, then simmer for

10 minutes. The sauce should be just thick enough to coat a wooden spoon, so thin with a little extra water if required. Set aside and keep warm.

❡ For the *enchiladas:* Heat the oil in a medium frying pan and immerse the *tortillas* one by one for a few seconds on each side until they fold easily. Then dip both sides in the chile sauce, fill with some chicken, fold in half, and place on a serving dish. Spoon the rest of the sauce over the *enchiladas* and top with the sour cream and cheese. Serve immediately.

Left: Chicken, Watercress, and Poblano Chile Salad; right: Tapatia-style Enchiladas

POULTRY AND GAME

Turkeys are usually cut up into bite-size pieces and cooked in their own stock to add to *moles* and other complex seed-, nut-, or chile-based sauces. In rural towns, *mole poblano de guajolote* (turkey in *mole poblano*) is traditionally the *pièce de résistance* at large celebrations: weddings, baptisms, and coming-of-age parties for girls of fifteen. It is made in vast quantities—everyone is invited—and the dark sauce is served in great earthenware casseroles sprinkled with toasted sesame seeds. The tradition of roasting sesame seeds whole, especially at Christmas, is a custom imported from the United States and Europe.

Other than steam-baking meat in a pit, ovens have not traditionally been part of the Mexican kitchen, where almost everything can be cooked on a stove top or *brazier*. In the Yucatán,

however, there is a famous dish called *pavo en relleno negro*, in which the turkey is stuffed with pork mixed with a black seasoning paste based on charred, dried chiles, ground *achiote* (annatto), garlic, and various seasonings, including the large-leaved Yucatecan oregano.

A great deal of chicken is consumed in Mexico. Cooks make stock with the backs and feet or wings as the base for soups, *moles*, casseroles, and rice dishes. For many of these preparations, the leg and breast meat are also cooked in stock to be added to the final dish in bite-size pieces, or they may be shredded into soups or layered *tamal* casseroles, onto *sopes*, or as the filling for *enchiladas* and *tacos*. In sophisticated households, the skin is always removed from the legs and breast before being added to a *mole* or sauce.

Breast meat is often pounded and quickly broiled (grilled), or stuffed with such delicacies as squash blossoms, *poblano* chiles, or sautéed mushrooms. (In Mexico, one breast means a whole breast or two half breasts; the recipes included here use the terms whole or half to avoid confusion.) In the Yucatán, leg and breast meat are wrapped in banana leaves and steam-baked with a seasoning paste of *achiote* and cumin. In Veracruz, they are served in an almond-, peanut-, or sesame-based sauce. In Oaxaca, they are accompanied by *tomatillo*-based green sauces, among many others, whole or wrapped as *enchiladas*.

The skin of raw chicken in Mexico may be either white or yellow, depending on whether *cempasuchil* (marigold flowers) have been added to the diet. Small, whole, wood-roasted chickens have become very popular in recent years in Mexico, and rotisseries are dotted throughout the streets of the cities and towns. The cost of a cooked chicken is virtually the same as that of an uncooked one in the market or supermarket—hence, their great popularity.

The quail in Mexico tend to be very small—about 3 to 4 ounces (90 to 125 g). They are excellent butterflied, marinated in a chile paste, and broiled flat, which is the most typical preparation. They are often threaded onto a spit for easy turning. Wherever they are sold, their small, blue, speckled eggs are also found. These are a delicacy added to salads.

Wild ducks, both native and imported, are available in Mexico. These are delicious substituted for

chicken or turkey in, for example, a *pipián verde* (green pumpkin-seed sauce). Many restaurants that specialize in contemporary cuisine—combining Mexican sauces and traditional ingredients in new and unusual ways, often using a mixture of Mexican and European techniques—roast the more tender imported ducks and serve them with unusual *mole*-style sauces: *chipotle* sauce or prune *mole*.

Smaller birds, such as pigeons and small gamebirds, may be prepared in the same way as quail, mentioned above, and broiled flat on an open fire or a *plancha* (a flat, metal grill).

1. whole chicken; 2. chicken breasts; 3. chicken breasts (skinned and boned); 4. chicken legs; 5. chicken wings; 6. chicken feet; 7. eggs; 8. quail; 9. quail eggs

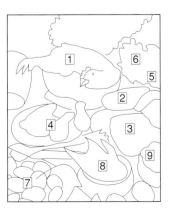

POLLO CON CHILE GUAJILLO Y HOJAS DE AGUACATE

CHICKEN WITH GUAJILLO CHILES AND AVOCADO LEAVES

In this recipe from Federico Siller, the use of fresh avocado leaves adds a distinctive flavor for which there is no substitute. Because the leaves can be difficult to find, they can simply be omitted; use sliced avocado as decoration.

½ cup (4 fl oz/125 ml) vegetable oil
6 pieces (2 lb/1 kg) chicken (legs, thighs, and half breasts)
1 teaspoon salt
2½ cups (20 fl oz/625 ml) chicken stock or water
14 medium guajillo chiles
½ onion
6 cloves garlic
¼ teaspoon cumin seed
20 avocado leaves

SERVES 6

❡ Heat 5 tablespoons (2½ fl oz/75 ml) of the oil in a frying pan. Season the chicken with the salt and brown lightly over high heat. Add ½ cup (4 fl oz/ 125 ml) of the stock, lower the heat, cover, and simmer until cooked, about 20 minutes.

❡ Meanwhile, heat a *comal* or cast-iron griddle and dry roast the chiles briefly on each side. Be sure to remove them from the pan before they begin smoking. Dry roast the onion and garlic, charring them lightly on all sides.

❡ Remove the stems from the chiles and cut open to seed and devein. Soak them in enough hot water to cover until soft, about 5 minutes. Drain.

❡ Put the chiles in a food processor with the onion, garlic, cumin, 2 cups (16 fl oz/500 ml) of the stock, and a pinch of salt. Process until smooth.

❡ Heat the remaining 3 tablespoons of oil in a frying pan over medium heat and heat the chile mixture briefly. Add the chicken with its liquid, lay most of the avocado leaves on top (reserving a few for garnish), cover, and cook over low heat until the chicken is heated through and the sauce thickened. Scrape the bottom occasionally to prevent burning. Discard the used avocado leaves.

❡ Transfer to a serving platter, using the unused avocado leaves as decoration (but don't eat them).

Chicken with Guajillo Chiles and Avocado Leaves

TLATONILE DE POLLO

CHICKEN WITH A CHILE AND SESAME SEED SAUCE

Another traditional dish from the book La Cocina Veracruzana, *tlatonile is a specialty of Huatusco. The comapeño chile, which flavors this sauce, is particular to Veracruz. This sauce is also delicious with beef.*

8 cups (2 qt/2 l) water
2 cloves garlic
½ onion
2 teaspoons salt, or to taste
6 pieces (2 lb/1 kg) chicken (legs, thighs, and half breasts)
15 comapeño chiles, chiles de arbol, *or medium-sized bright red chiles*
1 ancho chile
6½ oz (200 g) sesame seeds
5 tablespoons (2½ fl oz/75 ml) vegetable oil
epazote leaves, to taste, optional

SERVES 6

❡ Bring the water to a boil with the garlic, onion, and salt. Add the chicken and simmer for 30 to

Front: Chicken with a Chile and Sesame Seed Sauce; back: Coachala Chicken

40 minutes, or until tender. Drain, reserving the stock, and discard the onion and garlic.

❡ Remove the seeds and veins from the chiles and roast the chiles in a large pan with the sesame seeds. Put the mixture in a food processor and process with enough water to form a smooth paste.

❡ Heat the oil in a large saucepan, add the chile mixture, and cook for 20 minutes over low heat, stirring constantly. Add ½ cup (4 fl oz/125 ml) of the reserved stock and simmer. Add the chicken, *epazote* leaves, and 1 cup of the reserved stock. Simmer for 10 minutes, or until the sauce thickens slightly.

❡ Serve hot with white rice and *tortillas*.

POLLO COACHÁLA

COACHÁLA CHICKEN

This casserole, from the state of Colima, was given to me by Paloma, the wife of former Mexican President Miguel de la Madrid Hurtado. Coachála is traditionally served in a clay pot accompanied by tortillas.

1 whole chicken breast, with skin
2 chicken drumsticks, skinned
2 chicken thighs, skinned
8 cups (2 qt/2 l) water
1 onion, quartered
½ teaspoon oregano
1½ teaspoons salt, or to taste
1 guajillo *chile, lightly roasted*
2 ancho *chiles, lightly roasted*
1 lb (500 g) tomatillos, *husks removed (or use canned, drained* tomatillos)
2 cloves garlic, roasted
¼ teaspoon powdered cumin, or to taste
2 oz (60 g) tortilla masa (*see Tortillas de Maiz page 55*)
¼ cup (2 fl oz/60 ml) water
1 recipe chochoyotes (*see Texmole de Carne de Res page 181*)

SERVES 8–10

❡ In a large pot, combine the chicken pieces, water, onion, oregano, and salt. When the water begins to boil, cover and simmer over low heat for approximately 35 minutes, or until the chicken is cooked. Strain, reserving the stock and discarding the onion and oregano.

❡ When the chicken has cooled, bone and skin the breast, reserving the skin. Bone the drumstick and thighs, keeping the breast meat separate. Blend the breast skin and drumstick and thigh meat in batches in a blender with 4 cups (1 qt/1 l) of the reserved stock until smooth. Chop the breast meat into bite-size pieces and add along with the pureed chicken mixture to a large saucepan.

❡ Clean and devein the chiles. Soften them in hot water for 10 to 15 minutes and drain.

❡ Cook the *tomatillos* in enough water to cover for 10 to 15 minutes, or until soft, then drain. Put the chiles, *tomatillos*, garlic, and cumin in a blender and puree until smooth. Add the mixture to the saucepan with the remaining reserved broth and bring back to a simmer.

❡ Dissolve the *masa* in the water and gradually add to the casserole. Stir constantly with a wooden spatula for 25 minutes, or until the mixture is quite thick. Add the *chochoytes*, heat through, and serve with *tortillas*.

POLLO AL TEQUILA

CHICKEN WITH TEQUILA

This recipe is from Donato Ruiz, an authentic tequila producer from Tequila, Jalisco. The chilaca *chiles are long and dark green. Dried, they are called* pasilla *chiles.*

6 half chicken breasts, skinned and boned
1 teaspoon salt, or to taste
2 tablespoons (1 oz/30 g) butter
4 tablespoons (2 fl oz/60 ml) vegetable oil
¾ cup (6 fl oz/185 ml) tequila
4 chilaca *or* pasilla *chiles, seeded, and coarsely chopped*
1 tablespoon coarsely chopped onion
1 clove garlic, coarsely chopped
2 cups (16 fl oz/500 ml) chicken stock
1 teaspoon sugar
1 tablespoon cornstarch (cornflour), dissolved in
   2 tablespoons water

SERVES 6

❡ Sprinkle the chicken with the salt. Heat the butter and 2 tablespoons of the oil in a frying pan. Add the chicken and cook for about 20 minutes over low heat until done, turning once; do not brown.
❡ Remove the chicken from the frying pan and set the pan aside, reserving the fat. Transfer the chicken to a large saucepan, add the tequila, and ignite. Set aside.
❡ Reheat the fat in the frying pan and sauté the chiles, onion, and garlic over medium heat for 3 to 4 minutes, stirring occasionally. Put the mixture in a food processor along with 1 cup (8 fl oz/250 ml) of the stock and process lightly so that the ingredients are still coarse.
❡ Heat the remaining 2 tablespoons of oil in the frying pan and add the processed mixture. Cook over medium heat for 3 minutes. Add the chicken, sugar, the remaining stock, and the cornstarch mixture. Lower the heat and simmer until the sauce thickens, approximately 10 minutes. Serve.

POLLO CON AJOS EN VINAGRE

CHICKEN IN VINEGAR AND GARLIC

This scrumptious recipe by Mrs Carmen Ortiz de Ortiz is vaguely Northern European in make-up, with its combination of allspice, garlic, and vinegar. Soak pieces of crusty bread in the sauce that remains on the plate.

2 lb (1 kg) chicken pieces, (half breasts with bones, thighs, and wings)
1 cup (8 oz/250 ml) cider vinegar
2 heads garlic (2 oz/60 g each), cloves separated but unpeeled

Left: Chicken with Tequila; right: Chicken in Vinegar and Garlic

½ cup (4 fl oz/125 ml) vegetable oil
1 onion, quartered
5 allspice berries
5 black peppercorns, freshly ground
1½ teaspoons salt, or to taste

SERVES 6
¶ Place all the ingredients in a heavy saucepan over medium heat, cover, and cook for 1 hour, or until the chicken is tender. Serve the garlic cloves alongside the chicken or spread them on crusty bread.

POLLO EN SALSA VERDE CON PILONCILLO

CHICKEN IN GREEN SAUCE WITH PILONCILLO

The sweet-and-sour combination of the acidic tomatillos and the piloncillo (light molasses) in the sauce is unusual in Mexican cooking — and delicious.

½ cup (4 fl oz/125 ml) vegetable oil
1 whole chicken, cut into serving pieces
1 onion, sliced
1½ lb (750 g) tomatillos
5 jalapeño chiles
2½ oz (75 g) piloncillo, shredded, or light molasses
salt and pepper, to taste
3 plantains or bananas, sliced and fried, for garnish

SERVES 6

❡ Heat the oil in a large saucepan and cook the chicken until lightly browned. Add the onion and cook until translucent, stirring constantly.

❡ Roast the *tomatillos* and chiles on a *comal* or cast-iron griddle, then puree them in a blender with a little water. Add the *tomatillo* mixture and *piloncillo* to the pan and simmer until the *piloncillo* melts. Add the salt and pepper and simmer for 30 minutes.

❡ Serve hot, garnished with the plantains.

CODORNIZ ADOBADO A LA PARILLA

GRILLED MARINATED QUAIL

This recipe is from Manuela Cruz, the morning cook at La Circunstancia Restaurant in Mexico City. The trick to the marinade is to soak the ancho chiles in cold water. This marinade is also delicious with duck or pork.

12 quails
For the sauce:
6 ancho chiles
½ onion, coarsely chopped
2 large cloves garlic
1 rounded teaspoon cumin
1 cup (8 fl oz/250 ml) fresh orange juice
1 teaspoon salt, or to taste
3 tablespoons vegetable oil

SERVES 6

❡ Split the quails along the spine, butterfly, then place in a baking dish.

❡ To make the sauce: Open the chiles and remove the stems, seeds, and veins. Place them in a bowl and soak in enough cold water to cover for at least 1 hour. Drain the water and puree the chiles in a blender with the next 5 ingredients until smooth. The sauce should be

slightly salty, so correct the seasoning as necessary.
❡ Pour the sauce over the quail and mix thoroughly, massaging the marinade into the meat so the flavors penetrate. Marinate overnight in the refrigerator.
❡ Prepare a grill or barbecue, or heat a cast-iron frying pan. Brush the grill rack or pan with the

oil. Lift the quail out of the marinade, letting any excess marinade drip off, and grill over moderate heat for 15 to 20 minutes until cooked through. Turn the quail frequently so the sauce doesn't blacken too much and become bitter. Serve with *Frijoles Refritos* (see page 150).

Left: Chicken in Green Sauce with Piloncillo; right: Grilled Marinated Quail

Mole from Puebla

MOLE POBLANO

MOLE FROM PUEBLA

Of the many variations of this famous dish, this recipe is distinctive because it is not sweet; the large quantity of chipotle *chiles gives it its wonderful flavor. Note that the chiles must be fried* hasta carbonar, *until they are black and charred. In Mexico, after the various ingredients are roasted or fried, they are ground on a* metate *or grindstone to be turned to either a powder or paste. You can also process the spices in a coffee grinder and the rest of the ingredients in a food processor with enough stock to make a thick puree. This is traditionally a "special" dish and is geared for a large guest list.*

For the poultry:
30 serving pieces of chicken or turkey
2 onions, quartered
10 garlic cloves
salt to taste
For the *mole:*
1½ lb (750 g) chipotle *chiles (dried, not canned)*
1 lb (500 g) each mulato, pasilla, *and* ancho *chiles*
2½ lb (1.25 kg) lard
2 teaspoons aniseed
1 teaspoon peppercorns
15 whole cloves
3 (5-inch/12.5-cm) cinnamon sticks
8 oz (250 g) each almonds and pecans
1 lb (500 g) each sesame seeds and raisins

2 tablespoons cilantro (fresh coriander), tied in a small bunch and hung upside down to dry overnight, to concentrate the flavor
2 heads garlic, cloves separated but unpeeled
1 large (10-oz/315-g) white onion, coarsely chopped
5 tortillas
3 slices bread
4 lb (2 kg) tomatoes, cut into large pieces
1 tablespoon salt, or to taste
3 tablespoons lard
1 lb (500 g) Mexican or bittersweet (dark) chocolate

SERVES 25 GENEROUSLY

❡ To cook the poultry: Place it in a large pot with enough water to cover. Add the onions, garlic, and salt and bring to a boil. Simmer for 20 to 30 minutes, or until the meat is just cooked. Reserve the meat and stock.

❡ To make the *mole:* Remove the seeds and veins from all the chiles and discard. In a frying pan, heat enough lard to cover the bottom of a *cazuela* or casserole and cook the *chipotle* chiles until well charred. Discard the fat and place the *chipotles* into yet another large pot, where all the other ingredients will be held after they are cooked.

❡ Grind the aniseed, peppercorns, cloves, and cinnamon to a powder and set aside. Put enough of the lard in a wide casserole to reach ¾ inch (2 cm) up the sides. Cook the following ingredients one by one until they are fragrant, then transfer them to the pot containing the *chipotles:* the *mulato, pasilla,* and *ancho* chiles; the ground spices; almonds; pecans; sesame seeds; raisins; cilantro; garlic; and onion.

❡ Without adding more fat, cook the *tortillas* until well browned. Cook the bread, letting it soak up the lard, and finally cook the tomatoes. Add all the above ingredients to the pot with the *chipotles.*

❡ In batches, place parts of the chile/nut mixture in a food processor, using enough reserved stock with each batch to make a thick puree; add salt to taste. (The *mole* can be frozen at this stage if you wish.)

❡ In a large casserole, heat the 3 tablespoons of lard over high heat and cook the puree for about 10 minutes, stirring constantly. Add enough reserved stock to thin down to a consistency similar to poultry gravy (it should coat a wooden spoon thickly) and cook over low heat for 30 minutes. Add the chocolate, a few ounces at a time, letting it melt in the sauce, tasting as you go. Add more salt if necessary, and, if the sauce is too fiery, add some *piloncillo* (light molasses).

❡ Add the reserved cooked poultry and simmer for 30 minutes. Sprinkle with toasted sesame seeds and serve with rice, beans, and fresh, hot wheat *tortillas.*

NUTS, SEEDS, AND SPICES

The following nuts, seeds, and spices are all used as flavorings in different *mole* preparations, with either fresh or dried chiles, or in sauces and other preparations for meat dishes.

Pimienta negra (black pepper): Although chiles are more common than pepper as a flavoring in Mexico, ground pepper, which is native to India, is included in many *mole* preparations.

Canela (cinnamon): Two-thirds (or 2,000 tons/tonnes) of the world's production of true cinnamon, which comes only from Sri Lanka, is exported to Mexico. (When cinnamon trees are planted in other tropical countries, the flavor and aroma of the bark seem to degenerate in a matter of years.) It has a much thinner and more delicately fragrant bark than the *cassia* that is often sold in its place elsewhere. Inexpensive and sold in scrolls up to 2 to 3 feet (60 to 90 cm) long, it is used as a flavoring for desserts, hot and cold drinks, and *moles*. It is also used as a curative tea for a number of ailments, including diarrhea.

Almendras (almonds): Native to India, almonds were introduced to Mexico by the Spanish. They are included in most dark *mole* preparations and in an almond-based sauce called *almendrado*.

Cacahuates (peanuts): Actually the seed of a tropical legume rather than a nut, peanuts are indigenous to Mexico and South America. The Aztecs called them *cacahuatl*. They are often used in *moles* with equal parts of almonds and sesame seeds, and sometimes accompany sesame seeds in red *pipián* (a sauce of ground nuts or seeds and spices). They are used in many dishes from Veracruz, notably the sauce for meat or chicken called *encacahuatado* or "made of peanuts." Tlacotalpan, in Veracruz, produces an iced peanut-butter-based drink, *torito de cacahuete*, made with sugar cane liquor and milk.

Nuez de Castilla (walnuts): These are seen in Mexico only from July to September. Just the tender, fresh nut is used, with the fine skin removed, to make the famous sauce for *Chiles en Nogada* (see page 114), a dish that sports the three colors of the Mexican flag (green, white, and red).

Semilla de cilantro (coriander seeds): Originally from the Mediterranean region, the seeds are used in some *moles* but play a more important role in the flavoring of sausages.

Comino (cumin): A native of the Nile Valley, this spice is used with restraint in *moles* and other sauces in Mexico and is added only to provide a background note.

Clavos (cloves): A spice originally from the Orient, the unusually pungent flavor of cloves gives depth to many *moles*, *adobos* (chile pastes), and chile-based sauces.

Achiote (annatto) seeds: Used almost exclusively in the Yucatán Peninsula, annatto seeds, in paste or powder form, are the base of many seasoning *recados* (pastes) famous in Yucatecan cooking.

Pepitas de calabaza (pumpkin seeds): A variety of pumpkin seeds, green to white, large and small, is sold in Mexico. They may be bought hulled and salted, ready to eat; or unsalted; whole; powdered; or in a paste ready to be turned into a green *pipián* with the addition of green chiles, herbs, lettuce, and *tomatillos*.

Pimienta gorda (allspice): This pea-sized dried berry looks rather like pepper, thus its similar Spanish name. It is also called *pimienta dulce* (sweet pepper) and Jamaican pepper—it has been an important Jamaican export since the seventeenth century. The English name allspice reflects the combination of spice flavors found in this berry: clove, cinnamon, nutmeg, and pepper.

Ajonjolí (sesame seeds): Sesame seeds are toasted to use in *moles*, *pipiánes*, and other sauces, including the *tlatonile* of Veracruz. *Mole poblano* is traditionally served with a sprinkling of sesame seeds on top.

Anís (anise/aniseed): The seeds of the anise plant are used to make flavored liqueurs, sweets, sweet breads, dessert syrups, and also as a flavoring in some moles, including *mole poblano*.

1. pimienta negra (black peppercorns); 2. canela (cinnamon); 3. almendras (almonds); 4. cacahuates (peanuts); 5. nuez de Castilla (walnuts); 6. semilla de cilantro (coriander seeds); 7. comino (cumin); 8. clavos (cloves); 9. achiote (annatto seeds); 10. pepitas de calabaza (pumpkin seeds); 11. pimienta gorda (allspice); 12. ajonjolí (sesame seeds); 13. anís (aniseed); 14. achiote (annatto) seed paste

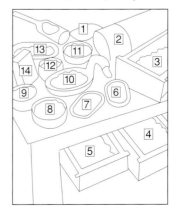

Tamarind Mole

MOLE DE TAMARINDO

TAMARIND MOLE

This recipe from Nushie Chancellor and José C. Marmolejo of Austin, Texas has the tangy acidity of tamarind pulp as the principal flavor of the dish. The use of tamarind in a mole is a recent innovation. As tamarind has a very strong flavor, it must be carefully balanced with the other ingredients to make a harmonious sauce.

For the meat:
32 serving pieces of chicken, duck, turkey, or pork
2 onions, quartered
6 garlic cloves
2 teaspoons salt, or to taste
For the *mole:*
8 oz (250 g) tamarind pulp
1 cup (8 fl oz/250 ml) water
12 ancho *chiles*
3 pasilla *chiles*
½ cup (4 fl oz/125 ml) vegetable oil
8 cups (2 qt/2 l) chicken stock
1 tomato, chopped
½ onion, chopped
3 cloves garlic, chopped
3 oz (90 g) sliced fresh bread
2 oz (60 g) each almonds, pecans, and peanuts
1 oz (30 g) each sesame seeds and raisins
8 oz (250 g) fresh peaches, peeled and pitted (or substitute
     drained canned peaches and reduce sugar to 1 teaspoon)
3 whole cloves
1 teaspoon cinnamon
3 tablespoons (1½ oz/45 g) sugar
2 teaspoons salt, or to taste
4 oz (125 g) Mexican chocolate, or bittersweet (dark)
     chocolate with a pinch of cinnamon

SERVES 16

❡ To cook the meat: Place it in a pot and add enough water to cover. Add the onion, garlic, and salt and bring to a boil. Simmer for 20 minutes, or until the meat is just cooked. Reserve the meat and broth; skin the poultry if using.

❡ For the *mole:* Soak the tamarind pulp in the water for about 1 hour. Meanwhile, remove the stems and seeds from the chiles and cook them lightly in the oil until very soft but not crisp. Remove the chiles from the pan and drain, but do not discard the oil. Soak the chiles in 2 cups (16 fl oz/500 ml) of the stock for 30 minutes.

❡ Reheat the oil and cook the tomato, onion, and garlic over medium to high heat for 5 minutes or until the fat rises to the surface. Puree the mixture in a blender, then pour into a large saucepan coated with a little vegetable oil.

❡ On a *comal* or cast-iron griddle, separately roast the bread, almonds, pecans, peanuts, and sesame seeds. Place them in a blender and puree, adding just enough stock to make a thick sauce. Add the mixture to the saucepan.

❡ Place the chiles and their stock in a blender and puree, adding more stock, if needed, to make a smooth sauce. Add this mixture to the saucepan.

❡ Blend the tamarind pulp and water with the raisins and peaches in a blender.

❡ Bring the mixture to a slow boil and cook for 5 minutes. Add the tamarind mixture and the cloves, cinnamon, sugar, salt, and chocolate. If the *mole* is too thick, add more stock. Simmer for 10 minutes, stirring constantly to avoid burning the sugar.

❡ Heat the meat in the sauce and serve, accompanied with rice or flour *tortillas.*

IGUANA
A type of lizard, the iguana can vary in color from green to almost black depending on the species, and, not including the tail, the body can measure up to about 18 inches (45 cm) long. The iguana has white meat, similar in taste and texture to chicken, and is part of a long culinary tradition in the tropical areas of Mexico. On the coast of Oaxaca, young girls walk along the tourist beaches with a bucket full of hot, banana-leaf tamales filled with chile- and tomato-stewed iguana meat. Less than 60 miles (100 km) south of Mexico City, in the direction of the famous colonial town of Taxco, women and children sell live iguanas, hanging by their tails, along the roadside. There are also many stands and restaurants in the region that sell iguana meat marinated and cooked with chile or in a broth.

PORK

The introduction of the domesticated pig by the Spanish following the conquest, transformed both the substance and the methods of cooking in Mexico. Hitherto, fat had not been used as a medium for cooking but, now, lard initiated a revolution of frying or sautéeing foods, enriching and flavoring them. For example, the spongy *tamales* of today owe their lightness to the addition of whipped lard to the corn *masa*.

The meat of the pig—literally, from head to trotter—is appreciated all over Mexico and is one of the most consumed of all meats in the country. Pork loin is served at elegant dinner parties, second in prestige only to beef tenderloin (fillet steak). This lean cut of pork can be boned, then seasoned with a chile paste or braised with fruit or vegetables. It is often flavored with *pulque* (the freshly fermented juice of the agave cactus) in central Mexico; broiled (grilled) in the Yucatecan manner, *poc-chuc*; or steam-baked in a pit, flavored with *achiote* (annatto) seed paste, as in the famous *pibils* from the same region. Pork chops are broiled, fried, or baked, and served whole or chopped for *taco* fillings. The spine may be cut into chops, and their high fat content gives an excellent flavor.

Pork meat (*pulpa*) from the rump or shoulder, cut into cubes for stewing, is prepared in countless ways. *Carnitas* (which can also include other cuts) are one of the most popular: the meat is seasoned with herbs and slowly boiled immersed in pork fat until tender and crisp. A little orange zest is added to give an intriguing flavor.

Moles are generally made for turkey, chicken, or cubed pork. The meat is simmered to make its own stock before being added to the hot *mole* so the flavors intermingle before serving. Equally, the meat may be bathed in *pipián verde* (green pumpkin-seed sauce), an *encacahuatado* (peanut sauce), or an *almendrado* (almond sauce), or stewed with chile or vegetables.

Cooked and shredded pork is put on many kinds of *antojitos*, such as the famous *chalupas* of Puebla—the flat *masa* base is covered with green or red sauce, pork, and chopped onion—or the *salbutes* of the Yucatán Peninsula.

One of the most famous kinds of *taco* prepared in Mexico City is the *taco al pastor* (shepherd's *taco*). Thin layers of pork are marinated and layered together on a vertical spit that revolves in front of a fire. The *taquero* (*taco* maker) is capable of preparing each *taco* in a matter of seconds. Getting a real rhythm going when the place is full, the *taquero* slices the meat into a small, hot *tortilla* along with some chopped onion broiled below the spit. He then flips on a little sauce and chopped cilantro (fresh coriander), and tops it off with a slice or two of the whole pineapple roasting on the top of the spit, which goes whizzing into the air with a quick swish of the knife.

Manitas de cerdo, pig's trotters, are also much appreciated in Mexico. They are boiled until very tender and pickled in a delicious vinaigrette (*manitas en escabeche*); batter-fried and stewed in a green sauce for a very hearty and very Mexican breakfast; or pressed into a terrine for a more modern dish.

Lest we forget the head, no *pozole* (pork and hominy stew) would be authentic without it. Another favorite preparation is *queso de puerco* (headcheese/brawn): the head is stewed and pressed inside a special basket (see Cured Meats and Sausages page 183).

1. head; 2. "spine" and rib chops; 3. chops; 4. lard; 5. loin; 6. manitas de cerdo (pig's trotters); 7. shoulder

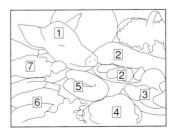

PIPIÁN ROJO DE ALMENDRAS

RED PIPIÁN ALMOND SAUCE

This dish is adapted by Alicia de'Angelia from a recipe in an old Yucatecan cookbook, with an important change for health-conscious cooks — the lard has been removed. You can also substitute hazelnuts, pine nuts, or walnuts for the almonds.

For the meat:
8 serving pieces of chicken, duck, turkey, or pork
1 onion, quartered
2 cloves garlic
1 teaspoon salt, or to taste
For the *mole:*
12 ancho *chiles,* deveined (1 tablespoon seeds reserved),
    soaked in water overnight, and drained
1½ cups (12 fl oz/375 ml) water
2 cups (8 oz/250 g) almonds
pinch of allspice
pinch of ground clove
salt and pepper to taste

SERVES 4 (MAKES 2 CUPS/16 fl oz/500 ml)

❧ To cook the meat: Place it in a pot and add enough water to cover. Add the onion, garlic, and salt, and bring to a boil. Simmer for 20 minutes, or until the meat is just cooked. Reserve the meat and stock; skin the poultry if using.

❧ Process the chiles with the water in a food processor until smooth. Lightly roast the almonds and the reserved chile seeds until golden on a hot *comal* or cast-iron griddle. Put the almonds and seeds in a food processor and process until combined.

❧ Combine the chiles and the almond mixture in a saucepan and simmer over low heat for 15 minutes. Season with the remaining ingredients.

❧ Reheat the cooked chicken, duck, turkey, or pork pieces in the sauce over low heat, and serve hot.

❧ The *pipián* sauce will keep in the refrigerator for 8 days in a sealed container.

ENCACAHUATADO

PORK IN PEANUT SAUCE

The thin yet creamy sauce in this recipe from La Cocina Veracruzana *is a specialty of Veracruz, where peanuts are cultivated. This dish works equally well with pork or chicken.*

8 cups (2 qt/2 l) water
5 cloves garlic

½ onion
1 teaspoon salt, or to taste
2 lb (1 kg) lean rump pork
6 tablespoons (3 fl oz/90 ml) lard or vegetable oil
2 potatoes
2 lb (1 kg) tomatoes
2 serrano *chiles,* or to taste, roasted
5 oz (155 g) peanuts, skins removed
5 oz (155 g) sesame seeds
ground clove, to taste
ground cinnamon, to taste

SERVES 8

❧ In a large pot, bring the water to a boil with 2 cloves of garlic, the onion, and salt. Add the meat and simmer for 20 minutes. Drain, reserving the stock and vegetables, and cut the pork into 1¼-inch (3-cm) cubes.

❧ Heat 4 tablespoons of lard in a heavy frying pan over medium heat and cook the meat for 15 minutes until cooked through and well browned. Drain on paper towels and set aside.

❧ Boil the potatoes until cooked but still firm. Peel and cut them into 1¼-inch (3-cm) cubes. Set aside.

❧ Roast the tomatoes with the remaining garlic on a hot *comal* or cast-iron griddle. Separately roast the chiles, peanuts, and sesame seeds; be careful not to burn the seeds or they will become bitter. Coarsely process the roasted ingredients in a food processor with ½ cup (4 fl oz/125 ml) of the reserved stock. Add the reserved cooked onion and garlic, the clove, and cinnamon, then process.

❧ Heat the remaining 2 tablespoons of lard in a large saucepan over medium heat and cook the processed mixture for about 5 minutes. Reduce the heat and simmer for 20 minutes. Add the meat, potatoes, and more of the reserved broth to thin the sauce. Simmer for 10 minutes; the consistency should be that of a light sauce or thin *mole,* that is, quite liquid.

❧ To serve, spoon the mixture around the outside edge of a large serving plate and fill the center with rice.

MANTECO DE CERDO

PORK LARD

Lard, rendered pork fat, remains an essential ingredient in Mexican cooking, particularly in the preparation of refried beans, tamales, *and many of the snacks made with* masa. *Both its cholesterol level and ease of use are better than*

Top left: Red Pipián Almond Sauce; center: Pork in Peanut Sauce; top right: Pork Lard

butter's but, purchased commercially, its price does not compare favorably with many oils. Make your own to save money and to give your favorite Mexican dishes an authentic flavor. The best pork fat to use is "leaf" from around the rib-bones and kidneys; it renders easily and is the most pure. Fat-back is almost as good; if neither is readily available, almost any pieces of pork fat will do.

1 lb (500 g) leaf fat, fat-back, or pork-fat pieces, cleaned of skin and meat, and finely diced

MAKES 1½ CUPS (12 oz/375 ml)

❡ Preheat the oven to 250°F (130°C/Gas ½).
❡ Place the fat in a ovenproof dish, adding enough cold water to partially cover, and put in the oven (or over a very low flame) for 40 minutes, or until the fat has liquefied, stirring from time to time to prevent it from browning or sticking.
❡ Remove from the oven (or stove) and strain through cheesecloth (muslin) into a heat-resistant container. Set aside.
❡ When the fat has cooled and set into a white, smooth shortening, cover and refrigerate. Lard will keep in the refrigerator for up to 3 months.

MOLES

The Aztec word *molli,* or *mulli,* refers to various sauces and preparations in pre-Hispanic Mexico, some of which are similar to those still made today (including the avocado-based *guacamole*). *Molli* is also the root of the Aztec word for the grinding stone called *molcajete.* Although we must assume

that this is the root of the word *mole,* it is curious that the Spanish verb *moler* also means to grind. The common denominator of these sauces is that their ingredients are ground together into a powder or a paste, and, according to *El Nuevo Cocinero Mexicano,* written in 1888, *tlemole* is the generic

term for this group of chile-based sauces.

The *moles* of today are a fascinating culinary expression of the cultural intermixing between the Old and New Worlds. We also find in *mole* ingredients the influence of the trade routes that crossed Mexico from Asia to Spain. While

chiles, chocolate (used in small quantities in *mole poblano* and some of the other dark *moles*), tomatoes, and peanuts are native to Mexico, the Spanish introduced almonds, sesame, and cumin. Spice-route commerce from the Orient brought in many of the key spices: black pepper, cinnamon, and anise.

include four types of dried chiles, almonds, pecans, sesame seeds, raisins, garlic, onions, spices, seasonings, and bitter (dark) chocolate. Although chocolate is an essential ingredient in *mole poblano*, it is not the principal one, so the idea that *mole poblano* is a chocolate sauce is erroneous. As in other *moles* and sauces, the ground ingredients are fried to make a well-seasoned paste. The paste is then thinned with the stock that the accompanying meat has been cooked in, and simmered until it has the rich consistency of a thick sauce. The traditional meat served with *mole poblano* is the native turkey of Mexico. The turkey (or chicken or pork) pieces are simmered gently with the *mole* so that the flavors penetrate the meat. When the dish is served, a generous helping of sauce, sprinkled with roasted sesame seeds, should cover the plate.

Oaxaca is the proud place of origin of seven *moles*: *negro* (black); *colorado* and *coloradito*, two different red *moles*; *amarillo* (yellow), which gets its name from a regional dried chile called *amarillo*; *verde* (green), made with fresh chiles and green tomatoes; *chíchilo negro* (also a black *mole*); and *mancha manteles* ("tablecloth stainer"), which would surely be an apt name for all of the above, not just this red *mole* with fruit and tomato.

There are other dishes referred to as *moles* that do not follow the above definition: *mole de olla* is more of a stock casserole with meat, vegetables, and corn on the cob. *Guazmole*, another casserole from the Sierra de Puebla, is flavored with *guajes*, long beans with strong-tasting seeds, and is made with young mountain kid nurtured on wild

oregano, when it is in season.

Pipián is the name given to *moles* that have seeds as their main ingredient. *Pipián verde* is made with pumpkin seeds, while *pipián rojo* has sesame seeds as its base.

Other pastes that are not *moles* but are sold in the same manner in market stalls are *adobos*, chile-based mixtures for marinating meat, and the *recados* of the Yucatán Peninsula, often based on *achiote* (annatto) seed paste. Other nut-based sauces are the *encacahuatado*, a thick, peanut-based sauce, and the *almendrado*, an almond sauce from Veracruz.

Tamarind is sold in its pod or in pulp. Although it is principally used for drinks and sweets, it is becoming popular as a contemporary mole ingredient.

Mole ingredients were traditionally ground on a *metate* or grindstone made of volcanic rock. Today, however, many cooks have the choice of taking their prepared ingredients to the local mill to be ground or using their own food processors. The markets also sell a variety of pre-prepared *mole* pastes and powders.

1. mole negro (black mole); 2. ground green pumpkin seeds; 3. pipián verde (prepared pumpkin seed sauce in powdered form); 4. adobos (chile paste of ancho chiles); 5. tamarind; 6. peanut butter paste (includes some pecans and almonds); 7. mole poblano in paste; 8. sesame seed paste; 9. pipián rojo (sesame seed sauce); 10. mole poblano in paste form

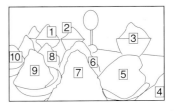

This *mestizaje* or intermixing is also evident in the processes employed for preparing *moles*. While toasting and grinding the ingredients are Aztec techniques, the addition of fat for frying sauces, whether lard or vegetable oil, is a legacy of the conquest.

The most famous of all

moles is *mole poblano*, said to have been invented in the eighteenth century in the Convent of Santa Rosa in the Spanish colonial town of Puebla. Tradition has it that the dish is the result of the combined efforts of the Spanish nuns and the indigenous servants. The fried and ground ingredients

CHULETAS EMPANIZADAS AL HORNO

BAKED BREADED PORK CHOPS

Breaded dishes such as chicken, beef, pork, and fish are very popular in Mexico. These traditional favorites are usually deep-fried, but in this contemporary recipe, no oil or frying is required.

8 pork chops, lightly pounded
salt and pepper, to taste
1 or 2 eggs, beaten
2 oz (60 g) fine breadcrumbs
4 slices regular or Canadian bacon
¼ cup (2 oz/60 g) butter
1 cup (8 fl oz/250 ml) boiling water
flat-leafed (Italian/continental) parsley, for garnish

SERVES 8

❡ Preheat the oven to 350°F (180°C/Gas 4).
❡ Sprinkle both sides of the pork chops with salt and pepper. Dip them in the beaten egg, then the breadcrumbs, and place them in a large baking dish in a single layer. Bake for 20 minutes. Turn the chops and bake for a further 15 minutes.
❡ Fry the bacon until almost browned. Cut the slices in half and drain on paper towels. Melt the butter in the boiling water and pour the mixture into the baking dish, but not over the meat. Place a bacon strip on each pork chop and continue baking for 20 minutes, or until the meat is fully cooked.
❡ Serve the chops with the bacon strips on a plate garnished with parsley and accompany with *Puré de Membrillo* (see page 122) or any spicy sauce.

CERDO CON CHILE

PORK WITH CHILES

This recipe comes from Silvia Figueroa de Llamas of Huitzuco, Guerrero. The original recipe calls for pulque, the freshly fermented juice of the agave cactus, which can be difficult to find, so use light beer as a substitute.

3 lb (1.5 kg) pork leg or loin, boned and cut into chunks
1 onion, halved and thinly sliced
2 cloves garlic, minced (finely chopped)
4 tablespoons (2 fl oz/60 ml) vegetable oil
2 pasilla *chiles*
3 arbol *chiles*

½ cup (4 fl oz/125 ml) water
1½ cups (12 fl oz/375 ml) flat light beer
½ teaspoon salt, or to taste

SERVES 8–10

❡ Cook the pork in salted water to cover for 50 minutes, or until cooked through and tender.

Strain and discard the stock.

❡ In a large flameproof casserole, sauté the onion and garlic in the oil until translucent.

❡ Lightly roast the chiles over an open flame. Remove the stems and seeds and blend them in a blender with the water until smooth. Add the mixture to the casserole. Rinse the blender with the beer and add to the casserole along with the chunks of pork and the salt.

❡ Cook over low heat for about 10 minutes, or until the sauce is reduced and thickened and the meat starts to fall apart.

❡ Serve at room temperature, in the casserole or on a serving platter with hot corn *tortillas* to make *tacos*.

Left: Baked Breaded Pork Chops; right: Pork with Chiles

PIPIÁN DE TERESITA

PUMPKIN SEED SAUCE WITH POULTRY OR PORK

The Fonda de Teresita Restaurant in Puebla is one of Mexico's great culinary centers, and owner Teresa Trigoyen Díaz is one of Puebla's best chefs. Her secret for making this classic mole *dish is to use the same oil to sauté the pumpkin seeds and to fry the sauce, thereby mingling the flavors. This recipe makes a large amount of sauce, but it freezes well.*

For the meat:
16 serving pieces of chicken, duck, turkey, or pork
2 onions, quartered
3 garlic cloves
2 teaspoons salt, or to taste
1 hoja santa leaf, optional
For the sauce:
1 cup (8 fl oz/250 ml) corn oil
1 lb (500 g) unsalted green pumpkin seeds, shelled
⅓ cup (2 oz/60 g) sesame seeds
2 lb (1 kg) tomatillos, fresh or canned and drained
½ small onion, coarsely chopped
4 cloves garlic
2 oz (60 g) serrano chiles
salt to taste

SERVES 8 (MAKES 4 cups/1 qt/1 l)

CHICHARRON
(Pork Crackling)

These great rectangles of puffed and crunchy pork crackling can be seen at markets or street stalls everywhere in Mexico. A piece is broken off and sprinkled with chile sauce or a few drops of lime juice as a popular snack. Small pieces may accompany guacamole, a delicious combination in which the chicharrón also acts as a spoon. The pork crackling may also be cooked in a tomato broth or green sauce until it becomes soft, and is then used as a filling for tacos with avocado or cheese. It is also good mixed in a salad with tomato, avocado, onion, serrano chiles, and cilantro (fresh coriander), tossed with a good dose of olive oil. To achieve the light, crispy texture of chicharrón, the raw pigskin is first salted and aired overnight. On the second day, it is cut into large rectangles and gently deep-fried in lard in great copper or other metal vats. The still-tough sheets of skin are left to cool until a brief second frying the following day; this is over a much higher heat, which makes the skin inflate and crackle.

---

§ To cook the meat: Place it in a pot and add enough water to cover. Add the onion, garlic, salt, and *hoja santa* leaf and bring to a boil. Simmer for approximately 20 minutes, or until the meat is just cooked. Reserve the meat and stock.

§ For the sauce: Heat the oil in a frying pan over medium heat and sauté the pumpkin seeds, stirring them constantly until they are roasted but not browned. Remove the seeds and set aside, reserving the oil. In a separate pan, dry roast the sesame seeds until golden and mix them with the pumpkin seeds.

§ Blend the seeds in a blender, with all the remaining ingredients, until smooth.

§ Reheat the oil used for the pumpkin seeds and cook the sauce over low heat, stirring occasionally, until thickened to a paste, about 10 minutes. (The sauce can be frozen at this point.)

§ To serve the sauce with the cooked meat pieces, thin it with enough of the reserved stock to achieve a creamy consistency. Add the meat and simmer to heat through; there should be enough sauce to cover the meat completely. Adjust the seasoning and serve.

LONGANIZA ESTILO DE LA COSTA

MEXICAN SAUSAGES COASTAL-STYLE

Like most Mexican sausages, these, from Jalapa, are flavored with ancho *chiles, cumin, and oregano. Traditionally, the* longaniza *is air-dried in the sun for twelve hours, which preserves it for up to ten days. Fried* longaniza *can be served with tortillas, sliced avocado, and any dried chile sauce. This recipe is from* La Cocina Veracruz.

4 lb (2 kg) lean shoulder or leg pork, ground (minced)
1 lb (500 g) pork fat-back, ground (minced)
8 ancho chiles, seeded, deveined, and soaked in warm water
10 cloves garlic
2 teaspoons cumin
1 teaspoon oregano
1 cup (8 fl oz/250 ml) white or cider vinegar, or to taste
2 teaspoons salt, or to taste
thin pork casing
2 tablespoons lard

MAKES 6 lb (3 kg) SAUSAGE

§ Mix the pork and fat-back in a bowl. In a *metate* or food processor, grind the chiles with the garlic, cumin, and oregano until coarse. Rinse the *metate* with the vinegar or pour into the hopper, and then add to the paste. Incorporate the paste into the meat, mix in the salt, and stuff the pork casing.

❡ Cut the sausages into 4-inch (10-cm) lengths. Heat the lard on a *comal* or cast-iron griddle, and fry the sausages over medium heat for approximately 5 to 7 minutes, turning occasionally to avoid burning.

❡ Serve the *longaniza* as an hors d'oeuvre or use the meat baked with dried beans.

Top: Pumpkin Seed Sauce with Poultry or Pork; bottom: Mexican Sausages Coastal-style

LOMO DE PUERCO CON FRUTA Y CHILE POBLANO

LOIN OF PORK WITH FRUIT AND POBLANO CHILES

This recipe has been in the family of Brenda Garza from Monterrey, Nuevo León, for several generations. It combines regional fruits with rajas, or strips of poblano chiles, in a delicious and unusual sauce. The pork can also be served just in its juices, with the sauce separate.

2 cloves garlic
¼ onion
1 teaspoon of salt, or to taste
½ tablespoon peppercorns
3 lb (1.5 kg) pork loin (de-boned if you prefer)
3 tablespoons vegetable oil
2 cups (16 fl oz/500 ml) water
For the sauce:
6 poblano chiles
2 tablespoons vegetable oil
4 (2 lb/1 kg) quinces, peeled, cored, and cut into wedges
4 (1 lb/500 g) small, firm peaches, peeled, pitted, and cut into wedges
1 cup (8 fl oz/250 ml) heavy (double/thickened) cream
salt and pepper, to taste

SERVES 8

❡ Grind the garlic, onion, salt, and peppercorns to a paste in a *molcajete* or spice grinder. Rub the mixture all over the pork and let rest for 20 to 30 minutes.
❡ Heat the oil in a pot and brown the pork on all sides. Add the water, cover, and cook over low heat until the meat is tender, about 1 to 1½ hours.
❡ To make the sauce: Roast the chiles over an open flame or under a broiler (grill), turning to char on each side. Seal immediately in a plastic bag for 10 minutes to allow to sweat.
❡ Wearing rubber gloves, peel the chiles under running water, removing the stems, seeds, and veins. Cut the chiles into strips.
❡ In a large frying pan, heat the oil and add the chiles and quinces. Cook, stirring constantly, over medium heat until the quinces begin to soften. Add the peaches and cook until the fruit is soft but still intact. Add the cream, and salt and pepper to taste, then cook for a further 5 minutes.
❡ When the pork is cooked, remove the meat from the pot, and spoon off the excess fat from the surface of the remaining liquid. Boil the liquid until reduced to ½ cup (4 fl oz/125 ml). Add the chile sauce to the juices and return the loin, sliced if you prefer, to the pot to reheat. Serve.

TEXMOLE DE CARNE DE RES

BEEF CASSEROLE WITH CHILE AND AVOCADO LEAVES

Texmole, from Coxcatlán, Puebla, is one of many varieties of mole de olla, a type of casserole with meat, chile, and vegetables simmered in broth. It is served in soup bowls as a main course. This adaptation of the traditional casserole is from Yaya and Alicia Herrera.

2¾ lb (1.3 kg) beef short ribs
5 cups (1¼ qt/1.25 l) water
1 teaspoon salt, or to taste
1 cup (5 oz/155 g) green beans, cleaned and cut into thirds
2 guajillo or cascabel chiles, stems removed
1¼ lb (625 g) tomatoes, halved and seeded
1 onion, chopped
2 cloves garlic
½ cup (4 fl oz/125 ml) water

PRE-HISPANIC GAME

Long before the Spanish conquistadors first set foot on Mexican soil, the indigenous people were hunters. Although they were advanced agriculturally, they had not domesticated many of the fauna native to their land, with the exception of the turkey and a small, hairless breed of dog. To supplement a diet of what basically consisted of tomatoes, corn, and pulses, they trapped and hunted wild deer (native to the Yucatán Peninsula and still one of the area's favorite meats, especially in barbacoa and dried in sheets similar to jerky), boar, pheasant, quail, rabbit, and duck. Various gamebirds—mainly of the duck and goose family—that migrated south from the United States and Canada to the lakes and marshlands of Mexico in search of warm weather, provided one prized food-source for the natives, who either harpooned or trapped them in nets spread over the water's surface. Cortés, writing to Carlos V from Veraruz in 1519, noted that "there is a street of game where are sold all manner of birds ... quail, partridges, owls, hawks and eagles, sparrow hawks and kestrels ... All kind of game is to be found, both animals and birds like those of our own country, among them deer, both red and fallow, wolves, foxes, doves of two or three kinds, and hare and rabbits." Many of the methods of preparation used then have survived through to today virtually unchanged—long cazuela simmering; salting and drying; and slow roasting, either over a low fire or wrapped in leaves and buried in a pit of coals.

Left: Loin of Pork with Fruit and Poblano Chiles; right: Beef Casserole with Chile and Avocado Leaves

3 avocado leaves, optional

20 squash blossoms, cleaned and chopped, optional

3 zucchini (courgettes), cubed, optional

*2 cups (10 oz/315 g) potatoes, peeled and cut into ½-inch
(1-cm) cubes*

For the *chochoyotes* (*masa* dumplings):

4 oz (125 g) prepared tortilla masa *(see Tortilla de Maiz
page 53) or mix ½ cup (2 oz/60 g) masa harina with
⅓ cup (2½ fl oz/75 ml) warm water to form a soft dough*

½ tablespoon lard

¼ teaspoon salt, or to taste

SERVES 6

❡ In a large saucepan, cover the short ribs with
the water and salt; cook until the meat is just
about falling off the bone, approximately 1 to
1½ hours. Just as it starts to cool, skim the fat off

the stock, and reserve. Remove the meat from the
bones, discarding the fat and tendons.

❡ Cook the green beans in boiling, salted water
until just tender, and drain.

❡ Puree the chiles, tomatoes, onion, garlic, and
water in a blender until smooth. Pour into a soup
pot with the reserved stock, avocado leaves,
squash blossoms, and zucchini, bring to a boil, and
simmer over medium heat for 20 minutes.

❡ To make the *chochoyotes:* Mix all the ingredients
together until well blended. Form ¾-inch (2-cm)
balls and make a small indentation on one side of
each with your finger.

❡ Add the dumplings and potatoes to the broth
and simmer for about 15 minutes until cooked.
Add the green beans and meat, then simmer for
10 minutes. Add salt to taste and serve.

Left: Holy Leaf Mole; right: Flambéed Salt-cured Beef

MOLE DE HOJA SANTA (ACUYO)

HOLY LEAF MOLE

This mole *recipe is from Chelo Arrubarena from Puebla. It is different from many of the other* moles *which feature in Mexican cooking because of the strong, anise-like taste of the* hoja santa *leaves (also called* acuyo *leaves) combined with the flavor of cumin and the sweetness of the plantain.*

1 lb (500 g) rump steak, cut into small cubes
5 cups (1¼ qt/1.25 l) water
1 small onion
1 clove garlic
½ teaspoon salt, or to taste
10 hoja santa *leaves (or fennel leaves with black pepper)*
6 serrano *chiles, or to taste, sliced*
¼ teaspoon cumin
1 (8 oz/250 g) plantain *or banana, unpeeled*
2 tablespoons vegetable oil
1 tablespoon all-purpose (plain) flour

SERVES 6

❡ Cook the meat in the water with half the onion, the garlic, and salt for 20 minutes, or until tender. Drain, reserving 1½ cups (12 fl oz/375 ml) of the

stock, and discard the onion and garlic.
❡ Devein the *hoja santa* leaves and tear them into small pieces. Process, along with the chiles, cumin, and most of the reserved stock in a food processor until smooth.
❡ Cut off the ends of the plantain and cut into 12 pieces. Boil in salted water for 10 minutes (the plantain should still be firm) and peel.
❡ Heat the oil in a small saucepan over medium heat. Chop the remaining half onion and cook in the oil until translucent. Add the flour and stir until browned. Add the meat, *hoja santa* mixture, and plantain, then heat through. The *mole* should be thick but not pasty; thin with a little stock if necessary.

CECINA FLAMEADA

FLAMBÉED SALT-CURED BEEF

Cecina, *salted, air-dried beef cut into thin strips, is usually bought already prepared in Mexico. This recipe for making it at home is from Graciela A. de Díaz from the Bancomer Volunteers' Group recipe book. It is grilled on a barbecue, flamed with tequila, and served with* salsa verde *and cream.*

For the *cecina:*
1 lb (500 g) beef tenderloin (fillet)
3 tablespoons oil
3 teaspoons salt, or to taste
¼ cup (2 fl oz/60 ml) aguardiente de caña, *white rum, or vodka*
¼ cup (2 fl oz/60 ml) lime or lemon juice, *or beer*
For the *salsa verde:*
5 large (14 oz/400 g) tomatillos, *skinned and washed*
2 serrano *chiles, or to taste*
1 garlic clove, peeled
1 small (2 oz/60 g) onion
½ teaspoon salt, or to taste
3 tablespoons oil
1 cup (8 fl oz/250 ml) heavy (double/thickened) cream, *optional*

SERVES 4

❡ To prepare the *cecina:* Cut the tenderloin into 4 pieces. Cut each piece into 1 strip about ½ inch (0.5 cm) thick by 16 inches (40 cm) long, following the grain. Apply very little oil to both sides of each strip and sprinkle with the salt. Hang the strips to dry in a cool place overnight. Roll up the meat, wrap in plastic, and refrigerate for 4 to 5 days. Cut each long strip into 2 or 3 pieces before grilling.

¶ Light a barbecue 1 hour before cooking or heat a *comal* or cast-iron griddle until very hot. Grill the meat for approximately 1 minute on each side. Remove from the flame and place the meat in a large, flat clay pan to one side of the grill to keep warm.

¶ Heat the *aguardiente* in another saucepan and pour it over the meat. Ignite, letting the flame burn until the edges of the meat are browned. Extinguish the flame with the lime juice or beer and then continue to cook until the liquid has almost completely evaporated.

¶ For the *salsa verde:* Puree the first 5 ingredients in a food processor. Heat the oil in a saucepan and pour in the pureed mixture. Lower the heat and simmer for 10 minutes, stirring occasionally. Add the cream, and set aside until cool. (The cream can also be served separately, if desired.)

¶ Serve the *cecina* immediately in its cooking dish, accompanied by the *salsa* and cream, if desired.

CURED MEATS AND SAUSAGES

Salt-curing and drying are two ways of preserving meat known the world over. In the north of Mexico, *machaca* (dried beef) is a specialty. The beef is salted and dried in the sun so it can be kept for any length of time without refrigeration. It is then pounded to break down the fibers, which makes it easy to shred. The dried beef can either be rehydrated before being cooked with tomatoes and vegetables, or sautéed as is with garlic and chile and scrambled with eggs for a delicious breakfast.

In the rest of Mexico, you are more likely to find *cecina* (called *tasajo* in Oaxaca), where the beef is only semi-dried after being salted and given a light coating of oil. It is sold in long, thin, folded sheets ready to be broiled (grilled) briefly or flambéed with tequila. *Cecina adobada* is pork meat in thin sheets that has been given a chile paste coating, or *adobo*, to flavor it.

Toluca (the capital of Mexico state) is famous for its sausages: *chorizo, chorizo verde,* and *longaniza.* The Spanish introduced the domesticated pig as well as techniques for making sausages to Mexico. The sausage-makers of Toluca are, however, proud of the traditions they have developed themselves over the centuries. There is the special taste of the pork, fed on corn, the addition of *ancho* chiles to color and flavor the sausages, and the well-guarded secrets of their spice mixtures. The meat should be allowed to marinate in white wine, or, failing that, a "pure" fruit vinegar, for just the right amount of time.

Longaniza is a chile-colored sausage that has not been sectioned off but is cut from one continuous piece. *Chorizo verde* (green sausage) is colored with fresh herbs and chiles and may contain pumpkin seeds.

Queso de puerco (headcheese/brawn) is another specialty of Toluca. The pig's head is simmered with flavorings, then cut up and pressed into a "pâté" inside a special basket, from which it is later sold. It makes a wonderful filling for *tacos.*

Carnitas is one of the most popular ways of cooking pork. The meat is seasoned with herbs and boiled slowly immersed in pork fat until tender and crisp.

1. machaca (dried, pounded beef);
2. cecina (salt-cured beef);
3. cecina adobada (salt-cured pork with chile); 4. chorizo;
5. chorizo verde (green sausage);
6. longaniza (chile sausage);
7. queso de puerco (headcheese/ brawn); 8. carnitas

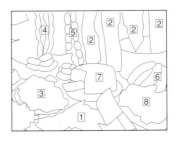

FILETE AL HORNO CON HONGOS SILVESTRES

BAKED FILLET OF BEEF WITH WILD MUSHROOMS

Fillet of beef is frequently served at formal luncheons and dinner parties. This recipe from Patricia Elías Calles is quick to prepare and redolent of the taste of wild mushrooms.

5 tablespoons vegetable oil
1 teaspoon salt, or to taste
4 lb (2 kg) beef fillet
2 teaspoons granulated chicken bouillon
½ onion, minced (finely chopped)
2 cloves garlic, minced (finely chopped)
3 lb (1.5 kg) mixture wild mushrooms, cleaned and coarsely chopped

SERVES 6

❡ Preheat the oven to 475°F (240°C/Gas 9).
❡ Rub 2 teaspoons of the oil and the salt over the meat, then sprinkle with the bouillon. Put the fillet in a large roasting pan and bake for 20 minutes. Turn the meat and cook for a further 20 minutes.
❡ Meanwhile, heat the remaining oil in a frying pan over medium heat. Add the onion and garlic, and sauté until transparent. Add the mushrooms, raise the heat, and cook for 10 to 15 minutes or until almost all of the liquid has evaporated.
❡ Remove the meat from the oven and allow to stand for 5 minutes before carving. Serve garnished with the mushrooms.

Baked Fillet of Beef with Wild Mushrooms

flank (skirt). It has a layer of fat around it that drips away when the meat is broiled, leaving a well-flavored but lean piece of meat, similar to that of *fajitas*.

Popular and inexpensive cuts of beef are *bisteces* (minute steaks) that come from the flank, the shoulder, or the top of the leg, and are sliced very thinly. These are broiled or breaded and fried as *milanesas*. *Costilla de res* is very thinly cut from the rib. Often broiled and chopped for *tacos*, its fat content gives a good flavor to the meat. Stewing meat may include *chambarete*, from the shank (shin); short ribs (top of skirt); and cubed meat from the leg or shoulder.

In the North, where beef is cut for export, many American cuts are popular, including rib-eye, sirloin (rump steak), New York, and T-bone.

BEEF

Chihuahua and Sonora, in the north of Mexico, are famous for the quality of their beef, but important cattle ranches also exist in the extreme south of the country, in Chiapas, and have been one of the sources of wealth for the coastal state of Veracruz.

Fillet of beef, in the highest price range, is either roasted whole or may be cut in the following way: the center is reserved for serving as tenderloin (fillet steak) or cut into filets mignons or the thinner medallions. The tips, called *puntas de filete*, are usually quickly browned and added to a stewed mixture of tomato, onion, and green chile (*a la mexicana*) or a dried chile sauce. The thicker top end may be cut into *filete a la tampiqueña*: the fillet is cut across the grain in a section four fingers wide (about 3 inches/8 cm) and roll-sliced, much like peeling an apple in one continuous strip gradually opening the piece into a long, thin strip. This is quickly broiled (grilled) and served with *guacamole*, beans, and an *enchilada* with a green sauce. The tips and the wings of the thick end of the fillet may also be cubed and skewered.

An interesting cut of beef, famous in the North, is *arrachera*. This is a thickly cut strip of meat from the

1. whole tenderloin (fillet);
2. filets mignons; 3. filete a la Taupiquéno; 4. beefsteak;
5. cubed stewing beef;
6. ground (minced) beef

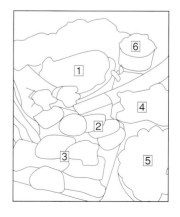

ASADO A LA PLAZA SINALOENSE

SINALOA-STYLE MEAT AND VEGETABLES

This dish is a unique combination of meat, fried potatoes, zucchini (courgettes), lettuce, cucumber, and red onion topped with a warm tomato and oregano sauce. The recipe comes from Yolanda Mercado de Lizárraga of Mazatlán, Sinaloa, and was first published in La Cocina Regiónal de México *by the Bancomer Volunteer Group.*

2 lb (1 kg) stewing beef
4 cups (1 qt/1 l) water
2 cloves garlic, unpeeled
1 small onion
8 black peppercorns
1 teaspoon salt, or to taste
4 tablespoons (2 fl oz/60 ml) vegetable oil
1 lb (500 g) potatoes, boiled but still firm, peeled, and cut
    into ¾-inch (2-cm) cubes
8 oz (250 g) zucchini (courgettes), cut into 1½- x ½-inch
    (4- x 1-cm) strips
1 red onion, sliced in thin rings
1 head lettuce, finely sliced
2 cucumbers, peeled and cut into ½-inch (1-cm) slices
For the sauce:
3 lb (1.5 kg) tomatoes
½ onion, chopped
2 cloves garlic
1 teaspoon oregano
½ teaspoon salt, or to taste
¼ teaspoon black pepper
2 tablespoons vegetable oil

SERVES 8–10

❡ Put the meat and water in a pot over low heat. Add the garlic, onion, peppercorns, and salt. Bring to a boil, then simmer for 1½ to 2 hours, or until the meat is tender. Drain, cool, and cut the meat into ¾-inch (2-cm) cubes.
❡ In a large frying pan, heat the oil and lightly fry the meat and brown the potatoes. Let cool.
❡ Boil the zucchini in salted water until cooked but still firm, approximately 3 to 5 minutes. Drain and set aside to cool.
❡ To prepare the sauce: Combine all except the last ingredient in a blender and puree until smooth. Heat the oil in a medium saucepan over low heat and fry the tomato mixture for 25 minutes. Remove from the heat, and keep warm or reheat before serving.
❡ Put the meat and potatoes on a serving plate and top with the zucchini, onion, lettuce, and cucumber. Pour the sauce over the mixture and serve with corn *tortillas.*

FILETE CON CHOCOLATE

BEEF TENDERLOIN WITH CHOCOLATE SAUCE

If you consider chocolate sauce to be an accompaniment to vanilla ice cream, you will be surprised by this dish which has chocolate as one of the main ingredients. Based on ancient Mexican recipes, this dish is from Joaquin Pinero and Miranda Quijano. While the recipe calls for rare beef, you can put the tenderloin (fillet) in the oven for ten to twenty minutes after browning and before saucing if you prefer it more well done.

2 teaspoons vegetable oil
¼ cup (2 oz/60 g) butter

Left: Sinaloa-style Meat and Vegetables; right: Beef Tenderloin with Chocolate Sauce

1 onion, chopped
1 clove garlic, minced
2 lb (1 kg) beef tenderloin (fillet)
1½ tablespoons freshly ground black pepper
2 cups (16 fl oz/500 ml) fruity white wine
8 oz (250 g) bittersweet (dark) chocolate, shredded
4 sprigs cilantro (fresh coriander)
¾ teaspoon salt, or to taste
cilantro (fresh coriander) leaves, for garnish

SERVES 10–12

❧ Heat the oil and butter in a small frying pan over medium heat. Sauté the onion until transparent, then add the garlic and fry for 2 to 3 minutes.

❧ Remove the onion and garlic, and pour the oil into a large, heavy casserole. Sprinkle the tenderloin with the pepper and brown on all sides in the oil. Remove the meat from the pan and keep warm while preparing the sauce.

❧ Pour the wine into the pan and raise the heat. Scrape with a spatula to dissolve any caramelized juices sticking to the pan. Add the chocolate and, when it has melted, add the cilantro and salt. Stir constantly until the sauce boils, reduce the heat, and simmer for approximately 5 minutes. Return the beef, onions, and garlic to the pan and simmer for a further 5 minutes, or until the meat is thoroughly warm.

❧ Remove the meat and carve. Serve with the sauce and garnish with the cilantro leaves.

MEDALLONES DE FILETE EN SALSA MEZTLI

BEEF MEDALLIONS IN MEZTLI SAUCE

This recipe from Patricia Quintana is a delightful dish that is special enough to serve at an important meal while at the same time being quite straightforward to prepare. It displays a quartet of Mexico's most important ingredients—cuitlacoche (corn fungus), epazote leaves, wild mushrooms, and several kinds of chiles—to their best advantage. Meztli means "moon" in Nahuatl, and the pale sauce atop the black one is meant to signify the moon shining on a dark night.

For the marinade:
2 cloves garlic, minced (finely chopped)
½ cup (½ oz/15 g) flat-leafed (Italian/continental)
    parsley, chopped
½ cup (4 fl oz/125 ml) Worcestershire sauce
¼ cup (2 fl oz/60 ml) soy sauce
1 teaspoon freshly ground black pepper
12 filets mignons (4½ oz/140 g each)
For the *metzli* sauce:
⅓ cup (3 fl oz/90 ml) olive oil
1½ onions, minced (finely chopped)
4 cloves garlic, minced (finely chopped)
6 pasilla *chiles*, minced (finely chopped)
4 arbol *chiles*, minced (finely chopped)
4 firm tomatoes, minced (finely chopped)
2 lb (1 kg) cuitlacoche (corn fungus), chopped
1 lb (500 g) wild or cultivated mushrooms, chopped
⅓ cup (⅓ oz/8 g) epazote leaves, chopped, optional
For the cheese sauce:
2 lb (1 kg) ricotta cheese
1 qt (1 l) heavy (double/thickened) cream
1½ onions, chopped
8 serrano *chiles*
¼ cup (2 oz/60 g) butter
For the meat:
⅓ cup (3 fl oz/90 ml) olive oil
¼ cup (2 oz/60 g) butter
salt and pepper, to taste
1½ cups (12 fl oz/375 ml) beef stock, boiled to reduce to
    ½ cup (4 fl oz/125 ml)
12 x-cat-ik or other fresh chiles, about 2 inches (5 cm)
    long, with tips cut into strips and soaked in ice water
    until they open like a flower

SERVES 12

❡ To prepare the marinade: Put all but the last marinade ingredient in a blender and blend for 2 to 3 minutes. Put the beef in a ceramic container, add the marinade, and set aside for 30 minutes.
❡ For the *meztli* sauce: Heat the oil in a casserole,

add the onions and garlic, and sauté until transparent. Add the chiles and tomatoes, and season lightly with salt and pepper. Cook over high heat until the sauce begins to thicken. Add the *cuitlacoche* and mushrooms, and season again as needed. Add the *epazote*, cover, reduce the heat, and simmer until thickened. Adjust the seasoning to taste. Keep warm.
❡ To make the cheese sauce: Combine all the sauce ingredients except the butter in a blender and blend until completely smooth. Heat the butter in a saucepan, and add the blended mixture to heat through, being careful not to boil. Keep warm.

BARBACOA

This technique for cooking meat is completely different from the American barbecue of meat grilled over the embers of an open fire. For a barbacoa, a fire is prepared in a pit in the ground, and the hole, food and embers, is completely covered. The fire is built on stones that retain the heat from the embers, and the result is a slow form of steam-baking or roasting, rather than open grilling. First, maguey cactus arms, which give the barbacoa its distinctive flavor, are grilled over the fire before it is reduced to embers. Then, a large, earthenware casserole is placed on top of the embers. The casserole contains a mixture of uncooked rice and chickpeas seasoned, perhaps, with guajillo chiles, garlic, and onion, depending on the region and the cook's preferences. A grill is placed on top of the casserole to hold the large pieces of salted mutton (in Mexico state, Hidalgo, and Tlaxcala) or goat (in Guerrero, Oaxaca, and Morelos). The animal's innards are seasoned and tied into a package in the stomach lining, placed with the meat. The maguey arms are then placed on top of the meat to completely cover it (sometimes avocado leaves are also added), and they, in turn, are covered with bricks and earth to seal the hole. The barbacoa is left to cook untouched for about four hours. The juices from the meat accumulate in the casserole, seasoning and cooking the other ingredients in a concentrated and delicious stock. When it is done, the meat is transferred to a large container that has been lined and covered with the maguey arms from the pit to keep it warm. The different cuts are chopped for tacos according to the diner's choice and served alongside the stock, rice, and chickpeas from the casserole. A salsa borracha (drunken sauce), made mainly from pulque, the fermented juice of the maguey cactus, is usually served with them. Fresh, chopped onion, cilantro (fresh coriander), and pieces of lime are put on the table to add either to the tacos or the stock.

Front: Beef Medallions in Meztli Sauce; back: Poor Man's Steak

❡ To finish: Heat a frying pan over high heat. When hot, add the oil and melt the butter. Brown the beef for 2 to 3 minutes on each side or longer if desired, season with salt and pepper, and remove from the heat. In a separate saucepan, heat the stock and drizzle it over the beef.

❡ Serve by placing 1 piece of meat in the center of each dinner plate. Top with the *meztli* sauce, then spoon on the cheese sauce. Garnish with an *x-cat-ik* chile "flower."

BISTECES DE POBRE

POOR MAN'S STEAK

This Mexican favorite from María Molina de Mantecón is delicious and easy to prepare. Bistec is an inexpensive thin slice of beef, very similar to a minute steak. The other ingredients to prepare this dish—potatoes, poblano chiles, tomatoes, and onions—are found in any Mexican kitchen.

⅓ cup (3 fl oz/90 ml) vegetable oil
1 lb (500 g) minute steak, or any thin, boneless beef slices

1 teaspoon salt, or to taste
1 teaspoon pepper
3 potatoes, cut in ½-inch (1-cm) slices
2 onions, sliced
3 poblano chiles, toasted, skinned, and cut into strips
4 tomatoes, cut in ½-inch (1-cm) slices
½ teaspoon thyme
½ teaspoon marjoram
1 cup (8 fl oz/250 ml) chicken stock or water, to cover

SERVES 6

❡ Heat 2 tablespoons of oil in a large frying pan over high heat. Sprinkle the steaks with the salt and pepper and brown them in the oil, turning once. Remove the meat from the pan and set aside.

❡ Reduce the heat and separately fry the potatoes, onions, and chiles, each for a few minutes, using the remaining oil as needed, and remove from the pan. Fry the tomatoes for a few minutes, then return the meat and the vegetables to the pan.

❡ Season with the thyme and marjoram, add the stock, cover, and simmer until the potatoes are completely cooked. Serve from the pan so the dish stays hot.

FISH AND SHELLFISH

FISH AND SHELLFISH

THE MEXICAN COASTLINE IS MORE THAN 6,000 MILES (10,000 KM) LONG, INCLUDING THE PACIFIC AND GULF of California coasts to the west, and the Gulf of Mexico and Caribbean coasts to the east. Lakes, rivers, and lagoons are also an abundant source of fish, although many of the lakes and rivers that existed in pre-Columbian Mexico have now dried up.

❡ Fish were eaten regularly from the time of the Aztec emperor Montezuma, as they were easily available from the freshwater lakes that surrounded the capital city. Sun-dried and salted fish were also sold in the marketplaces of Tenochtitlán (Mexico City). These fish can still be found: some in the city markets of Mexico, while others, butterflied for better drying, are only sold locally in the markets of the small country villages near lakes and rivers.

❡ One of the finest and most traditional fish in Mexico is the white fish *blanco de pátzcuaro* (white fish of Pátzcuaro) found in Lake Pátzcuaro in the state of Michoacán.

❡ Among the most sought after of the saltwater fish are red snapper and snook, which are esteemed for their succulent, firm, white flesh. *Pámpano* and *mojarra* are small enough to serve whole, as are the smaller red snapper.

❡ There is a multitude of fish dishes served, too many to describe here, but a few examples may indicate the huge range available. *Huachinango a la*

Previous pages: The early patron lands the best seafood at San Juan market in Mexico City.

Opposite: The morning's catch displayed on the beach in Mazatlan, capital of the Pacific coastal state of Sinaloa.

veracruzana (Veracruz-style red snapper) is prepared with fresh tomatoes, onion, olives, capers, and yellow chiles; *pan de cazón* is a *tortilla* casserole filled with refried beans and the shredded flesh of small-tailed, or baby, shark. *Mojarras* are small, broad, fresh- or saltwater fish that are fried so crispy that even their fins and toasted bones can be eaten. *Ceviche*, diced, raw fish marinated in lime juice, is served cold and can be prepared in a variety of ways with different ingredients including onions, tomatoes, and chopped green chiles.

❡ Many fish and seafoods are prepared in *escabeches*, served cold as an appetizer. Unlike the raw fish of *ceviches*, the fish is fully cooked before being marinated in a vinegar-based aromatic mixture.

❡ Fish roe can be fried for *tacos* with a little hot *serrano* chile, or scrambled with eggs. This is the whole egg sac, or hard roe, as opposed to caviar, which is made from the fish eggs.

❡ A surprising variety of shrimp (prawn) thrives in Mexico, from the tiny, freshwater *acociles* (½ inch/1 cm long), to the huge U-10 (10 to a pound/500 g) shrimp, one of Mexico's main exports. Other types of crustacean are two kinds of river shrimp—*acamayas* and *langostinos*—and two types of spiny lobster—the Caribbean variety and the larger, red spiny lobster from the waters of the Gulf of California.

❡ A great number of shellfish is also available. There are small to medium red clams, served live on the half-shell, and others that are steak-sized. Of the crab family, the most common is the blue crab (*jaiba*), followed by the stone crab (*cangrejo moro*), prized for its meaty claws. Oysters are also available, and, along with octopus and shrimp, are favorites for making *cockteles* (seafood cocktails).

OSTIONES EN SU CONCHA A LA MEXICANA

MEXICAN-STYLE OYSTERS

Guillermo Torres had the wonderful idea of serving fresh oysters seasoned with purely Mexican flavors — tequila and chipotle chiles.

4 cups (2 lb/1 kg) kosher salt
48 fresh oysters on the half shell, with a few drops of
    their liquid
1 cup (8 fl oz/250 ml) white tequila
1 cup (8 fl oz/250 ml) lime or lemon juice
liquid from a can of chipotle chiles, to taste

SERVES 6 AS AN APPETIZER

❡ Sprinkle 6 dinner plates with coarse salt, and place 8 oysters in their half shells directly on top of each plate. Sprinkle each oyster with a teaspoon of tequila, a teaspoon of lime juice, and a few drops of the chile liquid to taste.
❡ Serve on their own as an appetizer.

CLAPIQUES

FISH TAMALES

These fish tamales have been prepared since the time of the Aztec emperor Montezuma II, in the early sixteenth century. They have always been made with freshwater fish, and, after the Spanish conquest, new ingredients, including onion, garlic, lard, and black pepper, were also added. This recipe, from Florencio Mendoza's family, was given to me by Elena Amor de Lopez Portillo.

16 corn husks
3 teaspoons lard
6 mojarra, sardine, or fresh anchovy fillet strips
    (3½ oz/100 g each) or white fish fillet strips
2 cloves garlic, minced (finely chopped)
salt and pepper, to taste
6 thin slices onion
12 epazote leaves, optional
6 thin slices tomato with skin and seeds
2 serrano chiles, cleaned, deveined, roasted, and cut
    into 18 thin strips
18 strips nopal paddles (see page 116) cut into
    3½- x ¾-inch (9- x 2-cm) pieces, optional

MAKES 6

❡ Soak the corn husks in hot water for 10 minutes. Drain and dry well.

❡ Melt the lard in a small frying pan until it begins to smoke; set aside but keep warm.
❡ Lightly coat both sides of the fish with the garlic and sprinkle with the salt and pepper. Put ½ teaspoon of the lard on a husk and top with a fillet, onion slice, 2 *epazote* leaves, tomato slice, a

Left: Mexican-style Oysters; right: Fish Tamales

little salt, 3 chile strips, 3 *nopal* strips, and another ½ teaspoon of lard. Bring the sides of the husk together to cover the fish, then fold the tip down and bottom up. Repeat to make 6 *tamales*.

¶ Fill the lower part of a *tamalera* or steamer with water and bring to a boil. Put the rack or basket in place and line with some of the remaining husks. Stand the *tamales* in the steamer, filling the gaps with more husks. Cover with the remaining husks, plastic wrap, and the lid. Steam over high heat for approximately 25 minutes.

¶ Serve, still wrapped in the husks, on a platter.

SHELLFISH AND MOLLUSKS

A great number of *camarones* (shrimp/prawns) of all sizes are caught off Mexico's coasts. Some of the largest varieties are rarely seen in the markets, as they are fished for export, but a multitude of small, medium, and large shrimp abound. Every part of the coast has its regional specialties.

The *camarones para pelar* (shrimp for peeling) of Veracruz, are large shrimp boiled whole and given to the diner to peel, accompanied by nothing more than a few wedges of lime and some hot sauce. Shrimp broths are another favorite: Here, too, the shrimp are served whole in the broth, made from shrimp heads, and must be peeled by the diner, a messy but satisfying job.

Campeche, on the southeastern coast of the Gulf of Mexico, is famous for its shrimp and seafood cocktails.

A cocktail *campechano* is a mixture of shrimp, oysters, and octopus, although all of these are sold as individual cocktails as well. The cocktails are served in tall, cone-shaped soda glasses, and are usually made in full view at the seafood bar. The bar is laden with different kinds of seafood and the flavoring ingredients: freshly chopped onion, cilantro (fresh coriander), green chile, avocado, lime, and a spicy, red sauce. These ingredients are spooned or sprinkled into the glass together with the desired seafood.

Al mojo de ajo, a pungent sauce of fried garlic slices, is served on the Pacific coast with shrimp and with whole or filleted fish. Shrimp are also batter-fried, skewered, or cooked *a la plancha* broiled (grilled). In the cities, shrimp are sold either raw, with or without their heads, or cooked; small, peeled, cooked shrimp are called *pacotilla*, while a larger variety is sold cooked and whole.

Langostinos (river prawns) have a bluish-black shell like Maine lobster and range in size from about 2 inches (5 cm) to more than 6 inches (15 cm). They are found in the fresh waters and river mouths close to the sea; different varieties inhabit the Pacific and the Gulf of Mexico. Similar to these are the smaller and shorter-clawed *acamayas*, another type of river prawn. Both of these may be broiled, boiled, or sautéed, and served plain, in a green sauce, or *adobado* in a dried chile paste.

Langostas (spiny lobsters) have a large tail but, unlike lobsters, have no claws. They are often split in half and broiled under a grill and served with a spicy sauce.

Jaibas (blue crabs) are sold live, great bunches of them strung together by knotted green reeds. They are excellent stuffed, and their meat, *pulpa de jaiba*, which can be bought separately, is added to fillings or *ceviche*, raw fish marinated in lime juice. Blue crab is prepared in a soup flavored with *chipotle* chiles called *chilpachole*, a specialty of Veracruz.

Cangrejos moros (stone crabs) are found in the Gulf of Mexico and the Caribbean, and are sold whole or just as claws. The claws may be boiled and served whole or breaded and fried, out of the shell. The sweet meat is delicious in soups, and, like blue crab, is prepared as *salpicón*—a *botana*, or nibble, served as an appetizer in Veracruz. The cooked crab meat is added to a sautéed mixture of garlic, onion, pickled *jalapeños*, cilantro, carrots, and tomatoes and is served with hot *tortillas*.

Ostiones (oysters) are served on the half shell in coastal towns such as Tampico. They are added raw to cocktails in Campeche, and indeed, in the rest of the country, where they can be bought already shucked in glass jars sitting on ice at fish stalls. They may also be cooked in soups or breaded and fried.

Catarinas (red clams) are also known as *almejas rojas*. Of all the different kinds of clams found in Mexico, these are the most prized.

Boiled and chopped *pulpo* (octopus) is another favorite for seafood cocktails. It is also served as a main course. *Pulpo en su tinta* is octopus cooked with its own ink, while *pulpos enamorados* (octopus in love) is served in a dark sauce with chiles, raisins, and almonds.

Calamares (squid) from the gulf and the Caribbean are battered and fried, stuffed, or sautéed with onion, garlic, tomato, and chile. Cleaning them is rather complicated: it involves removing the hard, flat cartilage and the mouth in the center of the animal, and then peeling off the fine film on the skin.

1. camarones (shrimp/prawns);
2. langostinos (river prawns);
3. langosta (spiny lobster);
4. jaiba (blue crab); 5. cangrejo moro (stone crab claws);
6. ostione (oysters); 7. catarinas (red clams); 8. (calamares) squid; 9. pulpo (octopus)

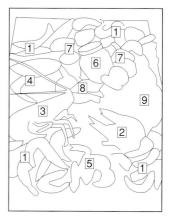

CALLOS DE ALMEJA CON SALSA DE CHILE ANCHO Y NARANJA

BAY SCALLOPS WITH ANCHO CHILE AND ORANGE SAUCE

Callos de almeja *from Mexican waters are not actually scallops, but a type of clam. Their size and shape, however, are similar to the small bay scallops, which can also be used successfully with this sauce from Analuisa Bejar.*

2 oz (60 g) ancho chiles
2 cups (16 fl oz/500 ml) clam juice
½ onion, peeled and quartered
1 clove garlic, peeled
½ teaspoon cumin
2 tablespoons olive oil
2 cups (16 fl oz/500 ml) fresh orange juice, strained
salt, to taste
1⅓ lb (615 g) bay scallops, or any scallop

SERVES 6

❡ Roast the chiles lightly on a hot *comal* or cast-iron griddle to soften them, but do not burn. Cut open and remove the seeds, veins, and stem.
❡ Boil the chiles in a small saucepan with the clam juice, onion, and garlic over medium heat for 10 minutes. Puree this mixture with the cumin in a blender until smooth.
❡ Heat the oil in a saucepan and strain in the chile mixture. Cook, stirring regularly, over high heat for 5 minutes. Add the orange juice and salt, then cook gently over low heat until thickened.
❡ Immediately before serving, put the scallops into the hot sauce. Cook for no more than 4 minutes, just long enough to soften the scallops without making them tough.

OSTIONES Y PAPAS EN JITOMATE

OYSTERS AND POTATOES IN TOMATO SAUCE

This recipe comes from the port of Guaymas, Sonora, on the Sea of Cortez. Whether from the Pacific or the Gulf, oysters are well appreciated in Mexico both on the half shell or in a seafood cocktail with tomato sauce, chile, and lime. In this dish, the breadcrumbs are used as a thickener, the cubed potatoes give consistency, and the paprika accentuates the red of the sauce. This dish makes an excellent appetizer.

1½ cups (12 oz/375 g) oysters
1 potato, cut into ¼-inch (0.5-cm) cubes
1 teaspoon salt, or to taste
10 oz (315 g) tomatoes, quartered
1 small onion, roughly chopped
2 cloves garlic
3 tablespoons vegetable oil
½ teaspoon salt, or to taste
freshly ground black pepper, to taste
2 teaspoons paprika
2 teaspoons breadcrumbs
6 small scallop shells

SERVES 6

❡ Put the oysters in a small saucepan and cook over low heat briefly, just until the edges curl. Drain and reserve.
❡ Boil the potato in salted water in a covered pot for 20 minutes. Drain and reserve.
❡ Put the tomatoes, onion, and garlic in a blender and blend until smooth.
❡ Heat the oil in a medium saucepan over medium heat and strain in the tomato mixture.
❡ Add the salt, pepper, and paprika and allow to simmer, covered, for approximately 10 minutes, stirring occasionally. When the oil rises to the surface of the sauce, mix in the potato, oysters, and breadcrumbs.
❡ Spoon into the scallop shells and serve immediately. This dish can be reheated later in a 300°F (150°C/Gas 2) oven for 15 minutes.

Top: Bay Scallops with Ancho Chile and Orange Sauce; bottom: Oysters and Potatoes in Tomato Sauce

CAMARONES CON CUITLACOCHE

SHRIMP WITH CORN FUNGUS

Cuitlacoche (corn fungus), thrown away as undesirable in most other countries, is one of Mexico's great delicacies. Although traditionally used with onion and chile as a taco stuffing, here Roberto Santibañez turns it into a sauce for shrimp (prawns), a surprisingly good combination. In his restaurant, La Circunstancia, he serves it with Mousse de Cilantro (see page 123).

⅓ cup (3 oz/90 g) butter
1 onion, chopped
1 clove garlic, minced (finely chopped)
2–3 serrano chiles, seeded and chopped
2 sprigs epazote leaves, chopped, optional
2 lb (1 kg) cuitlacoche, cut off the cob and cleaned of
    corn silk, or substitute canned and drained
salt and pepper, to taste
½ cup (4 fl oz/125 ml) chicken stock or water
4 lb (2 kg) large shrimp (prawns), peeled, deveined, and
    butterflied, with tails intact

SERVES 10

❡ Heat half the butter in a large frying pan and sauté the onion over medium heat until translucent with the garlic, chiles, and *epazote*. Add the *cuitlacoche*, season with salt and pepper, and cook for 8 minutes, stirring occasionally. Puree the *cuitlacoche* mixture in a blender, adding a little stock if necessary to thin the sauce. Reserve.
❡ In another large frying pan, heat the remaining butter. Season the shrimp with salt and pepper, and sear over high heat for 30 seconds only on each side. If necessary, cook the shrimp in 2 batches, returning the first batch to the pan before adding the sauce. Add the *cuitlacoche* sauce and simmer over medium heat for 5 minutes.
❡ Serve with rice and *Mousse de Cilantro*.

ESCABECHE DE CAMARONES

PICKLED SHRIMP

This dish from Patricia Prieto can be served either as an appetizer or an hors d'oeuvre. It should be made a day in advance to give the flavors a chance to develop.

For the shrimp (prawns):
¼ onion
2 cloves garlic, peeled

1 teaspoon salt, or to taste
2–3 lb (1–1.5 kg) large shrimp, heads removed but
    unpeeled
For the marinade:
¼ cup (2 fl oz/60 ml) olive oil
2 large onions, cut into thin rings
1 head garlic, cloves separated but unpeeled
4 bay leaves
2 teaspoons fresh marjoram
2 teaspoons fresh thyme
1 teaspoon oregano
15 whole peppercorns
1 tablespoon salt, or to taste
4 cups (1 qt/1 l) water
3 cups (24 fl oz/750 ml) white vinegar
1 teaspoon sugar, or to taste

SERVES 8–12 AS AN APPETIZER

❡ For the shrimp: Bring a pot of water to a boil and add the onion, garlic, and salt. Add the shrimp, and, once the water has returned to a boil, cook for 5 minutes. Drain and peel the shrimp.
❡ To make the marinade: Heat the oil in a large saucepan over low heat and sauté the onion and garlic until translucent, adding the herbs, peppercorns, and salt toward the end.
❡ Add the water and bring to a boil over high heat. Add the vinegar, bring back to a boil, then remove from the heat. Correct the seasonings, adding a little sugar if too acidic.
❡ Add the shrimp to the marinade, allow the mixture to cool, and refrigerate for up to 24 hours before serving.
❡ The shrimp can either be served with or without the marinade.

CEVICHES

Ceviches, raw marinated fish in lime juice, are not unique to Mexico but are also found in other Latin American countries and in the Philippines, where they are thought to have originated. However, the preparation methods do differ: For example, in a typical ceviche of Peru, the fish is marinated at the last minute, whereas in the ceviches of Mexico, the fish is usually allowed to marinate in the lime juice for several hours. This procedure is what "cooks" the fish, turning the flesh opaque. The raw, diced fish is mixed in the lime juice with various other ingredients, usually chopped, fresh tomatoes, onions, green chiles, and dried oregano. A little olive oil is also added. The list of seafoods prepared in this way is endless, but the most popular include mackerel, abalone, conch, and par-boiled octopus.

Top: Shrimp with Corn Fungus; bottom: Pickled Shrimp

CAMARONES CON CHILES JALAPEÑOS, CILANTRO, Y CEBOLLA

SHRIMP BAKED WITH JALAPEÑO CHILES, CILANTRO, AND ONIONS

The juices from the different ingredients produce a delicious combination of flavors in this recipe from Tinina Velasquez. It should be served hot, either as an appetizer or main course.

5 tablespoons olive oil
3 lb (1.5 kg) medium shrimp (prawns), washed and peeled with the tails intact
salt, to taste
2 medium onions, cut into wedges
3½ oz (100 g) canned jalapeño chile strips, drained
2 oz (60 g) cilantro (fresh coriander), chopped

SERVES 8

❡ Preheat the oven to 350°F (180°C/Gas 4).
❡ In a 10- x 14-inch (25- x 35-cm) baking dish, make 2 layers of each ingredient in the following order: olive oil, shrimp, salt, onion, chiles, and cilantro.
❡ Bake in the oven for 20 to 25 minutes, or until the shrimp are cooked through. Serve.

CAMARONES CON PEREJIL FRITO

SHRIMP WITH DEEP-FRIED PARSLEY

This is one of the signature dishes of the prestigious El Estoril restaurant in Mexico City. Chef Pedro Ortega Martinez introduced the technique of deep-frying parsley years ago in Mexico. Since then, deep-frying all kinds of herbs has become very popular.

For the shrimp (prawns):
⅔ cup (5 fl oz/155 ml) olive oil
30 large shrimp, peeled, cleaned, and dried
6 small serrano chiles, minced (finely chopped)
2 onions, minced (finely chopped)
6 cloves garlic, minced (finely chopped)
15 leaves epazote, minced (finely chopped), optional
juice of 3 limes or lemons, or to taste
For the parsley:
8 cups (2 qt/2 l) vegetable oil
6 cups (6 oz/185 g) parsley sprigs, leaves and fine stems only, well-dried and loosely packed
½ teaspoon salt, or to taste
lime juice, to taste

SERVES 6 AS AN APPETIZER

❡ For the shrimp: Divide the oil between 2 large frying pans and heat. Add half the shrimp to each pan and cook over medium heat for 3 minutes. Add half the chiles, onion, and garlic to each pan and cook for 1 minute. Season with

Top: Shrimp Baked with Jalapeño Chiles, Cilantro, and Onions; bottom: Shrimp with Deep-fried Parsley

the *epazote* and lime juice. Keep warm.

❡ For the parsley: Heat the vegetable oil in a deep fryer or deep pan. When hot, add half the parsley to the oil, pushing it down with a wooden spoon so that all of it submerges briefly. Remove from the oil after

7 to 8 seconds, drain on paper towels to remove any excess oil, and sprinkle with the salt and lime juice. Repeat this procedure with the second half.

❡ To serve, mound the parsley in the center of 6 plates, and encircle with the shrimp.

Top: Shrimp Sautéed with Guajillo Chiles and Garlic; bottom: Shrimp in Spicy Red Sauce

CAMARONES AL AJILLO

SHRIMP SAUTÉED WITH GUAJILLO CHILES AND GARLIC

This dish is made on the Veracruz coast with olive oil—because of the influence of Spanish commerce—and on the Pacific coast with vegetable oil. The shrimp (prawns) are boiled briefly before being sautéed, either with or without their shells, with the other ingredients. Be sure to use the large guajillo *chiles (about 4 inches/10 cm long), which are much milder than the small ones.*

2 lb (1 kg) medium shrimp (prawns), heads and tails intact
1 cup (8 fl oz/250 ml) olive oil

12 large cloves garlic, peeled and sliced
10 large guajillo *chiles, cut diagonally into ¼-inch (0.5-cm) slices, and seeded*
½ teaspoon salt, or to taste

SERVES 6

❡ Bring a pot of water to a boil and cook the shrimp for 1 minute until just pink; they should be slightly undercooked. Drain and reserve.

❡ Heat the olive oil over medium heat in a large frying pan. Add the garlic to cook lightly. Add the chiles and shrimp, and brown lightly.

❡ Season with salt and serve in individual earthenware dishes.

❡ For a variation, use small cubes of chicken instead of the shrimp, cooking it the same way.

CAMARONES ADOBADOS

SHRIMP IN SPICY RED SAUCE

This dish from La Cocina Veracruzana *can be made with shrimp (prawns) crayfish, or even scampi (yabbies). Although it may be messy to eat, it is delicious, and the chipotle chiles add fire to the garlic sauce.*

2 large heads garlic, cloves peeled
½ teaspoon salt, or to taste
⅓ cup (3 oz/90 g) butter
4 lb (2 kg) shrimp (prawns), crayfish, or scampi (yabbies)
  with heads

8 oz (250 g) tomatoes
1 can (2 oz/60 g) chipotle *chiles, drained, or to taste*

SERVES 10

❡ Grind the garlic with a little water and salt in a *molcajete* or mortar to make a smooth paste.
❡ Melt the butter in a medium frying pan and fry the shrimp with the garlic paste for 6 minutes, or until the shells change color.
❡ Place the tomatoes in a pot of boiling water for 15 seconds so that the skin peels away easily. Process in a food processor with the chiles.
❡ Pour the sauce over the shrimp and simmer until it thickens. Serve hot with *Arroz Blanco* (see page 148).

DRIED FISH AND SHRIMP

Salt cod, imported from the North Sea, is used for making many Spanish-style dishes, including *bacalao a la vizcaina* and *bacalao a la bilbaina*, or is prepared *a la mexicana*, with tomatoes, onions, and chile. It is traditionally a Christmas dish among the upper classes, although there is a less expensive substitute, salted *cazón* (small-tailed or baby shark), which comes from local waters.

These fish must first be soaked in water overnight to rehydrate them and then rinsed to remove some of their salt content. The meat of the fish is then shredded.

Different kinds of fish are dried in Mexico, from the minnow-like *charrales*, to salt- and freshwater *mojarra*, *jurel* (covally), *pámpano* (pompano), and sunfish. Many of these fish are flattish in form, which makes them easy to dry.

During the Second World War, drying techniques were refined by contact with the Chinese in the Pacific state of Nayarit. Experts in the ancient art of drying fish, the Chinese represent a huge market, and during the war, when sources closer to home ceased, Mexico became a new source of dried fish. The ensuing commerce was concentrated on the island of Mezcaltitlán, just off the coast. The area specializes in many preparations of dried fish as well as dried shrimp (prawns), including the local dried shrimp *tostadas*. (One of the varieties of fish in the area suitable for drying is the white fish of Nayarit, not to be confused with the smaller, more delicate white fish of Lake Pátzcuaro.)

Dried shrimp of all sizes are common in Mexico. They lend their rich flavor to many shrimp stocks and soups. A typical dried stock is made with dried chile and contains small cubes of potatoes. This is served piping hot in little cups as a *botana* ("little bite") with drinks in *cantinas*, popular Mexican bars, or at home at a party. The *tortitas de camarón* (dried shrimp patties), which form part of the festive dish known as *revoltijo*, are another favorite use for dried shrimp. The patties swim in a rich *mole* with cooked *romeritos*, a vegetable that looks similar to rosemary.

Although very small dried shrimp can be left whole, the head and tiny legs are usually removed and the skin is peeled off.

1. salt cod; 2. dried shrimp; 3. charrales and charralitos (dried small and very small fish/minnows); 4. dried mojarra; 5. dried white fish from Nayarit

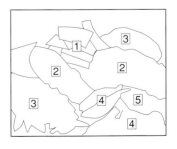

TRUCHA CON SALSA MEXIQUENSE EN HOJA DE TAMAL

TROUT TAMALES WITH MEXIQUENSE SAUCE

Trout is often prepared wrapped in a corn husk like a tamal and (broiled) grilled. In this recipe from Alejandro Heredia, the chef of the famous and beautiful Hacienda de los Morales Restaurant in Mexico City, the trout is stuffed with cheese and bathed in a Mexican tomato sauce

made with hot arbol chiles, before being wrapped in the corn husk. The result is a tasty and unusual fish tamal.

For the sauce:

4 arbol chiles, stems removed, or to taste

1½ lb (750 g) tomatoes, roasted on a comal *or cast-iron griddle*

4 cloves garlic, peeled and lightly charred

1 onion, thickly sliced and charred on a comal

⅓ cup (3 fl oz/90 ml) vegetable oil

¾ teaspoon salt, or to taste

Top: Trout Tamales with Mexiquense Sauce; bottom: Baby Eel, Abalone, and Shrimp Ceviche

For the fish:

6 trout fillets (10 oz/315 g each)

juice of 3 limes or lemons

salt and black pepper, or to taste

2 oz (60 g) Chihuahua or Oaxaca cheese, shredded

6 large dried corn husks, cleaned, soaked in hot water, drained, and dried with paper towels

SERVES 6

❡ To make the sauce: Boil the chiles in a small saucepan with a little water until tender. Combine

the chiles and their water with the tomatoes, garlic, and onion in a blender, and puree until smooth. Heat the oil in a separate saucepan and add the chile mixture. Cook, stirring, over medium heat for 15 minutes and season with the salt.

❡ For the fish: Preheat the oven to 325°F (170°C/Gas 3). Sprinkle the trout with the lime juice and salt and pepper, and rest for 5 minutes.

❡ Stuff the trout with the cheese. Lay a husk on a flat surface and place 3 tablespoons of sauce on it. Top with a trout and add 3 tablespoons of sauce. Bring the sides of the husk together and fold the tip downward. Repeat with the remaining trout and bake in a pan for approximately 30 minutes.

❡ Remove from the oven and serve with the husks opened but not removed.

CEVICHE DE ANGULAS, ABULON, Y CAMARONES

BABY EEL, ABALONE, AND SHRIMP CEVICHE

This is a different, sophisticated, and easy-to-prepare version of the popular ceviche from Patricia Elías Calles. Serve it as an appetizer to Cecina Flameada (see page 182) or Filete al Horno con Hongos Silvestres (see page 184).

3 cups (24 fl oz/750 ml) water

1 onion

2 cloves garlic

¾ teaspoon salt, or to taste

10 oz (315 g) whole baby shrimp (school prawns)

1 can (14 oz/440 g) abalone, diced or thinly sliced

3 cups (24 oz/750 g) seeded tomatoes, chopped

2 tablespoons minced (finely chopped) cilantro (fresh coriander)

2 onions, minced (finely chopped)

3 tablespoons canned jalapeño chile strips

1 tablespoon Worcestershire sauce

juice of 3 limes or lemons

1 tablespoon vinegar from canned jalapeños, or white or cider vinegar, or to taste

1 can (4 oz/125 g) baby eels in oil

SERVES 10 AS AN APPETIZER

❡ Put the water, onion, garlic, and salt in a saucepan over high heat. When the water boils, add the shrimp and cook for 2 minutes, or until they change color. Drain the shrimp, discarding the cooking liquid, peel, and cut into ½-inch (1-cm) pieces.

❡ Carefully mix the shrimp together with all of the remaining ingredients in a large glass bowl.

❡ Refrigerate for 2 hours before serving.

PESCADO CENTLI

FISH FILLETS SERVED IN CORN HUSKS

Centli is the Nahuatl word for fresh corn, one of the ingredients in the sauce. This is a modern creation from Roberto Santibañez, the chef of La Circunstancia Restaurant. The fish is steamed and served in a boat-shaped open husk unlike a traditional tamal which would be served closed.

10 dried corn husks
2¾ lb (1.4 kg) red snapper, sea bass, or sole fillets
salt and pepper, to taste
10 serrano chiles
10 small sprigs cilantro (fresh coriander)
For the sauce:
¼ cup (2 oz/60 g) butter
3 poblano chiles, charred, peeled, seeded, and cut
*   into strips*
¼ teaspoon powdered saffron
2 cups (16 oz/500 g) cooked fresh corn kernels
1 cup (8 fl oz/250 ml) heavy (double/thickened) cream
2 cups (16 fl oz/500 ml) fish, vegetable, or degreased
*   chicken stock*
1 tablespoon cornstarch (cornflour) diluted in
*   2 tablespoons cold water*

SERVES 10

❧ Soak the corn husks in hot water for 10 minutes, then drain. Cut the fish fillets into 10 serving pieces. If they are thin, as in the case of sole, roll them up. Season with salt and pepper on both sides. Place a piece of fish in the center of each husk and top with a *serrano* chile and cilantro sprig. Close the husk by bringing the sides together, folding up the bottom, and bringing down the top.

❧ Bring water to a boil in the bottom of a *tamalera* or steamer and stand the packages upright (with tips pointing up) in the steamer basket, packing them close together. Steam for 10 to 15 minutes, or until the fish is cooked through.

❧ For the sauce: Melt the butter in a saucepan over medium heat and sauté the *poblano* chiles for 1 to 2 minutes. Add the saffron, corn kernels, cream, and stock, and bring to a boil. Simmer for 10 minutes, or until the consistency is that of a thin sauce. Whisk the cornstarch mixture into the sauce until it thickens, and season with salt and pepper.

❧ Remove the fish from the oven and open the husks over the saucepan, letting the juices run into the sauce. Discard the *serrano* chiles and cilantro and place each open package on a dinner plate.

❧ Pour generous amounts of the sauce over the top of each package and serve.

ATÚN TIPO BACALAO

BACALAO-STYLE TUNA FISH

This easy-to-prepare and delicious dish bears some resemblance to the well-known bacalao a la vizcaína, the Basque dried salt-cod dish. In this version, devised by Miranda Quijano, the traditional fish has been substituted with canned tuna—something that can be found in almost everyone's kitchen the world throughout. While the taste may be different, it is every bit as good.

3 tablespoons olive oil
2 onions, chopped
2 cloves garlic, minced (finely chopped)
15 oz (450 g) tomatoes, seeded and minced (finely chopped)
2 teaspoons Worcestershire sauce
2 teaspoons Maggi sauce (or substitute any bottled liquid
*   flavor enhancer)*
dash of Angostura bitters
½ cup (2 oz/60 g) green bell pepper (capsicum), cut
*   into strips*
½ cup (2 oz/60 g) red bell pepper (capsicum), cut
*   into strips*
2 cans (6 oz/185 g) tuna in brine, drained
3½ oz (100 g) plantain or bananas, skinned and cubed
2 tablespoons (1 oz/30 g) raisins
1 oz (30 g) green olives, pitted and sliced
1 oz (30 g) blanched almonds, sliced
½ teaspoon salt, or to taste
1 teaspoon lime or lemon juice
½ cup (4 fl oz/125 ml) tomato juice, optional
4 güeros, banana, Hungarian, or other long yellow
*   chiles, canned*

SERVES 4–6

❧ Heat the oil in a casserole over medium heat and sauté the onion and garlic until translucent. Add the tomatoes, Worcestershire sauce, Maggi sauce, and Angostura bitters and simmer, stirring occasionally, for approximately 10 minutes, or until slightly thickened.

❧ Add the green and red bell pepper strips and cook them until soft, approximately 10 minutes. Add the tuna to the casserole and blend into the mixture.

❧ Add the plantains and cook for approximately 10 minutes, or until they become translucent.

❧ Add the raisins, olives, almonds, salt, and lime juice. Stir to mix and simmer until the flavors combine, approximately 5 minutes. If the dish is too dry, you can add some tomato juice.

❧ Serve the fish on a large platter, garnished with the chiles and, as a foil to its richness, plain steamed rice.

Front left: Fish Fillets Served in Corn Husks; back right: Bacalao-style Tuna Fish

FISH

Huachinango (red snapper) and *róbalo* (snook) from the Gulf of Mexico are probably the most esteemed fish in Mexico. Red snapper is fine-textured and white with a reddish tint toward the center line of the raw fillet. The size ranges from about 8 to 30 inches (20 to 75 cm) long. Small red snapper are cooked whole, often broiled (grilled), while the large ones are usually sliced into thick or thin fillets or steaks. Large ones may also be baked whole, as in Veracruz-style red snapper, or may be added to many of Mexico's fish soups. In the Yucatán, the fish is butterflied, marinated in the characteristic *achiote* (annatto) seed paste and spice mixture, blended with bitter orange juice, and grilled over an open fire for *pescado en tikin xic.*

content. Snook is commonly about 18 inches (45 cm) long, but the white variety can reach up to 4 feet (120 cm).

An interesting dish from the state of Tabasco is *mone de robalo*. A thick piece of snook fillet is baked wrapped in a banana leaf with tomato, onion, fresh chile, plantains, and the herb *hoja santa*. The combination of the anise-flavored herb and the sweetness of the plantain, along with the subtle flavors of the fish and the banana leaf it is cooked in, is truly intriguing. Robalo or pike would make good substitutes if snook is not available.

The flesh of *cazón* (small-tailed or baby shark) is white and firm, easily recognized by the white sinews that make it appear striped. It is popular in the Yucatán, Chiapas, and Campeche, where the meat is usually simmered in water and then shredded before being sautéed with a variety of seasonings (see *Zaragalla de Cazón* page 210). It is also made into meatballs for *albóndigas de cazón* and shredded into *panuchos*, typical of the southeast. These are small, fried, and puffed-up *tortillas* stuffed with black beans. Baby shark fillets are also prepared with a bitter orange and *achiote* seasoning paste, baked layered with tomatoes, green bell peppers (capsicum), and onions for *pan de cazón*.

The *mero* (red grouper or groper), a large fish weighing up to 40 pounds (20 kg), is caught and sold all over Mexico. Although the texture of the cooked meat is not as fine as that of red snapper, it is firm, white, and abundant, and the lower price makes it a popular substitute.

Pámpano (pompano) is a very flat, yellow-gray fish that is rather spiny but very popular. It is often baked whole in "paper" (*en papelado*), or more commonly today, in aluminum foil. Its small size is perfect for individual portions. Whole or in fillets, it may also be brushed with oil and broiled.

Blanco de pátzcuaro (white fish) are thin, small fish, about 6 inches (15 cm) long, from Lake Pátzcuaro of Michoacán; they have an almost translucent white skin when raw. They are excellent dipped into a well-beaten, light egg batter, fried, and served with a fresh sauce of chopped tomato, onion, and *serrano* chiles.

Sierra (mackerel) is long and thin, ranging from 12 to 24 inches (30 to 60 cm) in length. Its silvery skin has no scales and the meat is dark and oily. It is excellent for smoking and is often made into *ceviche* (raw fish marinated in lime juice).

1. sierra (mackerel); 2. mero (red grouper); 3. pámpano (pompano); 4. huachinango (red snapper); 5. cazón (small-tail or baby shark); 6. robalo (snook); 7. blanco de pátzcuaro (white fish from Lake Pátzcuaro)

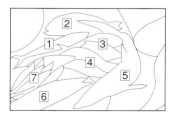

Of the two varieties of snook available from the Gulf of Mexico, the *robalo blanco* (white snook) has finer, whiter, and less fatty meat than the *robalo negro* (black snook). The flesh of both is very firm and tasty and is cut into steaks as well as fillets. Although snook lends itself to many fine preparations, it is particularly good for broiling, because of its fat

ZARAGALLA DE CAZÓN

SHARK WITH TOMATO AND HERBS

Zaragalla *means, literally, "tiny pieces of charcoal," and it is perhaps the fine shreds of shark meat in this dish that suggest the name. Despite the long list of ingredients, this recipe is surprisingly simple to prepare, especially if you do all the roasting and chopping while the shark is cooking. A specialty of northern Veracruz, this version from Guille Lárraga features a mixture of herbs, vegetables, jalapeño chiles, and the distinctive flavor of the small-tailed shark (dogfish/flake).*

½ medium onion, in 1 piece
1 clove garlic, peeled
1½ teaspoons salt, or to taste
2 lb (1 kg) shark (dogfish/flake) fillets or other firm-
    fleshed fish such as halibut, or cooked and mashed
    shrimp (prawns), or cooked blue crab meat
2 cloves garlic, unpeeled
10 whole peppercorns
¼ teaspoon cumin seeds
1 cinnamon stick (1 inch/2.5 cm) long
½ teaspoon coriander seeds
½ bay leaf
½ teaspoon fresh thyme
½ teaspoon fresh marjoram
¼ teaspoon dried oregano
3 tablespoons vinegar from a can of jalapeño chiles, or
    chile-flavored white vinegar
⅓ cup (3 fl oz/90 ml) vegetable oil
1½ lb (750 g) tomatoes, seeded and chopped
3 onions, chopped
3 tablespoons pitted and chopped green olives
3 tablespoons large capers, chopped
3 tablespoons raisins
20 blanched almonds, chopped
2 tablespoons canned jalapeño chiles, chopped
2 teaspoons salt, or to taste
½ teaspoon sugar
3 dashes Worcestershire sauce

SERVES 8–10

❧ Fill a large saucepan with enough water to cover the fillets and bring it to a boil with the onion, garlic, and salt. Add the fillets and cook over high heat for 30 minutes or until tender. Drain and finely shred the fish.

❧ In a small frying pan over medium heat, dry roast the garlic cloves until they are charred on all sides. Remove and peel. Dry roast the peppercorns, cumin, cinnamon, and coriander, shaking the pan, until the aromas are released. Remove from pan and reserve.

❧ Dry roast the bay leaf, thyme, marjoram, and oregano briefly so as not to burn. Remove from the pan. If you have a *molcajete*, grind together the garlic, spices, herbs, and vinegar. If using a spice grinder, grind only the herbs and spices, then mash them with the reserved charred garlic and vinegar in a small bowl.

❧ Heat the oil in a large casserole. Gently fry the spice mixture for 5 minutes. Add the tomatoes and onions, and cook over medium heat for about 10 minutes, or until the tomato liquid is slightly reduced. Stir in all the remaining ingredients, add the fish, then cook for another 5 minutes.

❧ Serve hot or at room temperature with a basket of warm corn *tortillas*.

CEVICHE VERDE DE BACALAO

GREEN SALT COD CEVICHE

This recipe from Arturo and Lila Lomeli, is an unusual twist on the classic ceviche. *Olives and capers are ingredients associated with Spanish cuisine, but it is not unusual to find them in dishes on the Gulf coast of Mexico where customs were influenced by Spanish trade. The use of basil, however, is very unusual, as in Mexico this herb is mostly reserved for medicinal purposes, often included in a spray of herbs that are brushed against the body of a sick person.*

2 lb (1 kg) tender, good-quality salt cod from the thick
    part of the fillet
2 oz (60 g) fresh parsley, thick stems removed
2 oz (60 g) fresh basil leaves
½ cup (4 fl oz/125 ml) olive oil
10 green olives, pitted
10 capers
2 large cloves garlic
½ cup (4 fl oz/125 ml) dry white wine
freshly ground black pepper, to taste
3 serrano chiles, or to taste

SERVES 10 AS AN APPETIZER

❧ Soak the salt cod in warm water for at least 24 hours to desalt and rehydrate. Rinse and shred the fish, discarding the bones, and place in a bowl; the shreds can be as large or fine as you prefer.

❧ Wash and dry the herbs and puree them in a blender or a *molcajete* with all the remaining ingredients until well mixed.

❧ Toss the mixture with the fish and refrigerate for at least 1 hour before serving, or longer if possible. The flavor will improve over 24 hours if prepared in advance.

Front: Shark with Tomato and Herbs; back: Green Salt Cod Ceviche

DELICIA DE ROBALO AL ACHIOTE

SNOOK AND ACHIOTE DELIGHT

This is a creation of chef Demetrio Colovalles of La Cava Restaurant in the southern part of Mexico City. Achiote (annatto) paste and bitter orange juice, common ingredients in Yucatecan cooking, give this dish its distinct flavor.

2 oz (60 g) achiote (annatto) paste
3 cups (24 fl oz/750 ml) bitter orange juice
6 snook, pike, or robalo fillets (6½ oz/200 g each)
18 shrimp (prawns), shelled and deveined
1½ cups (12 fl oz/375 ml) olive oil
2 onions, minced (finely chopped)
6 cloves garlic, crushed
3 large ripe tomatoes, peeled, seeded, and minced (finely chopped)
6 banana leaf rectangles (8 x 12 inches/20 x 30 cm),
   passed over a flame to soften
10 oz (315 g) fresh mushrooms, thinly sliced

SERVES 6

❡ Mix the *achiote* paste with the orange juice using a spoon or spatula. Marinate the fish fillets and shrimp in the mixture for 2 hours in the refrigerator. Remove the fish and shrimp and reserve the marinade.

❡ Heat the oil in a frying pan and lightly brown the fish and shrimp. Remove the fish and shrimp and set aside. Reheat the oil and fry the onions and garlic until translucent. Add the tomato and cook until creamy. Add the *achiote* marinade and cook until the sauce thickens.

❡ Preheat the oven to 350°F (180°C/Gas 4). Place the banana leaves on a flat surface, shiny side up, and put a spoonful of sauce in the center of each. Top with a fish fillet, the mushrooms, and shrimp. Top with more sauce and wrap the leaves to form little parcels. Place on a cookie sheet (baking tray) and bake for 20 minutes.

❡ Open the leaves, turn the sides under, and serve.

FILETES DE HUACHINANGO CON AJONJOLI EN SALSA DE CHILE CASCABEL

RED SNAPPER FILLETS WITH SESAME SEEDS AND CHILE SAUCE

This elegant dish is a creation of chef Rafael Bautista of Les Moustaches restaurant in Mexico City. Because of the restaurant's location near the embassies and the best hotels of the city, it serves both excellent Mexican and European food.

For the sauce:
1 large red bell pepper (capsicum)
½ onion, cut into 3 pieces
2 cloves garlic, peeled
8 oz (250 g) tomatoes
1½ oz (45 g) cascabel chiles
¾ cup (6 fl oz/185 ml) chicken stock or clam juice
1½ tablespoons vegetable oil
½ cup (4 fl oz/125 ml) heavy (double/thickened) cream
½ teaspoon salt, or to taste
pinch ground white pepper, or to taste
For the fish:
4 fillets (5 oz/155 g each) red snapper or other firm-
   fleshed white fish
½ teaspoon salt, or to taste
pinch ground white pepper, or to taste

Left: Snook and Achiote Delight; right: Red Snapper Fillets with Sesame Seeds and Chile Sauce

½ cup (2 oz/60 g) all-purpose (plain) flour
2 eggs, lightly beaten
½ cup (2½ oz/75 g) sesame seeds
½ cup (4 fl oz/125 ml) vegetable oil

SERVES 4

❡ To make the sauce: Heat a *comal* or cast-iron griddle and roast the pepper all over, until soft. Peel and discard the stem and seeds.

❡ Char the onion, garlic, and tomatoes. Also char the chiles for just a few seconds, being careful not to burn them, and carefully remove the stems and seeds.

❡ Combine the vegetables in a blender with the stock and puree until smooth.

❡ Heat the oil in a saucepan over medium heat and strain the sauce into it. Simmer for about

5 minutes, or until the sauce thickens, stirring occasionally. Add the cream to heat through and season with the salt and pepper. Keep the sauce warm while you prepare the fish.

❡ Sprinkle the fish fillets with the salt and pepper. Coat them with the flour and then dip into the egg. Spread the sesame seeds on a sheet of waxed paper and press one side of the fish onto the seeds.

❡ Heat the oil in a large frying pan and fry the fish on the side without the seeds for approximately 3 minutes. Turn carefully and then fry for a further 2 minutes.

❡ To serve, cover the bottom of 4 dinner plates with the sauce. Place a fillet on top of each, seed side up, and garnish with parsley. Accompany with *Arroz Blanco* (see page 148).

PESCADO MAÑANITAS

RED SNAPPER FILLETS, MAÑANITAS-STYLE

This recipe is a modern creation from the kitchen of one of the most famous restaurants in Mexico—Las Mañanitas, in Cuernavaca, Morelos. The restaurant has a sumptuous garden dotted with Zuñiga statues and strutting white peacocks. Corn, zucchini (courgettes), epazote, and serrano chiles flavor the creamy sauce for this fish, which is served with a medley of baby carrots, green beans, and new potatoes.

For the fish:
10 red snapper fillets (5 oz/155 g each), cut on the
    diagonal into about ½-inch (1-cm) slices
lime or lemon juice to taste
1 teaspoon salt, or to taste
For the sauce:
4 tablespoons (2 oz/60 g) butter
1 small onion, chopped
3 small zucchini (courgettes), washed and chopped in tiny
    cubes, about the size of corn kernels
kernels from 3 ears of corn
2 sprigs epazote or cilantro (fresh coriander)
2–4 serrano chiles, minced (finely chopped)
1 cup (8 fl oz/250 ml) milk
3 cups (24 fl oz/750 ml) heavy (double/thickened) cream
⅓ cup (3 fl oz/90 ml) white wine
squeeze lime juice
salt and pepper, to taste
4 tablespoons (2 oz/60 g) butter
serrano chiles or epazote, minced (finely chopped),
    for garnish

SERVES 10

❡ Sprinkle the fish with the lime juice and salt, and set aside.
❡ To make the sauce: Heat the butter in a large saucepan and sauté the onion until translucent. Add the zucchini, corn, *epazote*, and chiles, stirring for a few minutes.
❡ Add the milk and 1 cup (8 fl oz/250 ml) of the cream, and simmer until all the vegetables are tender.
❡ Add the remaining cream, and simmer until reduced and thickened to a sauce-like consistency.
❡ Season with the wine, lime juice, and salt and pepper. Keep warm and remove the *epazote* sprigs before serving.
❡ Melt the remaining 4 tablespoons of butter in a frying pan over medium heat and cook the fish about 3 minutes on each side or until done.
❡ Serve with the warm sauce and garnish with the reserved unused chiles or *epazote*.

HUACHINANGO EN SALSA DE JÍCAMA Y MANGO

RED SNAPPER WITH MANGO AND JÍCAMA SAUCE

This dish was developed by Roberto Santibañez, whose La Circunstancia Restaurant in Mexico City is located on Garibaldi Square—a gathering place for mariachis (Mexican musicians). In contrast to the traditional surroundings, Roberto offers a new Mexican cuisine which combines Mexican, and often foreign, ingredients in an untraditional way. This is one of his latest creations.

For the sauce:
2 tablespoons (1 oz/30 g) butter
1 small onion, minced (finely chopped)
1 clove garlic, minced (finely chopped)
2 large carrots (7 oz/220 g), peeled and cut into ¼-inch
    (0.5-cm) dice
1 small jícama (7 oz/220 g), peeled and cut into ¼-inch
    (0.5-cm) dice, or substitute water chestnuts
1 large green mango, peeled, seeded, and cut into
    ¼-inch (0.5-cm) dice
2 jalapeño chiles, seeded and cut into ¼-inch
    (0.5-cm) dice
½ cup (½ oz/15 g) loosely packed cilantro (fresh
    coriander) sprigs, washed and chopped
1 bay leaf
½ cup (4 fl oz/125 ml) dark mango chutney
salt and pepper, to taste
For the fish:
2½ lb (1.25 kg) red snapper or other firm white-fleshed
    fish fillets, cut in 8 thick slices
salt and pepper, to taste
1–2 tablespoons vegetable oil

SERVES 8

❡ For the sauce: Heat the butter in a large frying pan. Add the onion, garlic, and carrots, and sauté over medium heat for 2 to 3 minutes.
❡ Add the *jícama*, mango, chiles, and cilantro, lower the heat, and sauté for approximately 3 to 4 minutes, or until the ingredients are tender but still crisp. Add the bay leaf, chutney, and the salt and pepper, and simmer gently while searing the fish.
❡ To prepare the fish: Season the fillets with salt and pepper. Heat the oil in large frying pan over a very hot flame, and sear the fish rapidly, about 1 minute at most on each side.
❡ Transfer the fish to the pan with the sauce and cook over low heat, about 5 minutes. If the sauce becomes too thick, add a little water to thin.
❡ Serve with *Arroz Blanco* (see page 148).

Top: Red Snapper Fillets, Mañanitas-style; bottom: Red Snapper with Mango and Jicama Sauce

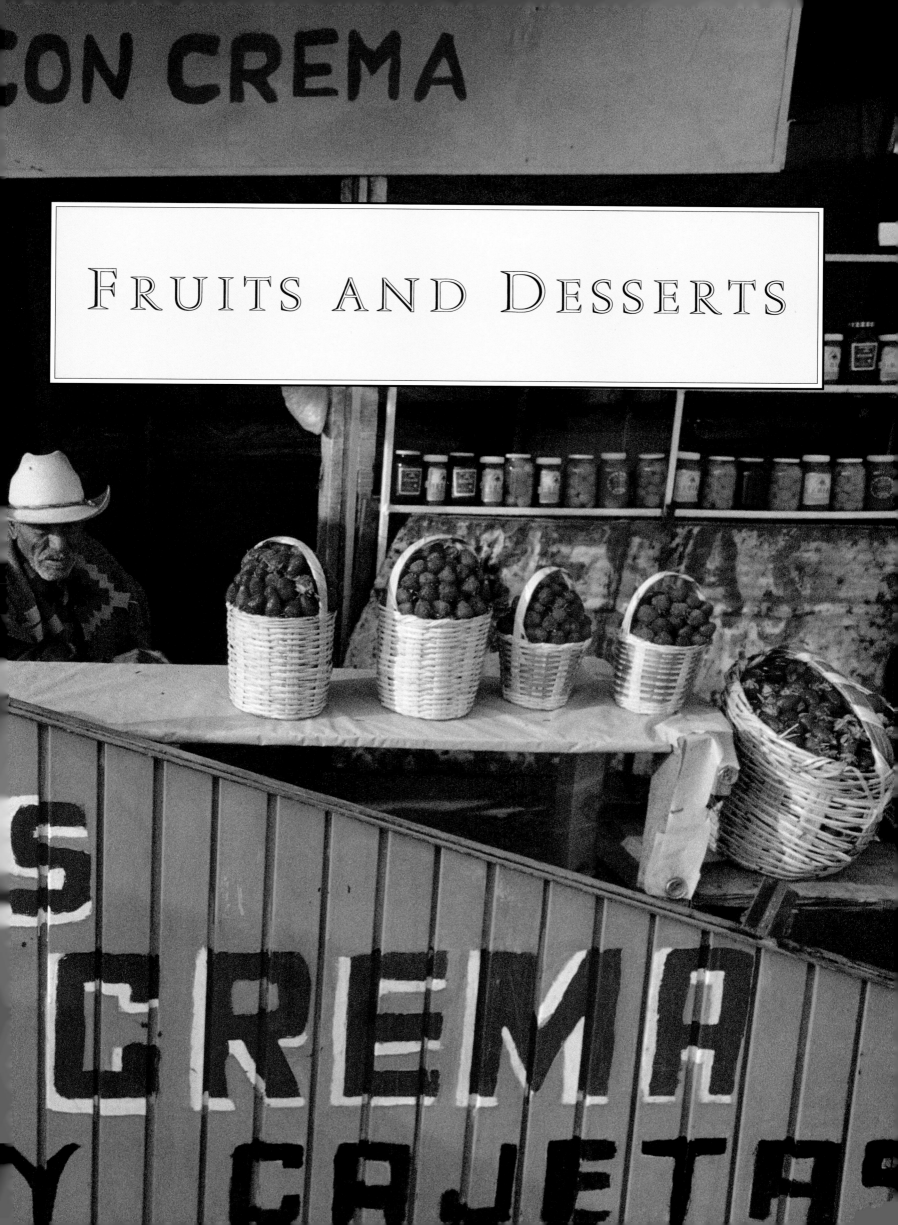

Fruits and Desserts

FRUITS AND DESSERTS

THAT MEXICANS HAVE A VERY SWEET TOOTH IS EVIDENT NOT ONLY IN THE ARRAY OF DESSERTS OR TROPICAL fruits that might end a meal, but also in the dizzying variety of sweets that can be eaten at any time of day. ❧ Not only does the country grow practically every fruit known to the world, but most of them are available the whole year through. Those most appropriate for dessert are the sweetest: mango, mamey, *chico zapote* (sapodilla), *chirimoya* (cherimoya/custard apple), or *granada china* (Chinese granadilla) from the passionfruit family, to mention a few. Other fresh fruits such as strawberries and bananas may be served with heavy (double/thickened) cream and sugar, while still others—guavas, peaches, or *tejocotes* (a fruit resembling a crabapple)—will be stewed whole in delicious syrups flavored with cinnamon, orange, or molasses. *Ates*, or fruit pastes of quince, apple, or guava, may be eaten alone or with slices of mild cheese, whether *panela*, *Manchego*-style, or *Chihuahua*. ❧ Gelatins are also a popular dessert, varying from a simple, fruit-flavored gelatin made with water, to a complicated production made in layers, some prepared with milk, *rompope* (an egg yolk-based liqueur), *cajeta* (burnt milk), or other liqueurs, and decorated with diced fruits, nuts, and raisins. ❧ Eating ice cream is an old custom in Mexico, and

Previous pages: Strawberries with cream provide a fresh counterpoint to rows of preserves at a roadside stall near Irapuato in the state of Guanajuato.

Opposite: Mexicans have a pronounced sweet tooth, satisfied by market offerings such as this array seen in the cloisters of Toluca, just south of Mexico City.

legend has it that during the centuries of the viceroy, ice cream and sherbets (sorbets)—called *nieves*, or snows—were prepared in the larger cities from ice brought down by mule from the peaks of the volcanoes. In addition to the flavors known to the rest of the world, Mexico prides itself on creams and ices made from indigenous fruits, such as guanábana (soursop), coconuts, guavas, mameys, mangoes, *tunas* (prickly pear fruit), and even sweet-corn. ❧ Many European-style desserts have been adopted in the last few centuries and transformed into uniquely Mexican creations with the addition of native fruits and seasonings, whether meringue, trifle, pastry cream, or cake based. Flan and rice pudding flavored with cinnamon are local favorites. ❧ The Mexican influence has also been exerted over the many sweets and candies prepared originally in the kitchens of the convents that were built in Mexico immediately following the conquest. Many of the techniques were of Arab origin, adopted by the Spanish over generations and brought to Mexico along with sugar cane. In time, each region—and, indeed, each town—in Mexico developed its own particular specialities, from the fine almond-paste sweets from Saltillo, in Coahuila, to the *borrachitos* (tequila jellies) from Guadalajara and the almond pastries filled with coconut from Durango. Crystallized strawberries are a specialty of Irapuato, in Guanajuato, and *camotes* (yam-based fruit pastes) are found in Puebla. In the central square of Toluca, under the *portales* (stone arches lining the square), a huge array of sweets is displayed in little baskets, while in the city of Puebla, a whole street is dedicated to sweet shops.

Left: Sapodilla and Almond Dessert; right: Mexican Trifle

ANTE DE CHICO ZAPOTE Y ALMENDRAS

SAPODILLA AND ALMOND DESSERT

Sapodilla, or chico zapote, *is the fruit of a tree called* chick *by the Aztecs. The tree's sap is known as* chicle *and is the basic ingredient of chewing gum.*

For the ladyfingers:
5 eggs, separated
¾ cup (6 oz/185 g) sugar
1 teaspoon vanilla extract
1 cup (8 oz/250 g) all-purpose (plain) flour
½ cup (3½ oz/100 g) confectioners' (icing) sugar
For the almond mixture:
½ cup (2 oz/60 g) whole, blanched almonds
¾ cup (6 oz/185 g) sugar
½ cup (4 fl oz/125 ml) water
2 lb (1 kg) sapodilla, or substitute mangoes, poached apricots
*   or peaches, peeled, seeded, and slightly pureed or mashed*
For the syrup:
1 cup (8 fl oz/250 ml) water
¾ cup (6 oz/185 g) sugar
½ cup (4 fl oz/125 ml) dry sherry
¼ cup (1 oz/30 g) toasted almonds

SERVES 10

❡ To make the ladyfingers: Preheat the oven to 325°F (170°C/Gas 3). Grease and flour 2 cookie sheets (baking trays). Beat the egg yolks and all

but 2 tablespoons of the sugar together until light in color and increased in volume. Add the vanilla. Sift the flour and fold into the yolk mixture.

❡ Beat the egg whites, adding the remaining 2 tablespoons of sugar gradually, until stiff peaks form, and fold into the yolk mixture. Put the mixture into a pastry bag fitted with a ½-inch (1-cm) nozzle. Squeeze 30 fingers of the mixture onto the cookie sheets, and dust with confectioners' sugar.

❡ Bake for 15 to 20 minutes in the upper part of the oven. Cool on a cake rack.

❡ To make the almond mixture: Grind the almonds and 2 tablespoons of the sugar in a food processor.

❡ In a saucepan, cook the remaining sugar and the water over medium heat for about 5 minutes to make a light syrup. Add the ground almonds and sapodilla, then cook, stirring constantly, to prevent sticking, until the mixture is the consistency of a thick puree. Remove from the heat and cool.

❡ To make the syrup: Combine the water and sugar in a saucepan and cook over medium heat for 5 minutes to make a light syrup. Let cool, then stir in the sherry.

❡ Dip the ladyfingers in the syrup one by one. Place half of them in a round 9- x 1½-inch (23- x 4-cm) serving dish, top with half the almond mixture, then place the remaining ladyfingers over the filling. Top with the remaining almond mixture.

❡ Decorate with the toasted almonds, and serve.

❡ Individual desserts can be assembled in 10 small sweet bowls by dividing the ladyfingers and almond mixtures equally among them.

ANTE DE YEMAS

MEXICAN TRIFLE

The European tradition of antes, *or trifle, came to Mexico in the nineteenth century. Recipe books and manuscripts from that era describe* antes *as a type of bread soaked in wine and layered with* natillas *(milk custard), fruit, or nuts. In this dish the candied* acitrón *is made from cactus, which is a typically Mexican touch.*

For the pastry cream:
1 cup (8 fl oz/250 ml) milk
3 egg yolks
½ cup (4 oz/125 g) sugar
3 tablespoons (1½ oz/45 g) cornstarch (cornflour)
1 tablespoon (½ oz/15 g) butter
1 teaspoon vanilla extract
For the syrup:
1 cup (8 fl oz/250 ml) water
¾ cup (6 oz/185 g) sugar
½ cup (4 fl oz/125 ml) dry sherry
30 ladyfingers (see Ante de Chico Zapote y Almendras *page 220)*
⅔ cup (3 oz/90 g) pine nuts

¾ cup (3 oz/90 g) acitrón *(crystallized* biznaga *cactus) or candied orange peel or pineapple, cut in ¼-inch (0.5 cm) squares*

SERVES 10

❡ To make the pastry cream: Heat the milk in a small saucepan over low heat. In a small bowl, beat the egg yolks with the sugar until thick. Mix in the cornstarch and slowly stir in the milk.

❡ Pour the mixture into a clean saucepan and cook over low heat, stirring constantly with a wooden spoon until the mixture comes to a boil and thickens (the lumps will smooth out as you stir). Remove the pan from the heat and add the butter and vanilla, blending until the butter has melted. Cover with plastic wrap until the mixture cools.

❡ To make the syrup: Bring the water and sugar to a boil and simmer for 5 minutes. Let cool, then stir in the sherry.

❡ Dip the ladyfingers in the syrup one by one. Layer half of them in a round 9- x 1½-inch (23- x 4-cm) serving dish and top with half the pastry cream. Sprinkle with half the pine nuts and *acitrón*. Repeat the layering with the remaining ingredients and serve.

Left: mango de manila; right: petacón or mango de oro

MANGOES

Originally from the Indo-Burmese region, mangoes grow abundantly in Mexico and are one of the most appreciated tropical fruits. Around April, trees laden with green mangoes can be seen along the roadside near Oaxaca, Veracruz, and further south. As they ripen, they are sold in great quantities, their season lasting through the rains to October or even November.

Many methods have been devised for eating mangoes, but one invariably gets covered with their sweet, sticky juice. In Mexico, they are lodged on a stick like a lollypop, peeled with the flesh decoratively carved like open petals, and sprinkled with lime and chile. Alternatively, the sides may be cut off the flat center pit, and the flesh scored to the skin and turned inside out, so juicy squares of mango flesh stand out, easy to eat. Genteel hosts often supply their guests with special mango forks.

There are several varieties available in Mexico. The *mango de manila*, which is yellow and medium sized at 5 inches (12 cm) long with a meaty but not fibrous flesh, has a wonderfully seductive smell. The *niño* (child) is a baby *manila* measuring about 3 inches (8 cm) long. Some argue that the *ataulfo* is the best; it is very similar in looks and taste to the *manila*. The large red to red-green variety is called *petacón* or *mango de oro* (golden mango). It is considerably less expensive than the *manila* and more fibrous, but it also has its supporters for the firmness of its flesh, which will not disintegrate into a puree.

When ripe, mangoes give slightly to the touch and should not have any black spots.

PASTEL DE ALMENDRAS

ALMOND CAKE

This delicious dessert from Toya Santos is reminiscent of the egg-based marzipans of Spain. If the almonds are not flavorful enough, add two or three drops of a top-quality almond extract along with the butter.

1 cup (8 oz/250 g) plus 1 tablespoon sugar
2 cups (8 oz/250 g) blanched almonds
4 eggs
½ cup (4 oz/125 g) plus 1 tablespoon (½ oz/15 g)
   butter, softened
⅓ cup (3 oz/90 g) apricot jam
3 tablespoons sliced, toasted almonds

SERVES 8

❡ Preheat the oven to 350°F (180°C/Gas 4).
❡ Reserve 3 tablespoons of sugar. Process the remaining sugar and almonds in a food processor until well ground and paste-like.
❡ With the motor still running, add the eggs one by one. Add the ½ cup of butter, scraping down the bowl when necessary. Process until thoroughly blended and smooth.
❡ Butter a 9-inch (24-cm) spring-form cake pan with the reserved tablespoon of butter. Pour the batter into the pan, and sprinkle the reserved sugar over the top.
❡ Bake for 35 minutes, or until a cake tester inserted in the center comes out clean.
❡ Let the cake cool on a wire rack for 10 minutes before unmolding. Remove the sides of the pan and transfer the cake carefully, using 2 spatulas, to a serving plate.
❡ To decorate, spread the apricot jam around the top edges of the cake and sprinkle with the sliced almonds so they stick to the jam.
❡ Slice and serve.

SOME PRE-HISPANIC FRUITS

When the Spanish conquerers explored the markets of the New World, they mentioned cherries as one of the many fruits they recognized. They were actually referring to capulines, *a kind of wild cherry that is much smaller than the European variety, with a large pit and an almost black, purplish-red color. These are still enjoyed today during their short season in late summer and early fall. Capulines are excellent for making jams, and are offered in the marketplace in areas where they grow in the central plateau as a* tamal *filling; they're cooked whole, seeds and all, with sugar to sweeten them. Another native fruit still found in the marketplace today but little known elsewhere is the* tejocote (Crataegus mexicana). *Although it is described as being like a crabapple because of its size, it belongs to another family altogether and has a large pit, instead of the seed pockets characteristic of the apple family. Its thin skin is a bright orange, while the flesh is yellowish with a texture between that of an apple and an underripe apricot. Tejocotes, one of the traditional fruits for stuffing a* piñata, *are eaten raw, or stewed, whole, in a flavored syrup for dessert.*

BUDÍN DE PIÑONES

PINE NUT CAKE

Pinenuts, although very expensive in Mexico, are frequently used both in desserts and meat fillings. The pink variety is the most common.

2 large eggs
1 can (14 oz/440 g) sweetened condensed milk
1¼ cups (5 oz/155 g) pine nuts
Confectioners' (icing) sugar, for dusting

SERVES 10

❡ Preheat the oven to 350°F (180°C/Gas 4).
❡ Put all the ingredients in a blender and blend, stopping to scrape the pine nuts off the sides of the blender as needed, until completely smooth.
❡ Butter a round 9-inch (24-cm) cake pan, place a wax-paper round on the bottom of the pan. Butter again and flour lightly.
❡ Pour the mixture into the pan and bake for 50 minutes, or until a cake tester inserted into the center comes out clean. Cool on a wire rack for 10 minutes, then unmold the cake, bottom-side up.
❡ Sprinkle with confectioners' sugar before serving.

Left: Almond Cake; right: Pine Nut Cake

EXOTIC FRUITS

Guanábana (soursop) and chirimoya (cherimoya/custard apple): These tropical fruits are both from the custard apple family. Soursop is the largest of the group, ranging in weight from 1 to 8 lb (0.5 to 4 kg). Its tough, green skin is more spiny than scaly, unlike the heart-shaped cherimoya, but they both have a perfumed, white flesh enclosing black seeds. Collectively, they are known as custard apples and are native to the American tropics. The seeds are removed from the flesh by hand, a time-consuming job but well worth it for the enjoyable flavor of the succulent, white flesh.

Soursop is used more often than cherimoya to make *nieves* (sorbets), *aguas frescas* (fresh fruit drinks), or pureed desserts. Some sherbets (sorbets) contain the seeds, and although the seeds are not eaten, the flesh clinging to them is satisfyingly chewy.

A ripe soursop or cherimoya should be soft all over and the skin should still be green rather than black. If overripe, the skin will be blackish and the flesh near the skin will have turned brown in spots and feel grainy. Don't use overripe fruit as you will find that your preparation will change color, oxidizing like a cut apple.

To prepare them, cut the fruit in half horizontally and pull out the tough heart. Scoop the flesh and seeds out of the skin (discard any brown or hard pieces), and squeeze the seeds out of the flesh (like skinning almonds).

Durazno (peach): The peach commonly found in temperate zones in Mexico is small and firm with a yellow-orange skin. It is eaten as a fruit and makes an excellent jelly (jam).

Granada (pomegranate): An ancient fruit of Asian origin, the pomegranate was brought to Mexico by the Spanish. The fleshy, red seeds are especially valued by cooks on Mexican Independence Day when they decorate the famous dish *Chiles en Nogada* (see page 114), which represents the three colors of the Mexican flag (green, white, and red). The stuffed, green *poblano* chiles are covered with a white sauce made from fresh walnuts. The pomegranate seeds provide the red color, as well as a bitter sweetness that balances the flavors of the dish.

Granada china (Chinese granadilla): While the granadilla is from the passion-vine family, originally from Brazil, it is sometimes confused with yellow passionfruit, which has a thinner skin and a stronger, markedly sour taste. The Chinese granadilla (actually one of several fruits referred to by the name of granadilla) has a smooth, yellow-orange skin covering a layer of white flesh that, in turn, encloses a host of slippery seeds, mildly sweet to the taste. It has a long, thick stem on one end of its egglike shape, which the passionfruit does not have.

While the most civilized way to eat a granadilla is to cut the fruit in half and eat the seeds with a spoon, some people prefer to slurp the seeds out after tearing a piece off the top.

Coco (coconut): Pictured here is a mature brown coconut with the green outer fruit removed. The liquid inside can be extracted by piercing two of the "eyes" with a nail and pouring it out. There will be less of it and the taste more watery than when the coconut is young. To remove the white flesh for eating or shredding, it is helpful to heat the coconut in the oven for about 15 minutes at 325°F (170°C/Gas 3). Then tap it with a hammer to break it open and prize the flesh from the hard shell. The soft, brown "skin" can be scraped or peeled off. To make coconut milk, soak the shredded flesh in about a cup (8 fl oz/250 ml) of warm water and squeeze it in a cloth—the resulting white liquid is coconut milk.

Chico zapote (sapodilla): Native to Mexico and Central America, sapodilla is the fruit of the tropical tree that produces *chicle* sap, used for making chewing gum. The skin is thin and matte brown, and the flesh, also a light brown, is sweet and soft. The fruit's oblong shape varies in size from about 3 to 5 inches (8 to 12 cm) long, and is soft to the touch when ripe. It is eaten peeled and sliced, the seeds removed, or pureed for a dessert.

Mamey: Not to be confused with the fruit of the West Indian tree of the same name (*Mammea* species), the mamey, or marmalade plum (*Calocarpum sapota*), is an oval-shaped fruit about 6 inches (15 cm) long (although sizes vary) with a tough, matte brown skin and meaty, deep orange to red flesh. A very large, smooth, dark brown seed lies at the center. The flesh is generally pureed in a variety of cooked or uncooked desserts, the most amusing of which is *mameyes fingidos* (fake mameys). The mameys are recreated with a colored almond-paste seed, around which a blend of mamey pulp, sugar, and cookie crumbs, cooked to a thick consistency, is formed into the shape of the mamey and rolled in cinnamon to form the crust.

Mameys are difficult to select as there is no external indication of whether the flesh has turned brown (this is usually nearer the seed). In Mexico, you will always see some partially peeled in an effort to convince the buyer of the fruits' freshness.

Zapote negro (black sapote): This plump, green-skinned fruit has a black pulp, reminiscent of a prune puree to the eye but with a surprisingly light, sweet taste. It is used uncooked; the flesh is simply scooped out of the skin and pushed through a strainer to remove the seeds. The puree is mixed with sugar, orange juice, and sometimes sherry to make a refreshing dessert served in a glass bowl. Black sapotes are ripe when they are very soft to the touch and look rather mushy.

Guayava (guava): The type of guava found in Mexico is small (1½ inches/3.5 cm in diameter) and light yellow. They can be eaten fresh or cooked, usually in a syrup with cinnamon and orange juice. There are also guavas that have a beautiful pink flesh inside.

1. guanábana (soursop);
2. chirimoya (cherimoya);
3. durazno (peach); 4. granada (pomegranate); 5. granada china (Chinese granadilla);
6. coco (coconut); 7. chico zapote (sapodilla); 8. mamey;
9. zapote negro (black zapote);
10. guayava (guava)

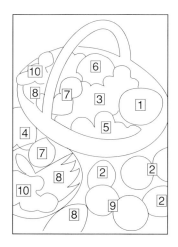

TURRON DE FRAMBUESAS

RASPBERRY MERINGUE

For years, the only place in Mexico where raspberries were cultivated was in San Jeronimo, in the south of Mexico City. When the berries were in season, people would come from great distances to buy them from roadside stands. The Fournier Amor family has had raspberry bushes in its home garden in San Jeronimo for generations, and this simple recipe is a family creation.

1 large egg white
1 cup (8 oz/250 g) sugar
1 cup (8 oz/250 g) raspberries
raspberries, for garnish
mint, for garnish, optional

SERVES 6

❡ Put all the ingredients in a large mixing bowl. Beat on high speed with an electric mixer for 6 to 7 minutes, or until firm, scraping down the bowl as necessary.

❡ Fill 6 long-stemmed glasses with the mixture and serve, decorated with whole raspberries and mint leaves, if desired.

❡ The meringue can be made up to 2 hours in advance and held at room temperature.

FLAN DE COCO

COCONUT FLAN

One of the many coconut desserts and sweets in Mexico, this recipe from the Molina Torres family is especially delicious.

2½ cups (1¼ lb/625 g) sugar
1 whole, mature coconut
2 whole eggs
8 egg yolks

SERVES 10

❡ Make the caramel by heating 1½ cups (12 oz/375 g) of sugar in a large, heavy-bottomed frying pan over medium-high heat. Start stirring when the sugar begins to melt and continue until it is amber-colored. Pour the caramel quickly into a round 10-inch (26-cm) flan mold or pie plate, and swirl to cover the bottom completely.

❡ Preheat the oven to 350°F (175°C/Gas 4).

❡ Make a hole through 2 of the black dots or "eyes" on the end of the coconut, using a screwdriver or a hammer and nail. Drain the coconut milk into a bowl, strain, and measure 1 cup (8 fl oz/250 ml) of milk, adding water to make up the quantity, if necessary.

❡ Break open the coconut with a hammer and put the pieces in the oven for about 15 minutes, until the meat comes off the shell when prized with the point of a knife. Remove any brown skin remaining on the meat with a vegetable peeler, and shred the meat using the medium grater of a food processor.

❡ In a saucepan, heat the coconut milk over medium heat. Add the remaining 1 cup (8 oz/250 g) of sugar and stir until it is completely dissolved. Add the coconut meat and cook, stirring, until it is translucent, about 5 to 10 minutes. Remove the pan from the heat and let cool slightly.

❡ Lightly beat the whole eggs and yolks in a bowl, add them to the coconut mixture, and mix well. Pour the mixture into the caramel-coated mold and place it into a larger ovenproof pan filled halfway up the sides of the flan mold with hot water. Bake for 1½ hours or until a toothpick inserted in the center comes out clean.

❡ Cool completely before gently turning out onto a serving plate.

ROSCA DE PASAS

RAISIN CROWN

This very old cake recipe from Sonora is an excellent and delicious example of making a few ingredients and a little money go a long way, as the Northern states did not share in the wealth of the coast or the tropics. The addition of the piloncillo (light molasses) and the pecan topping turns this simple dish into an elegant delight.

1 cup (8 fl oz/250 ml) boiling water
1 cup (6 oz/185 g) raisins
4 tablespoons (2 oz/60 g) butter
⅔ cup (5½ oz/170 g) sugar
1 large egg
1 teaspoon baking soda (bicarbonate of soda)
1 tablespoon cold water
1½ cups (6 oz/185 g) all-purpose (plain) flour, sifted
For the syrup:
14 oz/440 g piloncillo *cut into pieces or light molasses*
3 cups (24 fl oz/750 ml) water
2 tablespoons (1 oz/30 g) butter
2 teaspoons vanilla extract
½ cup (2 oz/60 g) chopped pecans

SERVES 8

❡ Pour the boiling water over the raisins to soak until soft. Drain, reserving ½ cup (4 fl oz/125 ml) of water, and cool to room temperature.

❡ Preheat the oven to 350°F (180°C/Gas 4).

❡ In a mixing bowl, cream the butter, beating in the sugar until well blended. Add the egg and the baking soda mixed with the cold water.

❡ Resift the flour and mix with the raisins. Fold the flour mixture into the butter mixture by thirds, alternating with the reserved raisin water.

❡ Butter and flour an 11-inch (28-cm) ring mold, then pour in the batter (it will seem like very little) and bake for 40 minutes, or until a cake tester inserted in the center comes out clean. Cool on a wire rack for 10 minutes and turn out onto a serving platter.

❡ To make the syrup: Heat the *piloncillo* and water in a saucepan, stirring constantly until dissolved. Remove the pan from the heat and then stir in the butter and vanilla until combined.

❡ Pour the syrup in the center so that it spreads over the top of the cake while the cake is still warm. Sprinkle with the chopped pecans.

❡ Serve warm or at room temperature.

Center left: Raspberry Meringue; back: Raisin Crown; front: Coconut Flan

LECHE FRITA

FRIED MILK

This custard-like dessert is called fried milk because, once set, the squares are sizzled in oil until they turn a golden-brown.

3 cups (24 fl oz/750 ml) milk
5 eggs, beaten, 1 reserved
½ cup (4 oz/125 g) sugar
1 piece cinnamon stick, 2 inches (5 cm) long
1 strip orange peel, (4 inches/10 cm) long
¾ cup (3 oz/90 g) cornstarch (cornflour)
flour, for coating
⅓ cup (3 fl oz/85 ml) vegetable oil
sugar and ground cinnamon, for dusting

SERVES 10–12

❡ Whisk together the first 6 ingredients, reserving 1 egg, in a medium saucepan and cook over low heat. Stir with a wooden spatula for 25 minutes until thick. Remove from the heat and discard the orange peel and cinnamon. Grease an 8- x 12-inch (20- x 30-cm) oblong mold and fill with the milk mixture. Cool, cover with plastic wrap, and refrigerate for 8 hours.
❡ Cut the mixture into 2½-inch (6-cm) squares. Dip each square into the reserved egg and then the flour. Heat the oil in a frying pan and fry the squares for 2 to 3 minutes on each side until golden-brown.
❡ Place on a serving dish and sprinkle with sugar and cinnamon. Serve warm.

CAJETA HECHA CON LECHE CONDENSADA

QUICK CONDENSED MILK CARAMEL

Cajeta, *also called* leche quemada (burnt milk) *or* alfajor, *is milk with sugar cooked in a copper pot for more than an hour until thick and condensed. This recipe is a quick method, made with sweetened condensed milk. The term* cajeta *refers to the little wooden box in which the sweet was traditionally sold (and still is, in Celaya, Guanajuato). Nowadays, however, cajeta is most often sold in glass jars. There are three types: vanilla, burnt, and wine cajeta. This very sweet dessert can be eaten by itself, with bread or cookies, or even as a filling for tamales.*

1 x 14-oz (440-g) can condensed milk

SERVES 4

❡ Remove the label from the can and scrub the can well, but do not open it.
❡ Put the can in a pressure cooker and cover three-quarters of the way with water. Close the lid and cook for 30 minutes following the manufacturer's instructions.
❡ Turn off the heat and let cool until the pressure subsides.
❡ Open the lid, remove the can, and place it in ice water until completely cool. Open the top and bottom of the can and push out the caramel.
❡ Serve immediately or store in the refrigerator, where it will keep for several days.

Left: Fried Milk; right: Quick Condensed Milk Caramel

SUGAR, SWEETENERS, AND FLAVORINGS

Sugar cane was one of the first crops the Spanish cultivated in the New World. Columbus introduced the plant to what is now Haiti on his second voyage, in 1493, and Cortés brought it to Mexico in the early 1500s. By 1550, the first plantations had been set up from Veracruz to Morelos, Guerrero and the Valley of Mexico, and refineries were built to process the cane. All this was to free the European colonizers from the Middle Eastern sugar monopoly.

Until the introduction of sugar cane, indigenous cultures relied on the sugar from the corn stalk and the maguey cactus, and honey from honeybees, to sweeten their dishes and drinks. But the cultivation of sugar cane grew rapidly, and its use took firm hold in the mixed culture that slowly developed between the native people and the conquerers.

Piloncillo, a hard molasses-like flavored sugar, is a byproduct of the process of sugar-refining. The liquid molasses that is spun out from the raw sugar is reheated and crystallized into small, conical molds the size and shape of pestles. The deep, rich flavor of this dark sugar characterizes many of Mexico's sweets and desserts. To turn it into a liquid syrup, it is simply heated with a little water until it dissolves. It can also be softened without the addition of water by heating it in the microwave for a couple of minutes, to the point where it will crumble easily. The light molasses available in many countries can be used as a substitute for *piloncillo*, as can brown sugar. Light molasses is from the first refining process and can be substituted by using equal weight.

Honey is still very common as a sweetener today in Mexico. While there is a large commercial production in Mexico that is exported worldwide, excellent honeys are also sold in towns and villages all over the country as a cottage industry.

Vanilla, like chocolate, is one of Mexico's great contributions to the culinary world. It is grown in Veracruz in the region near the town of Papantla, which is the name most associated with it in Mexico. Vanilla is the pod of a climbing vine in the orchid family. Its Nahuatl name is *ixtlilxóchitl*, meaning black flower. Vanillin, the component that gives vanilla its flavor, is developed by a long, slow process of alternately sweating the beans in the sun and then drying them. Vanilla's high price is due to the fact that the pods must be hand-pollinated, and a special bee must be introduced to the new habitat when transplanting vanilla, or it will not set fruit.

Pecans, almonds, and pine nuts are all used in the preparation of desserts and sweets in Mexico, as well as for making *moles* and other savory confections. Pecans are the most common nut (hence their name, *nuez*, or simply, "nut," in Mexico); they are principally cultivated in the North and are the only one of these nuts native to America. Pine nuts remain the most expensive; both pink and white varieties are available.

1. sugar; 2. powdered (confectioners' {icing}) sugar; 3. brown sugar; 4. piloncillo (brown cane sugar); 5. sugar cane; 6. honey; 7. pine nuts; 8. pecans; 9. vanilla beans

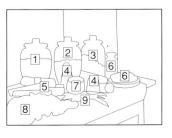

SALAMI DE CHOCOLATE

CHOCOLATE SALAMI

This chocolate confection from Lydia Leyzorek is ideal to give as a Christmas present or to offer to guests with coffee. The strong chocolate flavor and the aroma of the coffee liqueur make it a delicious treat, and the rolled-up sweet, with its chunks of cookies and walnuts, actually resembles a fat-flecked salami when it is sliced.

1½ cups (12 oz/375 g) sweet (unsalted) butter
5 oz (150 g) bittersweet (dark) chocolate, chopped
2 tablespoons cocoa
¾ cup (6 oz/185 g) sugar
5 eggs
¼ cup (2 fl oz/60 ml) Kahlúa or other coffee liqueur
1 teaspoon vanilla extract
3 packages (6½ oz/200 g each) any plain vanilla cookies,
   broken into small chunks
1 cup (4½ oz/125 g) chopped walnuts

MAKES 3 ROLLS

❡ Melt the butter in the top half of a double boiler over simmering water, then add and melt the chocolate. Add the cocoa and sugar and mix well. Remove from the heat. Lightly beat the eggs, and add one by one, whisking to incorporate. Add the liqueur and vanilla and stir to combine. Allow the mixture to cool slightly.
❡ Fold the cookie chunks and nuts into the chocolate mixture. Spoon the mixture into three 8- x 11-inch (22- x 30-cm) sheets of wax paper, and roll each tightly into a log, twisting the ends to seal.
❡ Place in the freezer immediately for about 3 hours or until frozen.
❡ While still frozen, finely slice (like salami), and serve. The rolls can be kept in the freezer for up to 4 months.

GELATINA DE MARRASQUINO Y UVAS

MARASCHINO AND GRAPE GELATIN

This gelatin dish is a wonderful excuse to eat grapes with the aromatic Italian liqueur maraschino. While it is tedious to peel the grapes, the job will be more fun if you enlist some helpers. You can also substitute canned tangerine segments or lychees for some of the grapes, and the dish should be made the day before. This recipe is from the Cuevas Lascurain family.

2 envelopes (½ oz/15 g) plain gelatin
½ cup (4 fl oz/125 ml) cold water
½ cup (3½ oz/100 g) sugar
1½ cups (12 fl oz/375 ml) water
½ cup maraschino liqueur
1½ lb (750 g) seedless green grapes, peeled
mint leaves or wild strawberries, for garnish

SERVES 6

❡ Soak the gelatin in the cold water to soften. Put the sugar and the 1½ cups of water in a small

saucepan over high heat, stirring lightly until the sugar has dissolved. Remove from the heat and immediately add the gelatin, stirring until dissolved. Let cool before adding the maraschino and stir well. Put the pan in the refrigerator for 30 to 45 minutes, or until the gelatin has just begun to set.

¶ Grease a 4-cup (1-qt/1-l) terrine with a little vegetable oil and put a sheet of plastic wrap on the bottom. Remove the gelatin from the refrigerator and pour one-third of it into the mold. Place in the refrigerator and chill for at least 4 hours, or until it

begins to set; also return the pan containing the remaining gelatin mixture to the refrigerator. Once the terrine is slightly set, spoon a layer of grapes on top and chill again, then add more gelatin. Repeat the procedure twice to complete the layers. If the gelatin in the saucepan begins to harden, soften slightly by heating on top of a double boiler.

¶ Put the terrine in the refrigerator and allow to set completely, at least 4 hours or longer if necessary. Unmold onto a serving plate and garnish with mint leaves or wild strawberries.

Left: Chocolate Salami; right: Maraschino and Grape Gelatin

Front: Baked Oatmeal and Apple Dessert;
back: Queretaro-style Dessert

POSTRE DE AVENA Y MANZANA

BAKED OATMEAL AND APPLE DESSERT

This traditional dessert is quite easy to make and tastes delicious. The lime and cinnamon bring out the flavor of the oats and apples. Prepare in the same ceramic dish in which the dessert is to be served.

1 lb (500 g) apples, peeled and finely sliced
3 tablespoons (1½ oz/45 g) plus ⅓ cup (2½ oz/70 g) sugar
¼ cup (2 fl oz/60 ml) water
½ tablespoon lime or lemon zest
1½ cups (6 oz/185 g) rolled oats
pinch baking soda (bicarbonate of soda)
¼ teaspoon salt
¼ cup (2 oz/60 g) melted butter

SERVES 8

❡ Preheat the oven to 350°F (180°C/Gas 4).
❡ In a frying pan, cook the apples with 3 tablespoons of sugar and water over medium heat until the water has evaporated and the apples are tender. Sprinkle with the zest and set aside.
❡ Mix the oats, the remaining sugar, baking soda, and salt in a bowl. Stir in the butter and mix thoroughly.
❡ Butter an 8- x 8- x 2-inch (20- x 20- x 5-cm) oven-proof dish. Spread half the oat mixture over the bottom and top with the apples. Cover with the remaining oat mixture.
❡ Bake for 35 minutes. Serve hot or cold.

DULCE DE QUERETARO

QUERETARO-STYLE DESSERT

Yams are native to the Americas and are particularly popular in Puebla and Queretaro. In Mexico they are called camotes, *a Nahuatl name, and they come with white, yellow, or purple flesh. Their sweet taste teams well with orange peel, spices, and raisins, and makes them suitable not only as a vegetable, but also as a dessert.*

3 yams (1½ lb/750 g), steamed and peeled
½ cup (4 oz/125 g) brown sugar
¼ cup (2 oz/60 g) butter
½ teaspoon cinnamon
½ cup (4 fl oz/125 ml) heavy (double/thickened) cream
grated zest of 1 orange
⅓ cup (2 oz/60 g) raisins

SERVES 6

❡ Preheat the oven to 350°F (180°C/Gas 4).
❡ Butter an 8-inch (20-cm) round baking mold. With a potato masher, mash the warm yams in a bowl. Add all but 1 tablespoon of the sugar, the butter, cinnamon, cream, and half the orange zest, and mix well.
❡ Spoon the mixture into the mold and sprinkle with the remaining orange zest and sugar. Bake in the oven for about 10 minutes or until warm. Remove from the oven and garnish with the raisins. Serve warm or at room temperature.

MEMBRILLO
Quince
Considered a native of Asia, this fruit is a member of the Rosaceae family, which also includes apples and apricots. Quince is similar to apples and pears in shape and texture but is more acidic and bright yellow in color. Its excellence for making jams and jellies has long been recognized, and, curiously enough, the word marmalade is derived from quince's Portuguese name, marmelo (in Spain and Mexico, it is called membrillo). It is primarily used in Mexico to make ate, a jelly-like fruit paste that is eaten for dessert, often accompanied by cheese, although it is also sometimes added to meat dishes along with other fruits. The quince grown in Mexico is smaller and considerably more acid than that grown commercially in the United States and elsewhere, and the latter is now imported to Mexico. You will probably find more of the imports in stores and markets, so sugar quantities in the recipes have been adjusted to suit the less acid variety.

Mexican Sweets

Many of Mexico's traditional sweets originated in convents populated by Spanish nuns. The nuns used techniques brought to Spain by the Arabs, who were the cultivators of sugar cane in the Iberian peninsula. The local produce of fruits, nuts, or seeds was used to produce the specialities of each area.

Necessity led to the imaginative use of egg yolks because so many whites were required to glaze altars and paint scenes inside the churches. Hence, the famous *rompope*, the yolk-based liqueur of Santa Clara, in Puebla, and the many yolk-based sweets called *yemitas* (little yolks) and *huevitos de faltriquera* (pocket eggs). *Yemitas* are a cooked mixture of yolks, sugar, and water beaten until white and thick. The mixture is formed into little balls, rolled in sugar,

and wrapped in brightly colored tissue paper. *Huevitos de faltriquera* are even smaller, marble-sized balls made with yolks, confectioners' (icing) sugar, and cinnamon. They used to be given to travelers to carry in their bag or pocket, hence the name.

Among the most famous of the sweets from Puebla are *camotes de Puebla*, the small, sugary logs made from white and purple yams and often flavored with other fruits; and *mueganos*, which are small pieces of a flour-and-molasses-based dough, deep-fried in lard to puff them, and then amassed into fist-sized balls with a crystallized molasses syrup.

Coconuts are the base for both desserts and sweets that go by the name of *cocadas*. A variety of the sweets based on egg yolks is made as follows: the shredded coconut is

cooked in a sugar syrup until translucent. Then, a mixture of milk and egg yolks is added, and the whole is boiled down to thicken and allowed to cool in small, round molds. The sweets may be flavored with cinnamon or sherry, and sometimes they are browned with the addition of butter at the end (*cocadas doradas*, or golden *cocadas*). *Veladores* is another type which contains a high proportion of egg yolks.

Cooked and caramelized milk and sugar are responsible for another whole gamut of sweets, from the *cajeta de leche* (a thick, caramelized milk sauce) from Celaya, to *mostachones* (small, round burnt-milk sweets topped with a pecan half), *macarrones* (small, ridged burnt-milk logs), and a large number of other *dulces de leche* (milk sweets), including *dulces*

de leche clara (light-colored burnt-milk sweets) from just about every region of the country. The famous *glorias* of Monterrey (made in Linares, Nuevo León, in the shape of small balls) are brought down to the capital to be sold in their characteristic red cellophane wrapping. From Linares also come caramelized milk sweets in great oblong blocks intricately decorated with pecans. When *dulces de leche* are covered with cinnamon, they become *encaneladas*. *Sevillanas* are another variety of burnt-milk sweet. In an almost flat, cookie shape, the caramel disk is sandwiched between two paper-thin wafers.

The tart pulp of the tamarind pod is another base for sweets. Whether made into balls covered with sugar (or sometimes salt and chile!), or flattened into sweet disks, these *dulces de tamarindo* (tamarind sweets) often still contain some of the tamarind seeds, keeping sweet-eaters on their toes.

Acitrón (candied cactus) is used both in desserts and as a meat stuffing.

1. camotes de Puebla (candied yam); 2. mueganos; 3. cocadas doradas (golden coconut sweets); 4. cocadas; 5. veladores (yellow coconut sweets); 6. dulce de leche clara (burnt-milk sweets); 7. encaneladas (burnt-milk sweets with cinnamon); 8. sevillanas; 9. acitrón (candied cactus)

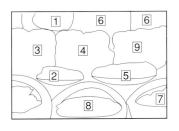

SOUFFLÉS DE CHOCOLATE A LA MEXICANA

MEXICAN-STYLE CHOCOLATE SOUFFLÉS

Oaxaca has long been considered the epicenter of the most delicious chocolate in Mexico. There, the cacao beans are first roasted, then ground with almonds, and next ground again with sugar and cinnamon to the cook's taste. The mixture is either patted into various shapes by hand or pressed into small, individual molds and set out to dry. Some Mexican varieties of chocolate are available in the United States, most easily found by mail order. However, the ingredients in this recipe will give a Mexican flavor to a plain bittersweet (dark) chocolate base. Substituting couverture, the chocolate most favored by professionals, will result in an especially glossy texture. This recipe is from Analuisa Bejan.

2 tablespoons (1 oz/30 g) butter
⅓ cup (2½ oz/75 g) confectioners' (icing) sugar
3½ oz (100 g) bittersweet (dark) chocolate, use couverture if available
2 tablespoons (1 oz/30 g) sugar
3 tablespoons milk
¼ teaspoon ground cinnamon
1 teaspoon vanilla extract
2 eggs, separated, plus 1 egg white extra
2 oz (50 g) almonds, toasted and finely ground

SERVES 4

❡ Preheat the oven to 400°F (200°C/Gas 6). Butter 4 individual soufflé molds (3 inches/7 cm) in diameter x 1¾ inches (4.5 cm) deep, and dust with half of the confectioners' sugar.

❡ Melt the chocolate in a microwave oven, or in the top of a double boiler over hot water with 1 tablespoon of the sugar, the milk, cinnamon, and vanilla extract. Remove from the heat and let cool slightly.

❡ Add the egg yolks, blending thoroughly. In a separate bowl, beat the egg whites with the remaining sugar until soft peaks form. Fold into the chocolate mixture, alternating with the ground almonds.

❡ Fill the molds to within ½ inch (1 cm) of the rim, allowing room for the soufflé to rise. Bake for 10 minutes or until firm but still soft in the center.

❡ To serve, unmold the soufflés by running a sharp knife around the sides of each mold, then turn upside down onto a dessert plate. Sprinkle the top of each soufflé with the remaining confectioners' sugar.

❡ For extra flavor, serve with a custard sauce (see *Gelatina de Vino Tinto* page 236), poured around the base of each soufflé.

BUDÍN DE SALTILLO

CHOCOLATE, PECAN, AND RED WINE CAKE

This scrumptious cake brings together three culinary ingredients associated with the northern state of Coahuila. Still a large producer of pecans (the only nut native to the Americas), Coahuila was home to the famous Oso chocolate factory as well as to the vineyards of the Madero family, which was among the first to engage in winemaking in Mexico. This recipe has been adapted from the one devised by Lydia Leyzorek which calls for milk rather than wine.

2 tablespoons (1 oz/30 g) butter
dry breadcrumbs, for dusting
3 oz (80 g) bittersweet (dark) or semisweet (cooking) chocolate, chopped, use couverture if available
½ cup (4 fl oz/125 ml) red wine
1¼ cups (4½ oz/140 g) pecans, finely ground
⅔ cup (5 oz/155 g) sugar
½ cup (1¾ oz/50 g) dry breadcrumbs
¼ teaspoon salt
¼ cup (2 oz/60 g) softened sweet butter, cut into small pieces
4 eggs, separated
2 tablespoons (1 oz/30 g) strawberry jam
2 tablespoons chopped pecans, toasted
sliced strawberries, to decorate, optional

SERVES 10

❡ Preheat the oven to 350°F (180°C/Gas 4).

❡ Butter a 9-inch (22-cm) cake mold, line the bottom with wax paper, butter the paper, and dust the bottom and sides with the breadcrumbs.

❡ Melt the chocolate in a microwave oven or in the top of a double boiler over hot water. Remove the pan with the water and place the pan with the chocolate directly over medium heat.

❡ Add the wine, pecans, sugar, breadcrumbs, and salt, then stir until thickened, approximately 3 minutes. Remove from the heat and allow to cool slightly.

❡ Stir in the butter piece by piece until fully incorporated. Stir in the egg yolks. In a separate bowl, beat the egg whites to stiff peaks and fold them into the chocolate mixture. Fill the mold.

❡ Bake in the oven for approximately 40 minutes or until a cake tester comes out clean. Let cool on a rack for 10 minutes before unmolding upside down on a platter. Remove the paper.

❡ To serve, spread the strawberry jam over the top of the cake and sprinkle the chopped pecans around the edge. Slice into 10 wedges and decorate each with a few fresh strawberries, if desired.

Front: Mexican-style Chocolate Soufflés; back: Chocolate, Pecan, and Red Wine Cake

GELATINA DE VINO TINTO

RED WINE GELATIN

This red wine gelatin is a light and delicious end to a meal. The gelatin can be served either with the custard sauce or surrounded by fresh berries.

2 envelopes (½ oz/15 g) unflavored gelatin
½ cup (4 oz/125 ml) water
1 cup (8 oz/250 ml) fresh orange juice, strained
1 cup (8 oz/250 g) sugar
3 cups (24 fl oz/750 ml) red wine
For the custard sauce:
2 cups (16 oz/500 ml) milk
4 egg yolks
⅓ cup (2¾ oz/80 g) sugar

pinch baking soda (bicarbonate of soda)
raspberries and mint for garnish

SERVES 8

❡ Soak the gelatin in the water.
❡ Heat the orange juice and sugar in a saucepan over medium heat until the sugar melts. Remove from the heat and add the gelatin, stirring until completely dissolved. Add the red wine and pour the mixture into a lightly oiled 1-quart (1-l) mold.
❡ Refrigerate for 8 hours before unmolding.
❡ To make the custard sauce: Beat the milk and yolks together in a bowl. Pour into a saucepan, add the sugar and baking soda, and cook over medium heat, stirring constantly, until the mixture thickens slightly; do not boil. Allow to cool.
❡ Serve either with the gelatin beneath it on a serving platter or separately, and garnish.

Just a few of the amazing forms gelatins can take in Mexico

GELATINAS

Gelatin-making is practically an art form in Mexico. The shapes may be a great source of amusement, as in the Volkswagen Bugs (Mexico has the only production line left in the world of this VW classic) and the dogs pictured here, or they may be a serious tour de force, demanding the patient layering of subtle flavors, bright colors, and carefully placed nuts, fruits, and raisins.

An exacting cook will use fine liqueurs or *rompope* (an egg yolk-based liqueur for which the Convent of Santa Clara in Puebla is famous), subtle extracts, or exquisite fruit purees and juices to flavor the *gelatinas* (gelatins). Care is taken that the correct amount of gelatin is used to solidify the creation and give it bite and texture. Indeed, it is amazing the heights these wobbly desserts can achieve!

A good bakery will display a variety of individual and large gelatins in its refrigerator case, ready to go while you pick up fresh *bolillos* (rolls), *pan dulce* (sweet bread), or even a birthday cake—in Mexico, cake and *gelatina* is a classic for birthdays.

Street vendors carry a specially designed case for displaying individual gelatins for sale. It is made of a hammered tin frame and glass doors, and its many shelves are encased in a box about 18 inches (45 cm) high by 12 inches (30 cm) long, with a handle on top for easy transport. The many-colored little gelatins gleam in the sunlight, each one placed on a small square of paper ready to be eaten from the hand.

Top: Soursop Gelatin with Mint Sauce; bottom: Red Wine Gelatin

GELATINA DE GUANABANA CON SALSA DE HIERBA BUENA

SOURSOP GELATIN WITH MINT SAUCE

The soursop has an intense aroma and a succulent white flesh so sweet that it is well worth the effort of removing its seeds to obtain the edible pulp. Traditionally used in Mexico as an agua fresca *(fresh fruit drink) or* nieve *(sherbet/sorbet), soursop is also excellent as a gelatin. Here, Shelton Wiseman has complemented the flavor of the fruit with a touch of mint in the sauce. Select a ripe soursop that is soft all over, and has a green, not black, skin; do not substitute the smaller cherimoya, as its pulp oxidizes.*

4½ lb (2.5 kg) soursop (1 to 2 pieces)
1½ cups (12 oz/375 g) sugar
1¾ cups (14 fl oz/440 ml) water
3 envelopes (¾ oz/20 g) unflavored gelatin
1½ tablespoons mint leaves, chopped and tightly packed

SERVES 8

❡ Lightly oil a 1-quart (1-l) gelatin mold.
❡ Cut the soursop in half lengthwise, pull out the tough heart, and scoop the flesh out of the shell, discarding any that is discolored. Push the black seeds out of the pulp with your fingers. There should be about 4 cups (1 qt/1 l) of pulp.
❡ In a small saucepan, bring the sugar and ¾ cup (6 fl oz/185 ml) of water to a boil and simmer for approximately 5 minutes to make a syrup.
❡ Process the soursop pulp with the syrup in a food processor until smooth, then push it through a strainer; there should be just over 4 cups (1 qt/1 l) of puree. Reserve 1 cup (8 fl oz/250 ml) for the sauce and use the rest for the gelatin.
❡ In a small saucepan, sprinkle the gelatin over ¾ cup (6 fl oz/185 ml) of cold water and let stand for 5 minutes to soften. Stir the gelatin over low heat until it is dissolved, without letting it boil. Add the gelatin to the puree and pour the mixture into the mold. Refrigerate for a minimum of 2 hours before unmolding.
❡ To make the sauce: Puree the mint with the remaining ¼ cup (2 fl oz/60 ml) of water in a blender. Add the reserved soursop and enough water (about ½ cup/4 fl oz/125 ml) to create the consistency of a sauce, and blend until smooth. Refrigerate until ready to serve.
❡ The gelatin and sauce can be made up to a day in advance.

NIEVE DE HIERBA BUENA

SPEARMINT SHERBET

This refreshing sherbet (sorbet) is a signature dish from El Estoril Restaurant in Mexico City. If you don't have an ice cream machine, you can make the recipe as a granita — just put the mixture in a metal tray in the freezer and stir it occasionally with a fork until it is frozen.

6 cups (6 oz/185 g) loosely packed spearmint leaves
1 qt (1 l) water
¼ teaspoon cinnamon
4 drops green food coloring
2 cups (16 oz/500 g) sugar
8 spearmint leaves, for garnish
8 strawberries or raspberries, for garnish

SERVES 8

❧ Blend the spearmint leaves with the water in a blender until completely smooth. Strain into a bowl and add the cinnamon, food coloring, and sugar.

❧ Put the mixture in an ice cream machine and carefully follow the manufacturer's instructions for making sherbet.

❧ To serve, decorate each dish of the sherbet with a spearmint leaf and a strawberry or raspberry and serve immediately.

Both the fruit and leaves from the banana tree are widely used in Mexican cooking.

BANANAS (PLÁTANOS)

Native to India and Malaysia, this ancient plant was introduced to Africa about AD 500, to Polynesia during the first millennium, and to the Americas with the Spanish conquest in the sixteenth century. Mexico alone now produces annually some two million tons (tonnes) of different varieties. These are cultivated primarily in the tropical regions of the southern half of the country, including both coasts, and from the isthmus down to the Guatemalan border.

The most common variety for export is the *Tabasco*, named after one of the states where it is cultivated, while smaller varieties, including the baby *dominicos*, or finger bananas, the *manzano* (slightly larger and a little fatter), and the medium-sized, red-skinned bananas, which have an orange tinge to their flesh, are very sweet and delicious but less suited to exportation.

Plantains are larger than the common banana, are blackish when ripe, and have a lower sugar content. They are usually eaten cooked or fried as a vegetable, especially on the coast of Veracruz, where the cuisine reflects the African influence originating from the Caribbean slave trade. Many chopped-meat fillings (*picadillos*) include plantains, as well as casseroles that mix fruits and vegetables with meat, such as the *manchamanteles* ("tablecloth stainer") of Puebla or the *mole coloradito* (red *mole*) of Oaxaca.

Banana leaves have many culinary uses in Mexico. They wrap *tamales* from Veracruz and Oaxaca to Chiapas and the Yucatán, as well as other foods, including fish for steam-baking and pork or chicken *pibil* in the Yucatán. Traditionally, the leaves would line an earthen pit oven, or *pibil*, although now it is common to wrap the food in the leaves and bake it in an earthenware casserole in a commercial oven. The leaves are not only used for their size but also because they impart a subtle flavor to the food.

Banana leaves should be bright green and fresh when you buy them. The central vein is cut out before the leaves are passed quickly over a flame to make them more pliable.

Left: Yam and Pineapple Dessert; right: Spearmint Sherbet

DULCE DE CAMOTE CON PIÑA

YAM AND PINEAPPLE DESSERT

This dessert from La Cocina Veracruzana *comes from the region around the border between Puebla and Veracruz. Yams are used a great deal in the former and pineapples in the latter.*

2 lb (1 kg) orange yams or sweet potatoes, washed, peeled, and minced (finely chopped)
1½ cups (10½ oz/300 g) sugar
4 slices fresh pineapple, cored and minced (finely chopped)
fresh pineapple wedges, lightly boiled, for garnish

SERVES 10

❡ Place the yams in a pot, add enough water to cover, and cook over low heat. When the water boils, add the sugar and minced pineapple. Boil without stirring for 20 minutes or until the yams are soft. Remove from the heat, strain, and reserve the syrup.
❡ Place the yams and pineapple in a bowl and mash with a wooden spoon or potato masher until smooth. Add the reserved syrup and mix well. Return the mixture to the pot and cook over low heat for 5 minutes.
❡ Turn out onto a platter or individual plates and let cool to room temperature or chill in the refrigerator before serving. Garnish with the pineapple wedges.

PLATANOS AL HORNO CON SALSA DE RON AÑEJO

BAKED BANANAS WITH DARK RUM SAUCE

This recipe from Tere Garcia Gayou calls for ingredients that are very easy to find in Mexico. There are many Seville orange trees, whose fruit is used for homemade marmalade, and bananas, brown sugar, and rum are so plentiful as to be considered native ingredients.

For the bananas:
1 tablespoon (½ oz/15 g) butter
2 tablespoons (1 oz/30 g) brown sugar
4 ripe bananas, cut in half lengthwise
For the sauce:
1 tablespoon grated lemon or lime zest
2 tablespoons lemon or lime juice
2 tablespoons (1 oz/30 g) sugar
3 tablespoons (1½ oz/45 g) orange marmalade
¼ cup (2 fl oz/60 ml) water
3 tablespoons dark rum, heated

SERVES 4

❡ Preheat the oven to 350°F (180°C/Gas 4). Grease a 8- x 8-inch (20- x 20-cm) ovenproof baking dish with the butter and sprinkle it with the sugar. Place the bananas in the baking dish.
❡ To make the sauce: Combine all but the rum in a saucepan and bring to a boil over medium heat. Remove from the heat and pour the sauce over the bananas. Bake for 10 to 15 minutes.
❡ Remove the baking dish from the oven, pour the rum over the bananas, ignite, and serve immediately.

BUÑUELOS

SWEET FRITTERS

Originally from Spain, buñuelos have become a national favorite in Mexico. During every important celebration or holiday, you can see street vendors with foot-high piles of these thin, crunchy fritters, some measuring 13 inches (32 cm) in diameter.

For the fritters:
1 lb (500 g) all-purpose (plain) flour
1 teaspoon baking powder
1 tablespoon (½ oz/15 g) butter
1 tablespoon (½ oz/15 g) lard
1 teaspoon salt
4 medium eggs, lightly beaten
¼ cup (2 fl oz/60 ml) sherry

2 cups (16 fl oz/500 ml) vegetable oil
For the syrup:
1 lb (500 g) piloncillo or brown sugar
3 cups (24 fl oz/750 ml) water
*1 or 2 fig leaves, 1 tablespoon orange peel strips, or
   1 teaspoon aniseed*

MAKES 36 FRITTERS

❡ To make the fritters: Sift the flour with the baking powder and salt onto a clean surface. Make a well in the center and add the butter, lard, salt, and eggs, incorporating them gradually with your fingers. Knead for a few minutes. Add the sherry and continue kneading until the dough is smooth and soft, approximately 3 minutes.
❡ Cover the dough with a damp kitchen towel and let rest for 30 minutes. Divide the dough into 36 balls, each about the size of a small egg (1 oz/30 g). Using a rolling pin on a floured surface, flatten each ball to a 7-inch (18-cm) disk, like a *tortilla*, or roll the dough as thin as you can.
❡ Heat the oil in a large frying pan and fry the fritters, one at a time. As each fries, press it down with a metal spatula to eliminate the bubbles that

AMARANTO
Amaranth

Amaranth has been around since the time of the Aztecs, who fabricated likenesses of their gods from the plant and used the seeds to make a kind of atole and a special tamal as a spiritual offering. They also used to eat the tender leaves from this member of the spinach family. The plant flowers every year in June and July, filling fields in Tlaxcala and Xochimilco (to the South of Mexico City) with its maroon-colored feathery blooms. Today, the tiny seeds, as light as popcorn, are used for making a variety of sweets called alegrias (happinesses), which are pressed into shapes with sugar syrup and sometimes decorated with nuts. To make alegrias, use the same amount (by weight) of amaranth seeds and piloncillo (a hard brown, unrefined sugar; substitute it with light molasses or brown sugar). Toast the seeds on a comal, keeping them moving constantly, until they pop like corn. Mexican cooks use a special whisk broom to control the seeds so that they neither burn nor pop off the comal. Melt the piloncillo (or brown sugar, if using), adding just enough water to make a thick syrup. If using light molasses (or even corn syrup), do not dilute. Add the seeds to the sugar liquid to form a paste. When cool enough to handle but still quite malleable, press the paste into molds, then remove and dry. Similarly, the mixture can be spread on a tray and when dry cut into shapes of your choice.

Bottom left: Baked Bananas with Dark Rum Sauce; top left: Sweet Fritters; right: Porcupine

form on the surface. Cook for 30 seconds on each side until golden but not browned and drain them on paper towels to remove the excess oil.

❡ For the syrup: Put all ingredients in a small saucepan and heat until the *piloncillo* has melted completely. Serve the *buñuelos* with the syrup at room temperature.

PUERCO ESPIN

PORCUPINE

This very rich dessert from Patricia Pintado Rivero of Guadalajara is traditionally served at formal dinners in Mexico. The elements are similar to those used for the traditional French Charlottes. The dessert is in the shape of a porcupine, with slivered almonds simulating the quills.

¾ cup (6 oz/185 g) butter
1 cup (6 oz/175 g) confectioners' (icing) sugar
3 egg yolks
1 tablespoon Kahlúa or other coffee liqueur

2 tablespoons instant coffee, dissolved in 2 tablespoons hot water and cooled
24 ladyfingers (see Ante de Chico Zapote y Almendras page 220)
¼ cup (1 oz/30 g) slivered almonds, lightly toasted

SERVES 18–20

❡ Cream the butter with an electric mixer, gradually adding the sugar. Add the egg yolks one at a time and continue beating. Add the Kahlúa and coffee to the mixture and beat until well combined.

❡ Place a little of the mixture on a serving dish and spread to make a 9- x 5-inch (22- x 12-cm) thin oval layer. Cover with 10 ladyfingers and add more mixture to fill the gaps. Place 8 ladyfingers in the center and add more mixture. Repeat with the remaining 6 ladyfingers in the center and cover all over with the remaining mixture. It should be roughly the shape of a porcupine or half an American football.

❡ Cover the oval with the almonds inserted upright to resemble porcupine quills. Chill in the refrigerator for about 3 hours. Present on the table, and cut into slices or wedges to serve.

DRIED AND CANDIED FRUITS

Dried fruits are very popular in Mexico, where they may be used in main course dishes as well as in desserts, or simply eaten alone. Many dried fruits are known as *orejonas*, or big ears, because of their shape, and the most common of these are apricots, peaches, apples, and pears. Raisins and sometimes even prunes are blended into *mole* sauces and added to meat *picadillos* (chopped-meat fillings) or sweet rice puddings, cakes, and flans.

Just about any fruit can be candied: whole oranges and limes, peel and pulp included, and the latter stuffed with grated coconut; figs; pears; *tunas* (prickly pear fruit); and slices of pineapple, not to mention nonfruits such as *acitrón*, which is actually a cactus; squashes; sweet potatoes; and yams.

Candied *acitrón* (*Echincactus grandis*) is bright yellow and sold in blocks or oblongs. It very often lends its chewy sweetness to *picadillos* as well as to salads.

The majestic *calabaza en tacha (tacha* is the name of a large casserole) is a large, green squash that is cooked whole, including the stem, or in pieces, with the seeds and flesh, in a *piloncillo*-based (light molasses) syrup. When whole, which is how it is usually sold in markets, the skin is perforated with large holes so the syrup will penetrate and flavor the flesh.

Most of these candied and crystallized fruits are available year-round, although they come out in full force around Christmas time for the festive occasions that surround the holiday.

Ates, or fruit pastes, a specialty of Michoacán, are an excellent way to use the guavas, apples, and quinces that grow in the area. The fruit purees are cooked to a paste with sugar, then allowed to dry for two weeks or so in their round or oblong molds in a cool, dry place, being turned periodically. Once dried, they will last several months stored in a cool place. They are usually thinly sliced to be eaten for dessert, often accompanied by a mild cheese such as *panela. Ates* of guava are an opaque mustard color, while those of quince are a gleaming, translucent, deep red-purple, and those of apple, a golden amber. Another popular *ate*, almost emerald in color, is made of *perón*, which is a type of green apple.

1. candied oranges; 2. candied limes filled with coconut; 3. acitrón (candied cactus); 4. candied chilacayote (with seeds)/candied spaghetti squash; 5. candied yams and sweet potatoes; 6. quince ate (paste); 7. guava ate (paste); 8. apple ate (paste); 9. calabaza en tacha (squash); 10. candied figs; 11. prunes; 12. raisins

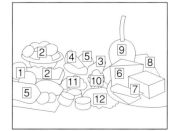

PONCHE NAVIDEÑO

CHRISTMAS PUNCH

This recipe is for making a hot Christmas punch for children, or for adults with the addition of rum. It is flavored with agua de jamaica, *or hibiscus water, and a variety of fruits. This recipe is from Analuisa Béjar, who writes for* Maria Orsini, *one of the best Mexican food magazines. It can also be made into a sherbet (sorbet) or served as a fruit sauce for ice cream or cake.*

5 qt (5 l) water
2 oz (50 g) flor de jamaica *(dried hibiscus flowers)*
3½ oz (100 g) piloncillo, *chopped, or light molasses*

Left: Christmas Punch; right: Fig Dessert

2 oz (50 g) pitted prunes, chopped
2 oz (50 g) dried apricots, chopped
2 cinnamon sticks, 2 inches (5 cm) long
5 guavas, 4 apples, 4 pears, or 2 ripe quinces
juice of 2 oranges
sugar to taste

MAKES 5 qt (5 l)

❧ Bring the water and *flor de jamaica* to a boil in a large pot. Remove from the heat and let steep for 15 minutes. Strain off the flowers and return the liquid to the pot. Add the *piloncillo*, prunes, apricots, and cinnamon. Return the liquid to a boil and add all the remaining ingredients. Simmer for about an hour over very low heat until the liquid is slightly thickened and the fruit is soft.

❧ For a punch, serve the mixture hot in earthenware mugs with or without a touch of rum.

❧ To make a sherbet (sorbet), pass the mixture through a sieve into a bowl, pressing the fruit to get as much pulp as possible. Stir to blend the liquid and mashed fruit. Add sugar to taste if necessary and let cool completely. Put the mixture in an ice cream machine, and carefully follow the manufacturer's instructions for sherbet.

❧ For a fruit sauce: Strain the liquid, discarding the fruit, add more sugar if necessary, and boil until it has the consistency of a thick syrup.

POSTRE DE HIGO

FIG DESSERT

This is a beautiful way to present fresh figs and mango puree. The flavors complement each other while the colors make a lovely contrast.

½ teaspoon vegetable oil
4 lb (2 kg) figs, ripe but firm
6 fl oz (185 ml) condensed milk
2 large mangoes, peeled and pitted
5 mint sprigs

SERVES 8

❧ Spread the oil on the bottom of a 10- x 4- x 2½-inch (26- x 11- x 6.5-cm) terrine and line the bottom with a piece of plastic wrap cut to fit.

❧ Peel the figs and cut them vertically into ¼-inch (6-mm) slices, or finer if possible. Place 1 layer of figs in the terrine, then pour 3 thin vertical lines of condensed milk across the figs. Continue layering with the remaining figs and condensed milk. Cover with another sheet of plastic wrap, pressing down slightly. Refrigerate for at least 12 hours.

❧ Remove the top sheet of plastic wrap and run a knife along the sides of the terrine to loosen the figs. Turn over the terrine and unmold on a dish with a raised rim. Remove the other sheet of plastic.

❧ Blend the mangoes in a blender until smooth, then pour around the figs.

❧ Garnish with fresh mint leaves.

FIESTAS

FIESTAS

MEXICANS ARE VERY FOND OF FOOD, NOT ONLY AS A BIOLOGICAL NECESSITY, BUT ALSO AS A special gustatory pleasure indulged in at the table, and, as we have seen, on the streets. This enthusiasm, almost bordering on the deadly sin of gluttony, is accentuated during fiestas, most of which are religious.

¶ The majority of Mexicans are Catholics, and each city, town, and village has its patron saint, on whose special day celebrations are prepared with traditional foods, fireworks, carnival rides, and religious ceremonies. Naturally, *tianguis,* or street markets, form part of the festivities. Although markets date back to pre-Hispanic times and are a normal weekly occurrence, they are more elaborate on these festive days, and stalls are often set up on the streets, amid the traffic.

¶ The calendar of festivities begins on January 6 with the celebration of *los Reyes Magos* (the Three Wise Men). The *rosca de reyes,* a kind of coffee-cake ring made with many egg yolks and decorated with strips of candied fruit, is shared on this occasion, accompanied by a frothy cup of hot chocolate or *atole.* Depending on the size of the ring, which can be as large as 3 feet (1 m) wide, a number of tiny dolls are baked in the cake. Traditionally porcelain but nowadays made of plastic, the dolls represent the baby Jesus. Guests cut their own slice of the crusty

Previous pages: Days of the Dead breads set on a trellis decorated with marigolds and placed at the head of a tomb for the night vigil on November 1.

Opposite: Toffee apples lend a sweet note to a fiesta day in the rich mining city of Zacatecas.

ring, and the person (or people) who finds a doll is obliged to offer a *tamalada,* or *tamal* party, for the rest of the group on February 2, the day of the *Candelaria* (Candlemas). It is on this day that the figure of the Christ child is taken out of the manger. (A nativity scene is traditionally set up in Mexican homes for the entire Christmas season.)

¶ The forty days of Lent, and, particularly, Easter week, are a time of deep religious devotion among Mexicans, and most people refrain from eating meat, especially on Fridays, restricting their diet to fish and vegetables. Dishes characteristic of this time of the year include *caldo de haba,* a dried, yellow fava (broad) bean soup made with mint or cilantro (fresh coriander) and *pasilla* chiles; *nopal* cactus paddles cooked in various ways, including the famous *nopales navegantes,* diced and "swimming" in broth; and *revoltijo,* "a mixture of everything," which has dried shrimp (prawns) patties made with egg and is served in a *mole.*

¶ Typical desserts during Lent are *capirotada,* made of slices of wheat-flour rolls, fried and served with a syrup of *piloncillo,* raisins, cinnamon, and shredded cheese; and *torrejas,* similar to *capirotada,* but dipped into beaten egg before frying and served with a syrup flavored with cinnamon and shredded lime peel. When a baby's first tooth appears, it is also a tradition to celebrate the occasion with *torrejas.*

¶ On September 15 and 16, Mexico celebrates the liberation from Spain in 1821. It is a commemoration of the dawn on which parish priest Miguel Hidalgo, now revered as the Father of the Country, sounded his *grito Viva Mexico,* the cry for independence. The entire month is recognized as Mexico's month, and for the full thirty days cities, towns, and villages are decorated with flags, tricolored paper chains, and twinkling colored lights. In the evenings, streets and squares are the venue for public fiestas at which much *pozole* is consumed; this is a pig's head and hominy soup served with chopped lettuce and radishes, ground *piquín* chile, oregano, and lime juice. *Pambazos*, Spanish-style wheat rolls filled with diced potatoes fried with *chorizo*, chopped lettuce, and *chipotle* chiles, are also much in evidence. The secret to a good *pambazo* is to dip the bread in the fat from the *chorizo* and potato filling before spreading with the chiles.

❦ The traditional sweets served during September are *buñuelos*, large, thin, wheat-flour *tortillas*, deep-fried in oil and covered with molasses syrup flavored with cinnamon; *alegrias*, toasted amaranth seeds pressed into blocks with a heavy syrup; and, finally, slabs of peanut brittle and halfmoon, paper-like wafers in purple, pink, or blue which cover a few candied pumpkin seeds.

The Days of the Dead

❦ Every country in the world has particular traditions, religious customs, and rites associated with death and the dead, but few celebrate the end of life the way the Mexicans do. Like the symbolic pre-Hispanic Aztec serpent that forms a circle without beginning or end, life and death form a continuous cycle, and death is seen as the renewal of fertility. To play with death and to give food and drink to the dead are profound and vital expressions to Mexicans.

❦ The *Dias de Muertos* (Days of the Dead) are celebrated from October 31 to November 2, and often mix pagan with Christian practices. On October 31, children who died unchristened are mourned, while November 1 is the day for babies who died after their baptism. This is known as the *Dia de Muertos Chiquitos*—the Day of the Little Dead. The main festival falls on November 2 and is dedicated to the *Fieles Difuntos*, the day of the faithful dead, or adults.

❦ The custom of making offerings of their former favorite dishes to the deceased, dates from pre-Hispanic times. These offerings may be displayed at the homes of the deceased or their graves, and, since they are intended not only to honor the dead but also to nourish them, a path is laid out in marigold petals to lead them straight to their destination. The *ofrenda* (offering) itself may include, in addition to food, pictures or statuettes of the Virgin Mary or of saints, votive candles, and, naturally, portraits or photos of the departed.

❦ Offerings for children usually include sweet *tamales* flavored with anise and tinted pink or any other favorite color of the young, or *sopa de fideos*, milk, sweets, and desserts. *Tejocotes* (a fruit that resembles a crabapple with a big seed) in heavy syrup, pieces of pumpkin candied with their own seeds (*calabaza en tacha*), and pieces of sugar cane are other temptations set out for the "little dead."

❦ Every offering, whether for children or for adults, includes salt, water, and a sweet bread known as *pan de muerto* (bread of the dead), which is made with egg yolks and orange water, topped with dough in the shape of human bones, and sprinkled with sugar before baking. Offerings for the adult dead are made up of both sweet and salty *tamales*, *moles*, and other favorite dishes, as well as the alcoholic drinks and cigarettes preferred by the deceased.

❦ A widespread custom during the Days of the Dead is to give a favorite person a little skull, made of sugar paste, that bears the name of the recipient on its forehead. These skulls, marked with popular names such as Guadalupe, Maria, José, Juan, and Jesus, are made by the hundreds for sale during this season. Foreign visitors are frequently puzzled by this custom, and even more so when they observe parents

During the Days of the Dead festivities, it's a widespread custom to give a favored person a little sugar skull bearing the recipient's name.

The Mexican fondness for sweets is indulged on festive occasions with special sweet breads or panes dulces *to commemorate the event.*

presenting their children with a little coffin with a sliding lid that releases a skeleton popping out like a Jack-in-the-box, or an orchestra of skeletons dressed in typical Mexican costumes, playing their instruments. Just as surprising to outsiders is when they discover that their Mexican friends write amusing verses, called *calaveras* (skulls), to or about each other, alluding to the subject as if she or he were recently deceased!

❡ Among the typical *tamales* prepared for the Days of the Dead is the *zacahuil*. Made in the Huasteca area, it is the largest *tamal* in the world, measuring 3 feet (1 m) in length and weighing as much as 150 lb (70 kg). The special corn *masa* is filled with several kinds of meat, including pork and turkey, and is assembled in a large pan covered with toasted banana leaves in which the *tamal* is enfolded.

❡ Another regional *tamal* for these festivities is the Yucatecan *mucbilpollo*, made in an earthenware casserole and flavored with *achiote* (annatto) seeds. *Mucbilpollo* sometimes contains *espelón*, a kind of bean that gives it a distinctive taste. Neither *mucbilpollo* nor the *zacahuil* is steamed like most *tamales*. Both are baked, either in the ground, like *barbacoa*, or in a bread oven.

❡ Different parts of the country have regional customs connected with their celebration of the *Días de Muertos*. In the state of Guanajuato, Otomi Indians living around San Miguel de Allende prepare green-, blue-, lavender-, or rose-colored *tamales* and little sombreros made of confectioners' (icing) sugar. The special *tortillas* of Comonfort are colored purple or black and have raised designs, while in Salamanca, figures of animals with human faces are made of sugar paste.

❡ The *mayordomo*, or chief steward, of the fiesta for the dead in Pajapan, Veracruz, must slaughter a bull for roasting. In Soteapan, housewives share their *nixtamal* (corn soaked in lime water) with their neighbors, symbolically offering the very substance of the *tortilla* to their friends. Bean *tamales* made with avocado leaves are characteristic of Zongolica, while in Jalapa, boiled *chayotes* form part of the offerings.

❡ It is the custom in Michoacán to prepare *mole* with little shrimp patties dipped in whipped egg batter and fried. In Tetela del Volcan, in Morelos, the people cook unripened beans with *epazote*, bake bread made with eggs, and prepare a strange drink, *chacualole*, a type of *atole* made of pumpkin, peanuts, and liquefied *piloncillo*. In Yucatán, *bolche*, a special wine that is made from tree bark, is prepared for the occasion.

❦ The day of December 12 marks another of the principal fiestas of the year: the anniversary of the appearance of the Virgin of Guadalupe, patron saint of Mexico and the rest of Latin America. Literally tens of thousands of pilgrims visit her shrine in Mexico City to honor her, and many perform native dances in the atrium of the basilica. Sweet *gorditas* of fine, cornmeal dough and lard, measuring barely 2 inches (5 cm) in diameter and ½ inch (1 cm) thick, are baked; they're sold in brightly colored tissue paper by the many women who always set up their little *anafres*, or braziers, around the shrine.

Christmas and New Year

❦ Joyous and animated are the *posadas*, the festivities organized on the nine nights preceding Christmas (December 16 to 24). *Posada* means inn or refuge, and the festivities take their name from the biblical account of Mary and Joseph being refused by the inns of Bethlehem. At these parties, the guests are divided into two groups: the one outside the house represents Mary and Joseph, while the other stays inside representing the innkeeper. The first group sings a request for admission which the second musically denies several times, until finally the weary travelers are admitted and the guests all sing together.

❦ Then comes the culminating moment: the breaking of the *piñata*, a clay pot in the shape of anything from a star to a locomotive, covered with brightly colored tissue or crepe paper and filled, traditionally, with pieces of sugar cane, *tejocotes*, oranges, tiny mandarines, *jícamas*, peanuts, and hard sweets. The *piñata* is hung from a rope that is fixed at one end and held on the other by someone on the roof, or strung over the branch of a tree, so it can be swung back and forth and up and down. The aim is to confuse the blindfolded guest who, armed with a sturdy pole, whacks the air until contact with the pot is made. When it breaks, the goodies it contains come cascading down. Blindfold and stick usually exchange hands after three fruitless attempts to smash the *piñata*, so young and old, toddlers (not blindfolded) and youths, parents, and grandparents, can enjoy their turn until the pot is broken. Special songs accompany the efforts to break the *piñata*.

❦ The four most traditional dishes served at the Christmas Eve midnight dinner are *revoltijo*; Spanish *bacalao a la Vizcaina*; the unusual Christmas Eve salad, traditionally made with beets (beetroot), *jícama*, orange sections, lettuce, peanuts, and sugar cane; and a roast turkey (a fowl indigenous to Mexico), baked according to the family recipe. Several desserts are generally served at the end of the meal, as well as dried fruits of many kinds and *peladillas* (sugar-coated almonds). Hard and soft *turrón* (made of almonds, sesame seeds, and egg yolks) from Alicante or Jijona are a Spanish contribution to the feast, and, of course, there are *tamales*. *Pozole*, that warming pork and hominy soup, is the mainstay on New Year's Eve, with its accompaniments of *tostadas*, fresh radish slices, oregano, and shredded lettuce.

Harvest Festivals

❦ There are many regional festivals that celebrate the local harvest. In Montemorelos, in Nuevo León, an important producer of oranges, the fountain in the central square is filled with orange juice instead of water during the orange festival at the end of January, much to the amusement of the participants. In Apan, Hidalgo, there is a *pulque* festival during the second week of April. The town is the most famous producer of this alcoholic beverage of pre-Hispanic origins, made from the juice of the maguey cactus. During the same period, sweet wines and liqueurs made from the many kinds of fruit grown in the area of Xicotepec, Puebla— especially that of the *acachul*, a kind of native mulberry—are the center of festivities.

❦ In October, the famous *Feria del Mole* (mole fair) takes place in San Pedro Atocpan, Milpa Alta, on the outskirts of Mexico City. Dozens of restaurants and *fondas* (eateries set up especially for the occasion) are open to serve the *moles* displayed out front, which include practically every type available in the country, but which specialize in *mole poblano*, the most famous of them all. The owners of the different stalls throw all their creativity into the displays of *mole* pastes and powders, and a prize is presented to the most beautiful creation.

❦ Weddings, birthdays, saints days (often the same day, as many Mexicans are named after the saint of their birth date), and that important rite of passage for all young girls of fifteen, the *quinceañera* (coming-out) party, are other moments of celebration. Large, elaborate cakes are obligatory; they are often tiered cakes large enough to feed all the neighbors, and can take any shape imaginable.

INDEX

ACKNOWLEDGMENTS

Recipe photography: Gerald Colley (photographer) and Kay Francis (food stylist): endpapers, pp 46–47 and 168. All other recipe photography by Andrew Furlong (photographer), Marie-Hélène Clauzon (food stylist), and Myles Beaufort (assistant food stylist).

Ingredients and location photography: Michael Calderwood.

Weldon Russell Pty Ltd would like to thank the following people for their assistance with the photography and supplying of props for this book:

Mela Szymanski (producer and assistant to Michael Calderwood), Jorge and Irene Szymanski, Martha Szymanski, Alberto and Bridget Estavillo, Maria Keirkuc, Monica Hernández, Giña Casteñeda, Mexican Imports, Pay Ban, Interentre, Artimex, Le Creuset, Home and Garden, Country Floors, Corso de Fiori, Pacific East India Company, Mexico.